Paranormal America

Paranormal America

*Ghost Encounters, UFO Sightings,
Bigfoot Hunts, and Other Curiosities
in Religion and Culture*

Christopher D. Bader,
F. Carson Mencken, and
Joseph O. Baker

NEW YORK UNIVERSITY PRESS
New York and London

NEW YORK UNIVERSITY PRESS
New York and London
www.nyupress.org

Library of Congress Cataloging-in-Publication Data
Bader, Christopher David.
Paranormal America : ghost encounters, UFO sightings, Bigfoot
hunts, and other curiosities in religion and culture / Christopher D.
Bader, F. Carson Mencken, and Joseph Baker.
p.   cm.
Includes bibliographical references (p.   ) and index.
ISBN 978-0-8147-9134-9 (cl : alk. paper) — ISBN 978-0-8147-9135-6
(pb : alk. paper) — ISBN 978-0-8147-8642-0 (e-book)
1. Parapsychology—United States. 2. Curiosities and wonders—
United States.   I. Mencken, Frederick Carson, 1964– II. Baker, Joe,
1965– III. Title.
BF1028.5.U6B34 2010
130.973—dc22   2010016525

New York University Press books are printed on acid-free paper,
and their binding materials are chosen for strength and durability.
We strive to use environmentally responsible suppliers and materials
to the greatest extent possible in publishing our books.

Manufactured in the United States of America

c 10 9 8 7 6 5 4 3 2 1
p 10 9 8 7 6 5 4 3 2 1

Contents

Acknowledgments

We have so many people to thank for their help in this endeavor that we fear the attempt. Someone will certainly be forgotten.

The quantitative data presented in this book are based upon the Baylor Religion Survey, Waves 1 and 2, collected in 2005 and 2007. The development and collection of these data involved the efforts of many people. The Baylor Religion Survey project was financially supported by a generous grant from the John Templeton Foundation. The development of survey content was the result of a collaborative effort with our colleagues in the Department of Sociology at Baylor University. Finally, the Gallup Organization provided valuable feedback on the final questionnaire and ultimately collected these data.

Throughout the book we frequently use pseudonyms for those we spent time with, and these names are in quotation marks for the first mention. We do so when the person has not publicly disclosed their paranormal beliefs and/or experiences, unless they have expressly stated a willingness to be identified.

Cheryl and Colleen of the Dallas Psychic Fair were quite welcoming and willing to answer our many questions about psychic readings. The late Datus Perry of Carson, Washington, spent many hours ushering the first author through the woods looking for Bigfoot. We greatly appreciate Laura Cyr's willingness to tell us of her many supernatural and paranormal experiences. We are equally grateful that the UFO Contact Center International opened its doors to our questions and to Paul Ingram for telling us his harrowing experience with the Satanic panic of the 1990s. Duane, owner of the Big Cypress Coffee House in Jefferson, Texas, proved a charming and puckish host. Depending upon your beliefs about ghosts, the psychics Gloria and Lee and the ghost hunter Victoria may have prevented us from being attacked by angry spirits at the coffee house. We enjoyed their company and appreciated their protection in theory. The

Texas Bigfoot Research Conservancy (TBRC) was extremely patient dragging three sociologists through the woods on one of their field operations, and we greatly enjoyed getting to know David, Craig Woolheater, and the many other members of the TBRC.

Numbers can only get you so far—we did not believe we could tell a story about American paranormal beliefs without hearing from people who have experienced the paranormal for themselves. We are greatly in debt to the many people who gave us their trust and their time.

Several people read drafts of this book. We must thank Jennifer Hammer of NYU Press, author and paranormal researcher Nick Redfern, and Kim Mencken for providing valuable suggestions, edits, and comments.

Finally, engaging in such a project requires support at home. The authors would like to thank their spouses—Sara Bader, Kim Mencken, and Amy Edmonds—for their love, patience, and understanding as we spent the night in haunted houses, chased Bigfoot, and delved into UFO abductions and psychic phenomena.

1

The House of 150 Ghosts

Situated on Big Cypress Bayou in the piney woods of northeast Texas lies the city of Jefferson, a haven for ghost hunters. Before the railroads moved into the northern part of the state, Texans were dependent upon boat traffic to receive goods and supplies. Jefferson was founded in 1840 at the perfect location for a port. Boats traveled up the Mississippi River to the Red River, which fed into nearby Caddo Lake. Even large stern wheelers could paddle through the lake to its eventual meet-up with Big Cypress Bayou.

By default the town held a monopoly on shipping for hundreds of miles around. Cotton moved through by the ton. During the Civil War, the Confederacy depended upon the Jefferson port to provide Texas troops with supplies. Stores, hotels, shipping companies, and other signs of a bustling economy competed for downtown real estate with taverns, cathouses, pool halls, and other necessary vices of a nineteenth-century boomtown. Indeed, the good and the bad appeared in equal measure during Jefferson's heyday. The population swelled to nearly eight thousand by 1872. Grand homes appeared on the hills. At the same time, fights at the local bars were frequent with an especially dangerous area near the river earning the nickname "Murder Alley."

As the railroad came and reliance on river traffic eroded, so did Jefferson's fragile economy.[1] Shipping companies folded; the population dwindled over the years to about two thousand citizens; houses sat empty and the taverns closed; a bayou formerly alive with the sounds of steamboats and dock workers, became silent. It's a familiar story of the American frontier: a boomtown gone bust. Jefferson today is bucking that trend. Its cobblestone streets are lined with quaint, locally owned shops, hotels, and bed-and-breakfasts, and on weekends the town center buzzes with activity. Even midweek a surprising number of people meander around the antique stores, restaurants, and gift shops.

Jefferson's resurgence is due—at least in part—to the ghosts of its sometimes violent past. Purported to be one of the most haunted locales in Texas, nearly every major downtown building and many of the surrounding homes claim spirit manifestations. Guests at the historic Jefferson Hotel, dating to 1851, report mysterious footsteps at night, faucets that turn on and off by themselves, and the laughter of unseen children. Visitors frequently request the most haunted rooms. Nearby is the Excelsior Hotel, where the filmmaker Steven Spielberg is said to have been frightened away by a ghostly child.[2] A "Ghost Train" operates from the depot during the tourist season. "The Grove," a historic home, provides tours on Sunday mornings for those hoping to spot its several resident ghosts, which include a woman and priest in the house as well as a sinister smiling man who roams the gardens. With few exceptions, the town has accepted its ghostly reputation. The Jefferson Hotel knows that spirits are good for business and proudly promotes each new reported encounter on its Web page.[3]

Jodi Breckenridge, a local resident, is one of the biggest beneficiaries of Jefferson's ghosts. For several years she has led a nighttime, walking ghost tour. On a busy weekend sixty people (more during the Halloween season) follow the affable Jodi through the city streets and into the surrounding residential areas. Christopher joined an excited group of about thirty on a November Saturday evening. Jodi led us past a two-story brick building with an iron balcony, where she reported that previous tours had captured pictures of a Confederate soldier and had heard sounds of a little boy singing. From there we wandered past the Excelsior and Jefferson Hotels, hearing tales about the most haunted rooms. A brisk walk uphill on darkened streets brought us to another historic mansion where the figure of a ghostly lady reportedly glides about the yard. From there we meandered to The Grove and learned about the spectral priest and his friends.

Surprisingly, Jodi readily admits that she is quite afraid of ghosts. It is part of her charm, and she reports several frightening encounters during tours. She claims she watched as a brash skeptic was hit in the back of the legs by a mysterious opening door. Ghostly voices and invisible hands on her back have led her to flee buildings at various times. One place frightened Jodi more than any other—a former tavern turned coffee bar by the name of Big Cypress Coffee House. "On a scale of one to ten this place is an eleven," she told our group, as she nervously led us into the building. We were warned against using the bathrooms where people report being grabbed by unseen presences and trapped by a door that sometimes refuses to let patrons exit. Upstairs, however, is where most of the action occurs. The tour previously included a visit to the second floor, before people reported being pushed by spirits on the stairs. Others heard voices ordering them to "get out!" and Jodi once felt something pull her hair. A visiting psychic declared the building home to 150 restless, sometimes angry spirits. These days, Jodi prefers to stay downstairs near the exit as she relates these tales.

The owner of the Big Cypress Coffee House, Duane L., and his wife moved to Jefferson a few years ago and bought the dilapidated building. They planned to open a coffee house with an Internet café upstairs, but they could never find workmen to complete the necessary renovations to the second floor. Construction crews complained of being pushed, pulled, and shouted at by invisible entities and fled the building—sometimes leaving equipment behind. Sadly, Duane's wife died during these difficult times. He moved a bed into the upstairs space and ignored the voices calling out his name in the dark. He awoke one night to a ferocious growling, and could hear—but not see—a dog pacing around his bed. Understandably, Duane quickly relocated to another part of the building.

The coffee house's sinister reputation is only magnified by Duane's self-described status as a Wiccan. The public often confuses Wicca with Satanism. Satanism focuses upon the worship of Satan or the devil. Wiccans worship the Earth in a personified form, typically referred to as "Gaia." The strong philosophical differences between Wicca and Satanism seem lost in Jefferson's rumor mill. Locals say Duane is a warlock. One told us that Big Cypress is "Satan's coffee house . . . where the witches hang out." The owner of another local shop simply said "Isn't that the place owned by the warlock?" At nearly seventy and more than six feet tall, with a thin build, snow white hair, and a pointy beard, Duane certainly looks the part. Jodi fears him. "I'm scared of that guy," she told me, "I think he wants the ghosts to be here." Indeed, she wondered why someone would even occupy the notorious building. "I won't ever go back upstairs again," said Jodi, "and he *lives* here!" The implication of local gossip was clear—the place is evil and Duane likes it that way. We soon left the coffee house and concluded the "ghost walk."

The next morning I returned alone to chat with Duane and hear more about the frightening building. He confirmed that no one who came to investigate successfully stayed the night. Some ghost hunters had run from the property at the prompting of angry voices. Another guest fled upon being locked in the bathroom and grabbed by an unseen entity. Others left with mysterious scratches on their arms and legs. Duane confirmed that he was a practicing Wiccan and that he holds gatherings of "like-minded" people. At times he performs rituals to bring the ghosts forth. Nevertheless, with the exception of the "invisible dog" incident, he has been unmolested by the spirits. "We have an understanding, the ghosts and I," said Duane, "Some of them really don't like me. But I keep out of their way and they don't bother me, for the most part."

The challenge and allure of seeing the second floor simply could not be resisted. I asked Duane if I could bring a team of sociologists to spend the night in the upstairs room. He gazed at me intently, paused, and leaned across the table where we sat. "You can come if you want to," he said, scratching at his beard, "but you will leave before the night is through."

In December I returned to Jefferson with the other authors and interested colleagues. Jodi was astounded when I phoned to tell her of my plans. "You are insane!" she exclaimed. Our team traveled to Jefferson and had dinner with Duane and two psychics he invited along, and our conversation centered upon the evening to come. One of the psychics stared at me with great concern before predicting that I would have a "ghost experience" before the night was through. The other simply suggested that we "would not make it." With a roguish grin, Duane announced that he would conduct a ritual that would "call something up" for us. "I want to make sure you get your money's worth."[4]

Paranormal America

In more than two decades of studying people who claim paranormal experiences, I have had many fascinating experiences. Some have been alone, others with my co-authors. I have observed support groups for people who report abductions by alien beings and visited with therapists who claim to have recovered memories of vast, Satanic conspiracies to control the planet. We have attended psychic fairs, heard all manner of outrageous conspiracy theories, and trolled the aisles of innumerable New Age and paranormal book stores. Over the years, I have often lectured to my students and community groups about these obscure belief systems. Many learned for the first time about claims that a giant ape roams the woods of the Pacific Northwest, or that little, gray aliens pull Americans from their beds for unspeakable scientific experiments.

We have noticed an interesting trend in how Americans relate to the paranormal: they are simultaneously fascinated and repulsed, intrigued and dismissive. The paranormal has permeated our culture, and the fascination Americans have with the paranormal appears to be growing. For example, by the late 1990s it was obvious that many students had developed a familiarity with paranormal beliefs. They could draw passable representations of the "gray" aliens reported by UFO abductees; some would raise their hands to describe their own UFO sightings, warn against playing with Ouija boards,[5] or tell me of an uncle's recent Bigfoot encounter. Over time my student and community audiences have become less interested in the makeup of people claiming the experiences than with the experiences themselves. In other words, many no longer wonder *why* someone would bother searching for Sasquatch. They only want to know if I've seen one during my field research.

Americans have been fed a steady diet of fictional shows with paranormal themes such as *The X-Files, Supernatural, Medium, Ghost Whisperer,* and many others. These shows may simply seek to entertain, but they also serve to disseminate paranormal beliefs. The public hunger for the paranormal seems insatiable. A host of so-called reality shows such as *Ghost Hunters* and *Destination Truth* (SCI-FI), *Most Haunted* (Travel), *Paranormal State* (A&E), and *MonsterQuest* and *UFO Hunters* (History Channel) seek to convince viewers as to the reality of their subject matter. In 2008 and 2009 alone even more new paranormal shows debuted, including *Ghost Lab* (Discovery), *Extreme Paranormal* and *Medium P.I.* (A&E), *Celebrity Ghost Stories* and *Psychic Investigators* (Biography), and *Ghost Adventures* (Travel). Occasionally even staid news channels join the discussion, as occurred when Peter Jennings hosted an ABC News special about UFOs ("Seeing Is Believing") in February 2005. If a viewer's interest is peaked by such fare, he or she can delve into the large New Age/paranormal book sections of Barnes and Noble or Amazon.com or join one of the three million regular listeners of *Coast to Coast AM,* a paranormal radio show carried on over five hundred stations.[6] Meanwhile the Internet allows like-minded individuals an open forum to discuss the paranormal.

A significant number of Americans spends their weekends at UFO conventions hearing whispers of government cover-ups, at New Age gatherings learning the keys to enlightenment, or ambling around historic downtowns learning about resident ghosts in tourist-targeted "ghost walks." Cities have learned to capitalize on their mysteries. Rumors of the 1947 crash of a flying saucer draw tourists to Roswell, New Mexico, which holds an annual UFO festival and sports its own UFO museum. New Mexico even entered a UFO-themed float in the 2008 Tournament of Roses Parade. Willow Creek, California, proclaims itself the "Bigfoot Capital of the World" and cashes in on the hairy beast through gift shops, museums, and festivals. And Jefferson, Texas, of course, has remade itself by focusing on its reputed haunted houses. It appears that the paranormal has become another tourist stop, another source of entertainment available in that vast consumerist marketplace. As the political scientist Michael Barkun observes, "[The] kinds of ideas that used to be really out on the fringe and tucked away in a subterranean subculture are now a part of pop culture."[7]

Whether belief in the paranormal is truly on the rise is difficult to determine due to the weakness of existing poll data, as different news polls and surveys have asked about paranormal subjects in many different ways over the years. It is possible that apparent differences are merely due to variation in sampling techniques, question wording, and interpretation. What we *can* state with confidence is that the paranormal is not going away any time soon. Since the 1970s the Gallup Organization has intermittently asked Americans if they have experienced a UFO sighting (see fig. 1.1). Most recently Gallup collected data for the Baylor Religion Survey 2005, which asked respondents if they have "ever witnessed an object in the sky you could not identify." We should not read too much into the recent spike to 17 percent of respondents answering in the affirmative, as

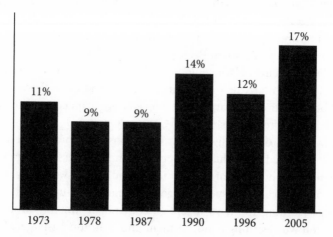

Fig. 1.1. Percentage of U.S. citizens claiming UFO experiences over time (Gallup Polls 1971–2005)

exact question wordings among these polls differ. The percentages rise and fall over time, but the trend reveals that over the last forty years at least 10 percent of Americans claim UFO sightings at any given time.

The media is attuned to the high level of interest in the paranormal. Every year during the week before Halloween the major news outlets release entertaining poll data on paranormal beliefs. For example, in late October 2007 an AP/IPSOS poll reported that 48 percent of Americans believe in ESP, and that 14 percent had seen a UFO. During that same week in 2005, a CBS News poll reported that 48 percent of Americans believe in ghosts, and that 22 percent had seen or felt a ghost. On October 26, 2007, *USA Today* referenced the Baylor Religion Survey in a story about how 33 percent of Americans believe in ghosts. Other surveys have shown that one-third of Americans believe that they can communicate with the dead.[8]

Who Are These People?

Curiously, the seeming fascination the American public has for the paranormal is tempered by negative attitudes about the people who experience it. When friends, family, co-workers, or students learn that we have been on a Bigfoot hunt or have spent the night with ghost hunters in a haunted house, the two questions they ask are: (1) Did you see a ghost/Bigfoot/UFO?, etc., followed by some variant of: (2) Who are these people anyway?

The second question is usually asked with a smirk or a giggle, but sometimes with concern. People wonder if we ever felt in danger when spending time with Bigfoot hunters in the woods or if we were afraid of UFO abductees because they might be "crazy." Such questions are asked of us because in our culture there are a number of prevailing attitudes about people who believe in or experience the paranormal. It seems that Americans want to explore the paranormal but also feel the need to reassure themselves and others that they have remained at a healthy distance from it. Are people who claim UFO sightings uneducated, rural folks who do not know the difference between a satellite and a flying saucer? Are people who study astrology or visit psychics a bunch of overprivileged, silly "New Agers" from California?[9] Paranormal believers are often perceived as a little bit "nutty," if not completely crazy. The Ohio congressman Dennis Kucinich learned as much after admitting to a UFO sighting during a 2007 presidential debate in Philadelphia, publicly reporting that a paranormal experience or belief invites scorn and concern for one's mental health.[10]

Unfortunately, existing coverage of the paranormal does not allow us to either confirm or deny such stereotypes. When the local news covers a nearby UFO sighting or haunted house, the reporters often pick the strangest people they can find to interview—because they offer the most interesting sound bites. The local anchors wink and smirk at one another after the story, before wishing their viewers a good night. Certainly such stories are interesting, but with the exception of the most cursory of demographics on occasion, we learn little to nothing about the typical paranormal believer or experiencer.

The goal of this book is to answer the simple question that has never been adequately dealt with: Who are these people anyway? Does holding an unconventional belief, such as believing in Bigfoot, mean that one is unconventional in other attitudes and behaviors? Do those who claim UFO experiences fit the popular stereotypes? Does religion provide a set of alternative beliefs that prevent experimentation with the paranormal? Or does being religious mean that one has a general supernatural orientation to the world, leading to greater paranormal belief among churchgoers? How do people who attend paranormal conferences or purchase related books differ from those who simply hold a belief? Do people who believe in paranormal things differ from those who are more selective? We have spent the last several years trying to answer these and many other questions about paranormal believers.

Chasing the Paranormal

The paranormal is frustratingly elusive. The more than sixty years of reported UFO encounters have still not produced conclusive evidence of extraterrestrials.[11] Purported films, hair samples, photos, footprint casts, and eyewitness reports have failed to convince scientists that the woods are home to a giant ape.[12] Ghosts remain as mysterious as ever, despite tales as old as the written word. Thankfully, people are the focus of our inquiry —and people are not as hard to find as ghosts or aliens. Consequently, we undertook two related investigations: survey research and field research.

First, we conducted two national random surveys of the American public in 2005 and 2007, called the Baylor Religion Survey (BRS).[13] These are mixed-mode (combination telephone and mail surveys) national random samples collected by the Gallup Organization. The BRS contains the most thorough battery of questions concerning the paranormal ever administered to a national sample of Americans.

Past research on the paranormal is informative, but such efforts are hampered by geography,[14] generalizability issues[15] or a lack of recent data.[16] Our survey asked respondents if they believe in the reality of things such as psychic phenomena, astrology, strange creatures, UFOs, haunted houses, fortune-telling, prophetic dreams, and the ability to talk to the dead. We also asked people if they have ever read a book on the paranormal, visited a Web site or a New Age bookstore, or otherwise researched a host of topics ranging from "UFO sightings, abductions, or conspiracies," to "the prophecies of Nostradamus." Further, we determined the extent to which Americans actually experience the paranormal by finding out if respondents consulted their horoscopes, called a psychic hotline, met in person with a psychic or palm reader, visited or lived in a home they believe to be haunted, used a Ouija board, or witnessed a UFO.

With a few exceptions, the phenomena we have discussed so far are reported outside of established religions. As of yet we do not have a church of Bigfoot. Scientology notwithstanding, churches developed around UFO tales and psychic phenomena are relatively rare.[17] However, Americans do claim experiences with unexplained supernatural forces inside established religious settings as well. Some Americans claim to have been granted access to a special language from God that allows a more direct line of communication with the Almighty, a phenomenon known as "speaking in tongues," or "glossolalia." Others report guardian angels saving them from harm, experiencing a miraculous physical healing, or even hearing the voice of God speaking to them. Previous studies have been unable to resolve how such experiences are related to the "paranormal." In order to examine this connection, we also asked our sample many general questions about religion, including an extensive series regarding religious beliefs and experiences. All told, our respondents answered dozens of questions that gave us a deep understanding of their encounters and beliefs about the world beyond, along with more than four hundred questions about other religious, moral, and political topics. With data from over three thousand Americans in two waves of the BRS, we can extensively examine the different views of the paranormal as well as the social, moral, religious, political, and cultural differences that accompany these beliefs.

Second, it is far too easy as academics to remain behind our desks and draw conclusions solely based on statistics and survey research. Paranormal experiences are highly personal, and often vague and abstract in nature. We therefore felt it necessary to supplement our national survey data with field research, and throughout this book we relay these experiences.

We return to the Big Cypress Coffee House, where one of the psychics collapsed to the ground, overpowered by the "presence of evil" in the room. We join the Texas Bigfoot Research Conservancy on a bitterly cold evening deep in the woods of east Texas as they search for the elusive Sasquatch. Purported Bigfoot screams echo through the woods as the TBRC attempts to lure in the creature with their call blaster, and the authors huddle in the bushes wondering if they made a wise choice. We observe a support group for people who claim to have been abducted by aliens. Psychics warn us of future peril, palm readings trace our life lines, and astrologers read our stars. We also explore extraordinary events that happen in church settings, such as speaking in tongues.

By combining information from our national surveys with extensive fieldwork, we hope to provide balanced and in-depth information from which to speak confidently about the paranormal in American culture.

Our Perspective on the Paranormal

Everybody has an angle. This is one of the primary reasons why experts in various fields may interpret the same occurrence in vastly different ways. For instance, in the case of a shooting in a public area, a psychologist, a ballistics expert, a criminologist, a bystander, a victim, and an offender could all offer knowledge of the event—but each from a different vantage point. The ballistics expert will provide a detailed report on the direction from which bullets were fired based on the victim's wounds and damage to the landscape. The psychologist will report on the trauma of the victim after the event and perhaps the inner turmoil that spawned the gunman's actions. The criminologist will report on trends in gun violence and how these reflect changes in neighborhood composition, policing strategies, and poverty rates. The offender may apologize for, attempt to excuse, or even deny his actions, while the bystanders will provide differing accounts depending upon their proximity to the events (and perhaps their relationships to the victim or offender). With the exception of flagrant lies one may tell, none of these "experts" is incorrect. They simply have different concerns and different areas of expertise, so their accounts of the same event differ.

In a similar vein, it is important that readers understand our perspective on the paranormal. Most books about Bigfoot, psychic phenomena, and other paranormal topics are focused upon presenting evidence for (and in rarer cases against) the reality of the phenomena in question. Bigfoot books often analyze the famous Patterson-Gimlin film (see chap. 5), catalog sightings or present the result of forensic tests of purported hair samples. UFO books recount sightings from pilots, police officers, and other figures believed to be credible witnesses.

To us the question of the factual, objective existence of paranormal phenomena is irrelevant to the purposes of studying belief in the paranormal. An analogy can be drawn between the sociological study of the paranormal and the social scientific view of religion. When studying religion, it is relevant to ask how religious beliefs affect the lives of believers. Do these beliefs affect other attitudes and motivate specific patterns of action? What types of groups organize around specific beliefs, and how do these groups operate? How are beliefs maintained and reinforced? The literature in the sociology of religion is replete with studies addressing such questions. The question of the validity of religious beliefs is, however, a matter that simply cannot be addressed with social scientific methods.[18] No survey we administer or interview we conduct will prove God's existence or nonexistence. No amount of fieldwork will grant us a picture of heaven. We can only address the effects that believing in God and heaven have upon *believers*. We use this same approach with regard to the paranormal.

This is not a book about evidence for or against the paranormal. We are not ghost hunters, Bigfoot experts, parapsychologists, or UFO field investigators. We are sociologists. Our research perspective guides our fieldwork in a number of ways. It means we are not seeking evidence for or against the existence of the paranormal. Thus even though we participate in activities surrounding the paranormal, our primary interest is in the believers, how their beliefs are perceived by others, and how these beliefs influence the lives of those holding them. During our Bigfoot hunt, the TBRC found a strange imprint in a creek bed, which they believed to be the track of a Bigfoot. We are not animal track experts and cannot assess whether the track is evidence of an undiscovered ape. Rather, we monitored how members reacted to the find and what it meant to them. We remain outside of debates regarding the existence of the paranormal, and we recognize that regardless of what exists "out there" in the world, paranormal beliefs show remarkable staying power. It is the formation and maintenance of such beliefs and their consequences that concern us as social scientists.

The Plan of the Book

This book attempts to answer the general question of who believes in and experiences the paranormal? To address such broad questions, we examine the paranormal from many different directions and from several different angles. Specifically we will assess survey data, draw on fieldwork observing and talking to participants in various aspects of the paranormal, and examine the narratives told within various paranormal subcultures. Groups of people cannot be properly understood on a cultural level without examining the stories they tell.

People use an astounding array of terms to refer to beliefs about UFOs, astrology, psychic phenomena, ghosts, and the like. Some people refer to such beliefs as "New Age." Others prefer the term we frequently fall back on, paranormal, or one of many others such as "occult," "mysticism," or "the supernatural." In chapter 2 we tackle the difficult issue of defining the paranormal. We visit a psychic fair in Dallas, Texas, where one can sample a wide array of the "products" of the paranormal in one easy shopping experience. By noting what is *not* present at the psychic fair, we can better differentiate between religion and the paranormal.

We also find that there are two distinct types of beliefs that fall under the broader rubric of the paranormal. First, there are beliefs and experiences focused on *enlightenment*: personal, internal, spiritual growth. The clients of psychics, intuitives, fortune-tellers, astrologers, and the like seek to become better people either by learning something about the future, understanding the past, or perhaps by gaining supernatural insight into the present. Such people are often unconcerned with unequivocally proving the "reality" of their experience; so long as something works for them they are happy.

Second, others become involved in the paranormal as a form of *discovery*; they hope to find compelling evidence for the existence of a phenomena not currently recognized by institutional science. In recent years the media has latched on to this form of paranormal interest (witness the spate of television reality shows); ghost-hunting clubs, UFO spotting groups, and Bigfoot research organizations have sprung up around the country to fulfill the desire for paranormal discovery. Some people state that they have already had a personal experience with Bigfoot or a UFO, and they seek concrete proof of its existence to prove to others that what they saw was real. Others dream of having their first experience with a giant, undiscovered ape by joining an expedition. Thus some seek discoveries because they hope to prove a new reality to science, while others are just out for an adventure.

The importance of direct experience was emphasized by Duane, the warlock and owner of the Big Cypress Coffee House. "You will never be the same once the ghosts touch you," Duane told us at dinner on the evening of our stay. Once we were scratched, pushed, prodded, or spoken to by the ghosts, our lives would be changed, echoed the psychics present. We could have no more doubts, no more comfortable skepticism. In chapter 2 we return to the Big Cypress and find out what happened when we spent the evening there. A key benefit of field research is its ability to reveal important features of an event that statistical techniques simply cannot capture, while providing access to situational and interactive factors of events as they occur. In this house of 150 ghosts we learned the importance of interpretation in a paranormal experience. According to the psychics present, we were under continual assault by spirits as the evening progressed. What we saw was quite enlightening.

Armed with a basic understanding of American paranormal beliefs, we move to examining the characteristics of believers. In chapter 3 we address the common stereotypes about people who believe in the paranormal or have related experiences. Unfortunately, information about the people who believe or who claim to have experienced the paranormal rarely goes beyond the anecdotal. To aid in our understanding of the paranormal we explore one example in depth, that of beliefs about UFOs in the United States and how they have evolved over time into tales of UFO abduction. Christopher spent several years observing the activities of a support group for people who believe they have been abducted by evil alien beings and subjected to medical experiments onboard flying saucers. Are UFO abductees just sick? Are they strange, marginalized people who have nothing left to lose in claiming a bizarre experience or ascribing to a weird belief system?

In chapter 4 we explore the connection between supernatural beliefs available in organized religion and those of the paranormal. Sociologists have long speculated upon the importance of the paranormal to mainstream religion in the United States.[19] The commonly used term "New Age" suggests a change in the way people practice religion, and scholars have attempted to document an increasing shift from mainstream to unconventional forms of religious belief.[20] The true significance of the paranormal may depend upon who believes in those topics. If paranormal beliefs, and the consumption of its materials and services, are primarily confined to those already outside of the religious mainstream, then its effects upon dominant religious traditions may be minimal. However, if, as part of a general cultural trend, members of all American religious groups are increasingly drawn to paranormal beliefs, goods, and services, then the movement may gradually draw people away from the mainstream. If the appeal of such "outside" materials depends upon the type of religious group in question,[21] then only certain religious groups or traditions may see more of their members gravitate toward astrologers, psychics, and seers.

The paranormal consists of a set of ideas and experiences, which have not yet been adopted, at least wholly, by the dominant religions in a given society. They lack the stability and organization that characterize successful religious groups. They lie on the periphery of American religion, spreading through conferences, the media, and the Internet rather than through sermons. And yet the paranormal comprises a pool of concepts from which new religions can draw a set of ideas that may prove to be the content of future religions.

At times a new form of religion has sprouted from this pool, as in the 1950s when several self-styled prophets built new religions around claims that they could channel extraterrestrials.[22] A short-order cook and self-labeled philosopher by the name of George Adamski was one of the first to report contact with extraterrestrial beings. On November 20, 1952, Adamski claimed an extended meeting with a "man from space" near Desert Center, California. The humanoid alien indicated that he was part of a friendly landing party from Venus that had come to Earth to teach humans to be more peaceful.[23] Adamski's tales, outlined in a series of popular books with titles such as *Inside the Spaceships* and *Flying Saucers Farewell*, combined UFO tales with Christian themes. The Venusians, for example, told Adamski that Jesus was also Venusian. Other hopeful prophets soon followed suit. The Englishman George King built a new religion, the Aetherius Society, around his claim of having met Jesus aboard a flying saucer. Ruth and Ernest Norman went a step farther, claiming to be advanced space beings themselves and the reincarnations of key religious figures of Earth history, such as Mary Magdalene and Confucius. So many people were claiming to be in friendly communication with aliens during the 1950s and 1960s that they were given their own specific name —UFO contactees.

But can a religious movement succeed by combining paranormal ideas with concepts from conventional religion? There are reasons for skepticism. Many paranormal beliefs are in conflict with the teachings of established churches, forcing one to choose between the two spheres.[24] There is, indeed, a rhetoric of "spiritual warfare" that pervades certain strands of Christianity. Some religious figures such as Billy Graham have seen the paranormal as Satan's work:

> The [paranormal] is, in fact, another storm warning indicating man's search for "transcendence" without regard for righteousness. Whether it's Dianetics, est, Unity, Gaea, Transcendental Meditation, Taoism, ufology, crystalology, goddess worship, reincarnation, harmonics, numerology, astrology, holistic healing, positive thinking, or any of a hundred "conscious raising" techniques of our day, the modern age is on a search for some mystical "divine unity."[25]

On the other hand, it is possible that holding any supernatural belief will make one more likely to hold another, no matter what its origin. As mentioned, we cannot "prove" or "disprove" the existence of God. The same is true of UFOs, and in a certain sense neither is more plausible than the other. Each requires faith and the willingness to suspend disbelief, and perhaps acceptance of one opens a person up to the other.[26] For example, is the Virgin Mary a "small step" from Sasquatch? Using our surveys and building upon previous research,[27] we determine which religious traditions and groups in the United States are the most and the least receptive to paranormal ideas. A careful, nuanced approach is necessary to understand the relationship between conventional religious and paranormal beliefs. Specifically, there may be different connections between these spheres depending on the type of beliefs (both religious and paranormal) in question.[28] Who expresses greater belief in the paranormal, Jehovah's Witnesses or Unitarians? Who is most hostile to ideas outside of the Christian mainstream, Southern Baptists or Episcopalians? Do people who frequently attend church also see UFOs? Does having a literal view of the Bible preclude one from believing in Atlantis, and ghosts, or does this view make one more likely to believe in such things? This chapter provides a detailed analysis of how conventional Christian beliefs interact with the paranormal.

In chapter 5 we begin to delve into people deeply interested in the various mysteries of the paranormal. For most people the paranormal is a relatively small part of life—stories come up at family gatherings and parties as conversation starters or as sources of amusement. A person might watch the occasional episode of *Ghost Hunters,* go out to see the latest UFO invasion movie, or perhaps recall fondly an aunt who claims prophetic dreams. For others a paranormal topic (if not the paranormal in general) becomes an intense interest, a hobby, and for some even an obsession. Here we examine the world of people who devote themselves to the "quest."

The authors have engaged in extensive fieldwork observing the Texas Bigfoot Research Conservancy, a nonprofit organization dedicated to finding the elusive primate. Unlike the popular image of Bigfoot hunters, many members of the TBRC are highly educated people in professional fields. We joined a business professional and a doctor for a weekend excursion to search for Sasquatch in the woods of southeast Texas. Despite their enthusiasm for the subject, members of the TBRC manage their Bigfoot beliefs carefully. "Steven," the doctor, is very cautious about revealing his activities to certain people. We asked if his colleagues knew what he did on the occasional weekend. He was emphatic that they not find out, as it could potentially cause some serious problems for him in the workplace. Such instances speak to the fact that while prevalent in popular culture, paranormal beliefs still hold a place as stigmatized views for many Americans. Are people who research the paranormal, purchase its goods and services, or enter the field in the hunt for Bigfoot or ghosts really that "different" from the rest of us?

In chapter 6 we address the issue of involvement in the paranormal from a different perspective. There is considerable speculation within the Bigfoot community, on message boards, blogs, and in books that connects Bigfoot to other paranormal mysteries. There are stories of Bigfoot creatures emerging from landed flying saucers. Some speculate that the outstanding elusiveness of the creature may be due to its ability to jump between dimensions, or perhaps it has psychic powers that it can use to confuse its pursuers. The paranormal author Nick Redfern claims that Bigfoot, the Loch Ness Monster, Mothman, and other mysterious creatures are demonic entities that manifest in particular forms to frighten people and leech their emotional energy.[29] And we talked with the late paranormal enthusiast Jon-Erik Beckjord, who held that creatures such as Bigfoot were interdimensional entities.

Such claims are infuriating to members of the Texas Bigfoot Research Conservancy. Most members we spoke to were singular in their interest: they care about Bigfoot and Bigfoot only. To them the existence of Sasquatch is a realistic proposition. It is merely an undiscovered ape. Indeed, the TBRC's entire approach and protocol is based upon this understanding. They place camera traps near rivers, natural pathways, and other animal "highways," hoping to catch a clear photo of the beast as it goes about its daily business. They play primate sounds in the woods because other monkeys and apes are known to respond to such calls. They leave pheromone chips high in trees to entice the creature to investigate the presence of a possible mate because this works for bears.

One member, David, did not hesitate to call things like UFOs, ghosts, and other psychic phenomena "stupid" flights of fancy. He stated that every time someone makes the Bigfoot subject look "kooky" by connecting it to UFOs or other strange things, their work becomes that much harder. Scientists will refuse to listen to them if they think the TBRC is just a bunch of nuts. Besides, why place camera traps if Bigfoot can elude such cameras with its psychic abilities? Why would an alien care about pheromone chips? And how will they ever bring a specimen to the doors of the Smithsonian if it can slip into another dimension at will?

In our travels and research we have encountered many who are the exact opposite of David and the TBRC, people who are interested in exploring the paranormal in all of its varied forms. Laura, who claims to have frequented an alien mothership hovering above Earth (see chap. 4) is one such person. She is a UFO contactee and abductee who has been on the craft numerous times. But that is not all she is. She also considers herself a Buddhist and occasionally attends a Roman Catholic Mass. She likes to read about Bigfoot and talk to witnesses, believes she may have had past lives, and routinely visits a Native American shaman. Laura is as experimental and diverse with her beliefs as David is singular and focused. People such as Laura are truly treating religion and the paranormal as a great spiritual cafeteria, piling onto their trays any and all beliefs that appeal to them.[30]

Robert Short, a UFO contactee and founder of the alien-based Blue Rose Ministry, claims to be able to "channel" messages from extraterrestrials. When he wishes to receive a communiqué, he sits in a chair, relaxes his body, and "opens himself up." Before long, his head rocks back and forth, his shoulders tense, and a deep voice emerges from his body, punctuated by occasional, bizarre noises. Short's experience is strikingly similar to a phenomenon that occurs in some Pentecostal Christian churches. Visit any particular Pentecostal church on Sunday, and one will witness members writhe, twist, and ultimately begin speaking in strange tongues, whispers, squeals, and noises. They are not channeling messages from

Venus. Speaking in tongues for these practitioners is a sign of deep devotion, and those who engage in "glossolalia" believe that God has gifted them with a special language, a direct line of communication with the Almighty. The difference lies in *where* those who have these experiences attribute the source—and how others view the validity of this source.

Chapter 7 explores this contested ground between religion and the paranormal; those beliefs and experiences that are closely connected to Christian beliefs yet not fully accepted in many Christian settings. In addition to including a thorough set of questions on the paranormal, our surveys asked Americans of all types if they have ever spoken in tongues, witnessed or experienced a healing they believe to be miraculous, heard the voice of God speaking to them, or had religious visions. Additionally, we asked extensive questions about perceptions of supernatural religious evil. Chapter 7 provides an entrée into this "normal" version of the paranormal—those supernatural experiences that are associated with the dominant religious traditions in American culture. We find out how many of these surveyed Americans claim such experiences, what they are like, and whether people speak in tongues *and* report UFO sightings.

First we explore Christian beliefs about evil. Who believes in Satan and demons? Who believes that humans can be possessed by the devil? Who fears an upcoming Armageddon? Sometimes such beliefs about evil coalesce into widespread panics as occurred in the 1980s when the FBI began to receive reports from therapists across the country that their patients had "recovered" memories of hideous abuse perpetrated by secretive, underground Satanic cults.[31] The victims claimed to have witnessed animal and human sacrifices. Some reportedly were forced to kill their own children after being impregnated by cult members, and victims often alleged that high-ranking members of society, such as doctors, lawyers, and judges were cult members. Around the same time, reports surfaced of Satanic cults using daycare centers as a source for children to abuse in their rituals.[32] A chorus of sociologists, psychologists, and some critical journalists exposed the claims as the latest outbreak of Satanic panic.[33] They noted the suggestive techniques used by therapists and a complete lack of physical evidence.[34] But before the hysteria died down, several accused Satanists were forced to endure long and costly trials to defend themselves. Obviously one did not have to believe in the reality of Satanic conspiracies to be impacted by them. Similar Satanic panics have emerged at periodic intervals in U.S. history, and in each case many innocent people have been significantly affected before the panics eventually died down.[35] Chapter 7 profiles a man who was, himself, accused of being the ringleader of a secretive, underground Satanic cult.

Emerging from the darkness of Satanism tales, we then explore religious experiences. We learn in here that Pentecostals are among the least accepting of paranormal beliefs and experiences, and yet they are the most likely to claim other supernatural experiences—healings, glossolalia, and so forth—that outsiders would consider equally strange.

In the course of exploring the paranormal in the United States, we cover who believes in the paranormal, who has paranormal experiences, how the paranormal relates to mainstream religion, how paranormal beliefs vary by status subgroups, and the impact that such beliefs have upon society. Chapter 8 attempts to answer the question: What will happen to paranormal beliefs and experiences in the future? Our statistical data provides us with a key tool in this regard; we know who currently believes in the paranormal. Consequently, by analyzing data on which societal groups are growing and receding, and which religious groups are facing growth or decline, we can predict which paranormal beliefs may experience the greatest increases in popularity in coming decades.

Our journey begins in the realm of all things psychic.

2

The Truth Is Within

Sometimes it is easier to recognize a phenomenon than it is to define it. So it is with the loose association of beliefs, ideas, phenomena, and experiences variously labeled "new age," "paranormal," "the supernatural," "occult," "unexplained phenomena," "metaphysics," "pseudoscience," "mysticism," and a host of other terms. Depending upon one's personal definition, crystal balls, Bigfoot, ghosts, and palm reading are similar things; by other definitions they are vastly different. Adding to the confusion, researchers and retailers often label the same phenomena using different terms than do the general public. For example, scholars of religion often use the term "New Age" to refer to a social movement that started in the 1960s, which focused on the development of personal enlightenment and freedom from conventional thinking and religion.[1] To bookstores, New Age is simply a section in which employees shelve books on ghosts, the Loch Ness Monster, UFOs, psychic powers, Atlantis, and books about a host of other beliefs or experiences.

We do not wish to add to such confusion here by coming up with new terminologies, but we hesitate to use a term such as "New Age." First of all, the term refers to a specific movement that emerged at a particular time. Further, it suggests that our phenomenon of interest is something "new." This is far from the case.

Consider the following tales:

Seattle, Washington

Sara and her husband moved into a rental house near the University of Washington, sharing with an old friend, Jason, to save money. Sara fell in love with a room on the main floor; Jason happily took one of two rooms on the upper floor. About a month after they moved in, strange things started to happen. Sara was the first to get up in the mornings. Oftentimes while getting ready for work, she would hear the unmistakable sounds of someone walking down the stairs. The footsteps ceased at the landing, but no one was ever there. Sara learned to ignore the sounds, becoming flustered only when her two cats would on occasion stare and hiss at the stairs. She even put up with the lights in her bedroom, which sometimes switched on and off by themselves. The experiences were irritating but never felt menacing.

Jason was not so lucky. He worked a swing shift at a warehouse pulling orders for grocery stores. One evening he arrived home at around 11 p.m. and went up to bed. He had just turned off his light when he felt a weight at the end of the bed. In the darkness a hazy form slowly took shape near his feet. What looked like an old man with a hunched back was facing away from Jason, its head in its hands, seemingly distressed. As if it could feel Jason's eyes upon its back, the "man" turned and looked directly at him. Jason shrieked upon seeing the wrinkled, balding visage with completely black eyes, and he flipped on the light. The spirit faded away, but an impression remained for several minutes where it had been sitting on the bed. Jason slept with a light on after that.

Charleston, South Carolina

Before moving its location in 2007, the Orange Grove Elementary school in Charleston, South Carolina, was surrounded by woods that backed up to the Ashley River. John and his brothers attended Orange Grove as children. After school they would often enter the woods to play (sometimes even sneaking into the periphery during recess). Near the center of the wooded area in a small clearing was an old cemetery with weathered headstones from a prominent Charleston family dating back to the 1600s. The local kids told tales of specters and spooks that walked among the graves, and they dared one another to enter the cemetery. Later, developers purchased the land and immediately made plans for a new subdivision. The graves were dug up, and the coffins were moved to another graveyard nearby. In the process, however, many of the old grave markers were broken, and the careless workers simply threw them into a pile. One day John and his brothers found the pile. He grabbed a broken tombstone and brought it home, thrilled to have a gruesome souvenir to use as a doorstop for his room.

From the day he brought the headstone home John was uncomfortable. He felt someone was watching him and sometimes heard a whispering voice that was too faint to make out. Worst of all, he felt something following him. Shuffling footsteps and a prickling sensation in his back constantly had him looking over his shoulder. Every once in a while, if he turned fast enough, he thought he spied an extra shadow. After months of escalating fear, John finally revealed the broken tombstone to his mother.

She was horrified and told John to return it to where it was found. John cajoled his two brothers to help him, and they hesitantly walked the ghostly door stopper to the edge of the new development. The other broken headstones lay in a heap next to a partially completed home. John felt a presence over his shoulder as he carefully placed the stone on top of the pile. The "followings," as John called them, immediately stopped.

Auxerre, France

Germanus and a few of his friends decided to have a little adventure, traveling the region around his town on foot so he could get to know the landscape and people better. Perhaps unwisely, they chose to begin their travels in the dead of winter and found themselves in a rural area with no place to stay one bitterly cold evening. Running out of options, they entered a dilapidated building on the side of the road, which locals believed to be haunted. The building's fearsome reputation did not bother Germanus, and he quickly drifted off to sleep. One of his fellow travelers was reading when he shouted an alarm. A specter was slowly rising up through the floor, and at the same time the walls were pelted by a shower of pebbles. The assailant was nowhere in sight. The alarmed traveler begged Germanus to protect him from the ghost. A deeply religious man, Germanus invoked the name of Jesus and commanded the spirit to provide its name and purpose. It told Germanus that he and a friend had been chained together and killed as punishment for some unrevealed crime, their bodies denied proper burial. The next day the men dug at a spot identified by the spirit and found two bodies tied together with chains. Germanus arranged for a proper burial, and the haunting ceased.

More than likely the reader has heard stories like these before. Most people have a ghost story, if not more than one: an aunt, uncle, parent, grandparent, or other relative who claims a ghost sighting as a child, or a best friend who insists his home was haunted. Some of us have seen a ghost ourselves. As testament to the ubiquity of such tales, the first two stories above are from the authors of this book. The Seattle ghost story is from 1990, when Christopher Bader and his wife, Sara, shared a home with their friend Jason near the University of Washington. It was Carson Mencken's brother who absconded with a broken tombstone from the old Charleston cemetery in 1975.[2]

Although ghosts have been reported for three thousand years, the basic elements of such stories often remain the same, seemingly reflecting time-less human concerns.[3] The belief that a ghost may result from a violent death or improper burial, or that the ghost of a relative might appear to warn of impending danger were favorites of medieval times and are still with us today. Indeed, the tale of Germanus occurred in 488 CE and the Germanus in question was bishop of Auxerre at the time and is now a Roman Catholic saint. His traveling companions consisted of clerics under his command.[4] Barring such details (and the anachronistic name Germanus), this story could easily pass for one that would be breathlessly reported on the latest television installment of *Paranormal State* or *Ghost Hunters*.[5] Ghosts are anything but new, nor is astrology nor the belief in psychic phenomena, or even belief in the possibility of apelike beings living in the woods. Many beliefs stubbornly persist on the edges of mainstream culture, believed in by many but never fully accepted. These often violate our taken-for-granted understanding of the "nuts and bolts" working of the world and mundane experience. They are not normal, but *paranormal*.

But what is the paranormal? Despite our jest about bookstores earlier, the analogy works well here.[6] If a prospective book buyer wants to read about a phenomenon that is at least partially understood and recognized by science, she should visit its respective section of the bookstore. The "health and medicine" section will have books on heart health, chemo-therapy, and other topics "owned" by modern medicine. For information on investing, taxes, market conditions or retirement, one must wander to the economics or "business" shelves.

But if our shopper wants to read about a topic not currently recognized by scientists, she must hunt the fiction aisles for horror, fantasy, or science fiction, or browse the bookstore's New Age and religion stacks. If the topic of interest is the resurrection of Jesus, healing through prayer, being "saved," or another concept closely associated with Christianity or another world religion, the religion stacks are the best bet. Those scientifically dubious topics that are not tightly connected to mainstream religion, such as crystal balls, ghosts, and UFOs fill the New Age shelves.[7] Here one would also find books that might belong in another section, were they to one day become accepted by science.[8] Books on the healing power of crystals are consigned to the New Age section, waiting for a scientific discovery to facilitate a call-up to the legitimacy big leagues in the medicine section. Volumes that promote the power of positive thinking in acquiring fame and fortune sit here also, rather than in the business stacks.

Following what bookstore owners already know, we group together a wide assortment of beliefs and experiences under a single banner labeled "paranormal." Such beliefs and experiences are dually rejected—not accepted by science *and* not typically associated with mainstream religion in the United States.[9] Thus, the belief that a crystal ball can foretell the future would be paranormal in nature, as would be the belief that an unidentified ape roams the Northwest woods.[10] Both of these beliefs refer to unexplained phenomena and neither is associated with mainstream religion in the United States.[11] Belief that Jesus Christ was resurrected from the dead would not qualify as part of the paranormal per this definition, since Jesus is associated with the majority religion in the United States —Christianity. The distinction is important, but we do not make it for theological reasons. Previous research and theory by sociologists and our own findings indicate that believers *themselves* make this distinction. Different types of people are interested in mainstream versus nonmainstream beliefs. A certain type of person tends to be attracted to paranormal beliefs and experiences. This is not the same type of person, in general, that tends to be attracted to more mainstream religious beliefs. We realize that some people may combine the two elements, but overall the distinction remains relevant.

Paranormal phenomena	Beliefs, practices, and experiences that are not recognized by science and not associated with mainstream religion.
	Examples: *Extrasensory perception, ghosts, and spirit phenomena, astrology, crystal therapy, belief that extraterrestrials have visited earth, Bigfoot*
Religious phenomena	Beliefs, practices, and experiences that are not recognized by science but associated with mainstream religion.
	Examples: *Belief in the divinity of Jesus, belief in the power of prayer, faith healing, Satan, and demons*

Fig. 2.1. Definitions of paranormal and religious phenomena

Unfortunately, definitions are never perfect, and the paranormal rests on ever-shifting sands. Does a book on aromatherapy belong in the "self help" section or is it part of the paranormal? It depends on whom you ask. Does a book about visions of the Virgin Mary end up in the paranormal section or religion section? It often depends upon who published it or the perspective taken toward the topic. A book from a Christian publisher that uses the Marian visions at Lourdes as a testimonial will be filed with the religion books. An author who discusses visions of the Virgin Mary as another manifestation of the same phenomena that produces faeries and ghosts, or that de-emphasizes the Christian aspects of the Marian visions, may find his book filed under the paranormal.[12] On a recent visit to a local bookstore, the authors found books about angels in *both* the religion and paranormal sections.

We must also be clear that labeling of a belief, practice, or experience as "paranormal" is not meant here as judgmental or pejorative. It is possible that Extra-Sensory Perception (ESP) is a legitimate phenomenon that science is simply too stubborn to recognize. It is also possible that the many dedicated Bigfoot hunters will one day capture the beast, moving Bigfoot from paranormal status to nature status in one fell swoop. But until and unless such things occur, Bigfoot and ESP inhabit the fringes. To express belief in such phenomena in certain circles may prompt scorn or concern about one's mental health.

We took a tentative step into the world of the paranormal on a wintery Sunday afternoon, hoping to better understand the appeal of its dizzying array of beliefs and practices.

Dallas, Texas

Cheryl, a friendly, soft-spoken woman in her early forties moved from San Diego to Dallas in 1990. A self-described "intuitive," she was frustrated to find limited opportunities to pursue her interests.[13] In early 2008 Cheryl and her sister, Colleen, purchased the aging Dallas Psychic Fair with the hopes of providing a resource for "like-minded people seeking to understand greater truths."[14] The fair currently meets on the first Sunday of each month in a breakout room of a Holiday Inn in north Dallas. The sisters believe that with the year 2012 approaching, people will become more and more open and accepting of psychic phenomena.[15] Indeed, they have ambitious plans:

Our immediate plans . . . include expanding the manner in which we support the community in their spiritual growth by securing a permanent location to operate all month long and maintaining the Fair as a once a month "showcase" of individuals and the services they offer. The permanent location would include offices for lease to our Readers, Wellness Practitioners and even others who offer like-minded services. We plan to offer classes, workshops and seminars as well. The space would also be able to host larger special events—book signings, national guest speakers, etc. The vision we currently hold is in response to the demand we recognize is currently unmet in our community . . . support of individual's interest in expansion of conscious awareness which will lead to a stronger community.

We traveled to the Holiday Inn and arrived a bit after noon. A short chat with Cheryl and a five-dollar admission fee later, we were browsing the amazingly diverse selection of beliefs, products, vendors, and practitioners that comprise the paranormal.

Ringing the edge of the large conference room were tables lined with colorful wares. An older woman displayed ceramic statues of doors. Each about six inches high, some of the statues looked as if they might be doors to a castle or medieval keep. Others seemed to be the rounded doors of a hobbit's home. Less fantastical statues seemed to be doors to a standard suburban home. "They represent doorways to different states of being," she told us. Next to her sat "the Pixie Chicks," who specialize in small, plush dolls of faeries, pixies, and elves bedecked in sequins and ribbons. Four different vendors, "Rock n Jewels," "Crystal Quartz Depot," "Power of the Rainbow," and "Stone Maven," competed for the crystal and jewelry market. Each sold an assortment of gems, minerals, spices, stones, and jewelry, some labeled as having health or healing benefits. For example, amethyst purportedly strengthens psychic abilities and increases dream recall; geodes help with mathematics and aid in "astral travel."[16] Kunzite dispenses negative energy and promotes positive thinking and well-being. Appropriately the New Age and paranormal sections of most bookstores carry catalogs of the magical powers of various gems and stones.[17]

Next to a booth of candles, flowers, and incense, we watched a Reiki practitioner tend to a female client. Lying facedown on a massage table, with a blanket draped over her, the client rested peacefully as the masseuse alternated between touching her shoulders and back, and gesturing in the air above her. A chiropractor had set up shop at a nearby table, but a disturbing banner of a curved spine and a stack of business cards were its sole occupants. More lively was a table displaying an astounding variety of tarot card decks for sale. The nearby bookseller offered *Wicca for Dummies* and a host of other manuals and self-help books related to paranormal practices.

To this point, we had simply circled the booths, fascinated but wary. It was time to dip our toes into the paranormal. In a corner next to the book exhibit, Daniel Weatherbee calmly watched the crowd.[18] A Vietnam veteran in his early sixties, Weatherbee sported a black baseball hat partially hiding even blacker hair. Sunglasses masked his eyes.

According to some New Agers, the human body is surrounded by an invisible "aura" of energy. This aura takes on different colors depending upon one's mood and state of well-being. Some believe that the aura has a stable base color. Some people have green auras, others blue, black, red, orange, and so on. This stable color will provide insight into a person's general personality and outlook, while changes within the spectrum will reflect current concerns.

For twenty-five dollars Daniel offered to photograph one's aura using a special camera and analyzed the resulting image.[19] Corporations frequently hire him, he told us, to take aural photographs during company parties. I handed over the fee and sat on a stool in front of a boxy camera resting on a tripod. He instructed me to smile and stare at a sticker of Tweetybird affixed near the top of the camera. The resultant picture showed my face swimming in a sea of orange.

Noting that most of the sample photographs posted in his booth displayed a rainbow of colors, I expressed concern about the singular color of my photo. Thankfully, orange was not indicative of severe physical or emotional problems. Orange was "Sexual, Creative, Cheerful, Flowing," according to a handout on Weatherbee's table. There were no "bad" colors in the bunch. White was described as "Purity, Innocence, Faith, Peace," black as "Mysterious, Protecting, Absorbing, Seductive." The overwhelmingly orange color of my photo, Daniel noted, was simply indicative of the strength of my "orange nature." When pressed for greater detail, Weatherbee pulled another flyer from his briefcase that gave a longer summary of life with an orange aura:

ORANGE: This is the color of warmth-energy with mental direction; creativity and emotions—courage, joy and pride-reflects an opening of new awareness—can sometimes indicate emotional imbalances, agitation, worry, and vanity. In healing it stimulates optimism, hope, and is good for exhaustion and weakness. Orange is activity generating. You are alive, artistic, perceptive and creative. Constructive self-expression is important to you. People see you as happy and willing to work. You like to get out and have fun.

Browsing these more detailed descriptions of each color we found that most were entirely positive. Red, pink, yellow/gold, blue/indigo, purple/violet, and white provide the benefits of good circulation, warmth, love, comfort, joy, and a host of other upsides, with no apparent downsides. Other colors, including orange, mixed the positive with concerns. Green reflects success, growth, teaching, and endurance but may also indicate jealousy and mistrust, self-doubt and possessiveness. Gray reflects an "awakening of energies," and an unfortunate tendency toward secretiveness.[20]

Weatherbee concluded the reading by noting two variations in my aura. A halo above my head suggested "strong spiritual protection." Meanwhile an "orb of energy" he saw in the black area near the bottom of the photograph revealed the presence of a protective spirit.

A Spiritual Cafeteria

Vendors at the Dallas Psychic Fair claimed to provide services of great spiritual value such as knowledge about one's place in life, information about what the future holds, guidance for personal transformation, and spiritual meaning. Clearly, these are some of the same benefits offered by more conventional religious groups, even if they might be referred to in different terms. Yet, access to the benefits provided by a religious denomination often requires membership in the organization or at least some commitment to its beliefs. Scholars have long noted that the paranormal has a strong focus upon personal spiritual transformation over devotion to a particular belief or practice.[21] Personal fulfillment and exploration trumps singular commitment.[22] Those interested in the paranormal can freely select from a variety of "tools" in their hunt for transformative experiences and may explore their interests via the media, by attending conferences, lectures, and fairs, or by developing relationships with psychics.[23] The metaphor of a spiritual buffet provides an apt description of these patterns.

The Dallas Psychic Fair had a remarkably organized system in place, which allowed precisely this form of experimentation and exploration. While the tables ringing the room were manned by the various sellers, two long rows of card tables in the middle of the room held twenty-eight different types of "readers." These readers used a variety of different methods and techniques to serve their clients, but the general purpose was the same. Each aimed to provide information that the reader could not know by any means other than the supernatural. Sometimes this was information that the client might already know. For example, some readers focus upon giving an extensive breakdown of one's current personality, or they may note the importance of an event that occurred in the client's past. Other readers provide predictions about the future, warning of dangers in the coming months or congratulating impending fortune. Most use a combination of such information to provide general life guidance.

How the readers claim to acquire their information varies greatly. Some use tools such as crystal balls, tarot cards, or handwriting samples, to facilitate their readings. Others claim to receive their information by reading their client's mind or by pulling data from the cosmos without the need for such tools (see fig. 2.2).

To sample these wares, visitors stopped by a scheduling booth near the entrance to the fair. Behind the booth a large whiteboard with a grid written on it rested on a tripod. Each psychic had her own column on the grid. Rows marked off fifteen-minute intervals from noon to 5 p.m., and a series of purple magnets with names and times written on them indicated when readers were available, e.g., "Leighton Haverty: 12:15 p.m." By scanning the board, visitors could quickly determine who was available and at what times. The attendant handed over each magnet for a fee of ten dollars. It was a clever system for allowing visitors to schedule their entire day of readings at once, if desired, and to facilitate the sampling of a variety of different psychic services.[24] We walked away from the booth clutching our tickets to readings from an astrologer, a psychic, a clairvoyant, and a handwriting analyst.

At 12:15 I visited Leighton Haverty. A kindly, grandmotherly woman in her early sixties, she sported tussled hair, multiple earrings, and a ready smile. With thirty-plus years of experience, Leighton is convinced of the power of astrology. As her flyer asserted:

There is no better tool than your Birth Chart for helping you to be the best you can be. Your Horoscope is a road map for this lifetime and gives a greater understanding of yourself and others. Use it as a tool for Self-Awareness as it gives great insights to the person who is seeking within.

As the planets make their way through the heavens, they affect your natal chart and can bring unexpected delights and/or debilitating crises,

	Readers Available
Angel cards	The reader uses a set of cards with stylized paintings of angels each with its own message. The client selects cards at random (usually three) and the reader interprets their meaning. Similar to tarot cards (below)
Animal communication	A reader who specializes in psychic communication with animals. Clients may bring their current pet and ask for help in understanding its moods or behavior. Or they may ask the reader to communicate with a beloved dead pet.
Astrology	Astrology assumes that the position of stars and planets at the point of one's birth will have effects throughout life. The reader provides insight into one's personality and information on how the current position of stars and planets will impact the near future.
Clairvoyant	A reader who claims to receive psychic knowledge about the past, present, and future through touch or feeling. They read the "vibrations" of clients or an object such as a watch or piece of clothing.
Crystal ball	The reader gazes into a crystal ball, which reveals images (visible only to the reader) of the client's past, present, and/or future. The reader must interpret these images for the client.
Dreams	The reader interprets the client's dreams and nightmares, providing insight into the past, present, and future.
Handwriting analysis	The client provides a writing sample to the reader. Based on the writing style, the reader provides insight into the client's personality, strengths, and weaknesses.
Mah Jongg	The reader uses a set of cards with images based on Chinese symbols; as with Angel and Tarot Cards, the client selects random cards and the reader interprets their meanings.
Medical intuitive	A reader who claims to be able to "read" the client's energy to determine the potential for illnesses or disease.
Numerology	Similar to astrology, numerology readers assume that the date of one's birth impacts personality and future. Rather than focusing on the alignment of stars, numerologists focus upon the numbers in one's birth date.
Palmistry	The reader examines the lines, marks, and patterns on the hands of a client to gain insight into personality and the future.
Past lives	A past-life reader claims to be able to intuit previous incarnations of the client. It is thought that difficulties in previous lives may cause problems or "imbalances" in this one.

Fig. 2.2. The New Age cafeteria: readers available at the Dallas Psychic Fair

which is where the Astrologer comes in. A good Astrologer can guide you through these Karmic challenges and help you understand the lessons to be learned. Most people do not seek an Astrologer when things are going good!!![25]

Readers Available (continued)	
Psychic	A general term for a reader who claims to receive information about the client's past, present, and/or future through supernatural means, generally without the use of tarot cards, crystal balls, or other accessories.
Runes	The reader uses stone "runes" to intuit the client's past, present, and/or future. The client may draw a single stone from a bag or the reader may throw the runes and interpret the resulting pattern.
Spanish deck Tarot	See tarot cards, below. The reader uses a special Spanish-language tarot card deck with "pictoral [*sic*] cards from Spain."[a]
Spirit readings	The reader receives her information about the client from spirits. These may be the spirits of the client's departed loved ones. Some spirit readers claim to have "spirit guides," or spiritual entities that provide them with guidance and information on a regular basis.[b]
Tarot cards	The reader uses a set of cards with stylized characters such as "the Fool," and "Death." The client or reader shuffles the deck and lays out a number of cards in a spread (numbers vary). The reader interprets the meaning and layout of the cards.

Additional Services and Products Available from Vendors	
Aura photography	The vendor takes a photograph of the client that shows their colorful, surrounding aura. The vendor will typically offer an interpretation of the aura as well.
Aromatherapy	The vendor provides candles, incense, or other scented materials. It is believed that the scents can produce relaxation, healing, and/or heightened states of awareness.
Chiropractic	Chiropractors focus upon the muscles and skeleton, in particular the spine, as the source of many health problems. It is believed that manipulation of the spine can cure many disorders.
Healing crystals/stones	The vendor provides stones, crystals, and often jewelry made from same. It is believed that certain stones and crystals can positively influence mood and health, improve psychic abilities, and/or ward of negative influences.
Reiki massage	A massage/relaxation technique in which the masseuse alternates between physically massaging the client and manipulating the client's "energy."

[a] Quote is from handout provided at the psychic fair titled "Dallas Psychic Fair—December 7, 2008."

[b] We have put a more general description of a spirit reader here. At this particular fair, the self-labeled spirit reader used a less common technique. He selected a passage from the Bible based on input from his "Higher Self." He then interpreted this passage in light of the client's life.

I took a seat in front of Leighton. To my immediate left and right, other visitors were receiving readings from a clairvoyant and a crystal ball reader. I waited for Leighton as she fiddled with her laptop. After a long silence, she smiled, looked at me intently, and asked "So, what do you want to know?" It was a surprising question. I assumed that a reader would simply attempt to tell me what I needed to know. Leighton patiently explained that her reading would be more detailed if I provide her with a focus or topic. I thought a moment and told her that I was currently co-authoring a book. How would that go? She asked for my birth date, gave a knowing wink in response, and typed on her laptop.

Thankfully the stars were in this book's favor. Sort of. At first Leighton reported that the book would begin to generate returns more than a year before it was actually slated to see print. In addition to her laptop, Leighton frequently consulted a thick stack of paper charts lined with columns of numbers. Each number represented the position of a planet in the heavens on a particular date. Based on the charts she revised her estimates by several months to a seemingly more likely time frame. The stars also informed her that I was prone to writer's block, but inspiration would strike over the upcoming Christmas holidays. "Some sort of friend or mentor" would also help open doors for this book. Its chances for success would further improve should I take a writing class sometime in March. What followed was a quick succession of observations, statements, and predictions, some of which were true . . . some less so.

- Leighton asked if I was a teacher or in higher education. True.
- She asked if I was divorced. False. She quickly changed the subject.
- She asked if I had children. True. Is one a teenager? False.
- She asked if one of my children had continuing health problems. False.
- She continued that she could see expenses related to a child's health in December. Indeed, a son had braces put in during December.

American Belief in Psychic Powers

As we completed appointments with different readers, we could see the appeal to believers. The readings are, quite simply, fun. One could not help but attempt to impart meaning to the possible futures and current insights produced by the readers. We are not so jaded that we did not feel a glimmer of hope when told that this book would be successful. Our skepticism returned in full force once we had left the fair and reported to our families, however. We had fun with the paranormal, but we did not want our family and friends to think we *believed* the psychics we visited.

Indeed, the paranormal has a curious relationship with the "mainstream." Too much expressed interest in the paranormal will prompt concern from others. Yet television shows with such themes flood the airwaves. Horoscopes appear in our daily newspapers and have made the move to the digital age, with prominent placement next to email and the latest weather forecast on Yahoo.com. Many of us have a grandmother who saw the ghost of her father, a "nutty" uncle who claims the occasional premonitions, a neighbor who fancies herself a psychic, a brother who never misses his horoscope. Indeed, in our experience it is the rare person that does not have a friend or family member who claims some sort of paranormal experience or at least an intense interest in a related subject.

This conflict is apparent when Americans are asked about such topics. Fully 14 percent of Americans believe that astrologers, palm readers, fortune-tellers, and others who claim psychic abilities can see the future (see fig. 2.3). Another 15 percent are not sure; they are not ready to admit belief but remain open to the possibility. But this tells us that the majority of Americans (71%) remain skeptical about the ability to foresee the future (at least as far as these types of readers are concerned).

We find a similar pattern when we ask more specifically about astrology (see fig. 2.4). Americans are slightly more open to the idea of communication with the dead (see fig. 2.5), and most are convinced of the benefits of alternative medicine (see fig 2.6).

There are reasons for the mixed feelings Americans seem to have about the paranormal. On one hand, our readers scored some impressive "hits." One of us was pegged as a teacher by two of them. Braces for my son indeed made Christmas a little tight. On the other hand, correct statements were surrounded by many more incorrect ones. The Temple University mathematician John Allen Paulos recognized this phenomenon and labeled it the "Jeane Dixon effect."[26] When presented with a large amount of information, some true and some false, we are naturally more interested in the true statements, Paulos argues. People tend to forget statements that are clearly false, leading them to wildly overestimate the accuracy of psychics. Skeptics argue that psychics use the Jeane Dixon effect to their advantage.

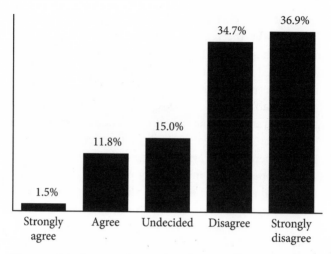

Fig. 2.3. *Astrologers, palm readers, fortune-tellers, and psychics can foresee the future.* (Baylor Religion Survey, 2005, n = 1641)

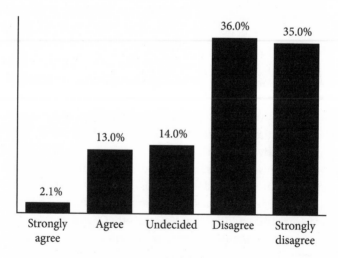

Fig. 2.4. *Astrology impacts one's life and personality.* (Baylor Religion Survey, 2005, n = 1627)

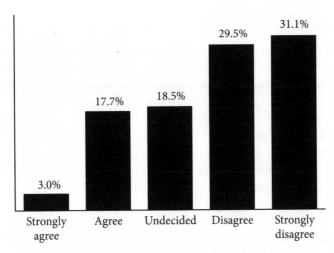

Fig. 2.5. *It is possible to communicate with the dead.* (Baylor Religion Survey, 2005, n = 1636)

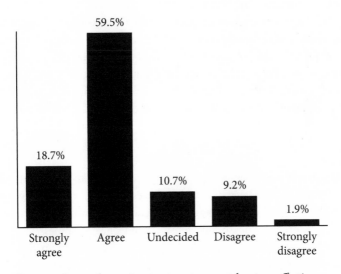

Fig. 2.6. *Some alternative treatments are at least as effective as traditional medicine.* (Baylor Religion Survey, 2005, n = 1638).

Note: A series of items on the Baylor Religion Survey, 2005, ask respondents, "To what extent do you agree or disagree with the following statements." For more details on the methodology behind the Baylor Religion Survey, see the appendix.

Readers pummel their clients with predictions, counting on the few hits to be recalled with reverence and the many misses to be forgotten. We can attest to this phenomenon. One cannot help to feel a slight thrill whenever an accurate statement is presented. The inaccurate statement immediately previous is much less interesting.

Skeptics have noted other processes at work in such readings. Readers often make vague statements that have a high probability of success, such as "I see that you have suffered a great loss in the last year." One who has recently lost a parent to illness will connect with this statement, as will someone who recently had to put their beloved pet to sleep, suffered great losses in the stock market, or recently broke up with a boyfriend, and so on. Such vague statements are often coupled with observations that the client *wants to be true*. We were told by different readers that we "don't follow the crowd," and "think for ourselves." One of us was labeled a "generous lover" (your guess who); another was complimented for his kindness and tendency to "think more about others than your self." We "refuse to be pushed around," "have a great sense of humor," and "keep friends for life." We choose to believe that all of these things are true.

We could continue by discussing the possibility that many psychics are master "cold readers," but to do so is somewhat missing the point.[27] Neither the readers nor the clients were at the fair in the hopes of proving the reality of paranormal phenomena to a skeptical public. People attend because they desire help and guidance and have not found the answers they seek through other means. Behind the use of crystal balls, palm reading, aura photography, attempts to contact dead relatives, psychics and clairvoyants, crystals, aromatherapy, past-life regression, and handwriting analysis is the desire to better oneself. As Cheryl told us:

> We see people attending our fair because they desire to live a better life. The contrast in their lives (that which causes discomfort) encourages one to find better ways, better experiences, deeper relationships, more money, etc. . . . in order to do so, one must expand one's awareness. They are looking for answers. They are looking for understanding so they may make healthier choices or so they can forgive, or let go, or shift direction.

At the Dallas Psychic Fair we met people who were primarily interested in the paranormal as a source of personal enlightenment, improved health, discovery, and/or growth. They hoped to learn more about themselves by determining the color of their aura or gain supernatural insight

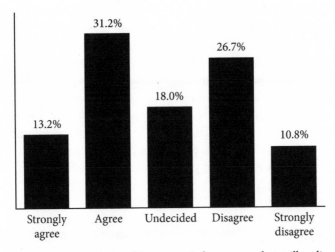

Fig. 2.7. *We are approaching an entirely new age that will radically change our view of science, spiritual knowledge, or humanity.* (Baylor Religion Survey, 2005, n = 1637)

into their future through the use of tarot cards or by communicating with dead relatives. That the methods being used at the psychic fair to elicit change or improvement remain unaccepted by science was of little concern to those involved. Leighton Haverty's clients are happy if her readings work for *them*, not whether her techniques would pass a double-blind test in laboratory conditions. Personal enlightenment trumps scientific proof.

As the sociologist Jeremy Northcote notes, many paranormal believers "privilege experiential knowledge over empirical validity and the power of the imagination over the authority of physical reality."[28] Indeed, a significant number of Americans truly do envision a "New Age on the horizon that will trump our current notions of reality (see fig. 2.7).

Enlightenment vs. Discovery

As we wandered the Dallas Psychic Fair, we noted the absence of materials on several popular aspects of the paranormal. Bigfoot was in hiding, ghosts were invisible (perhaps this is to be expected). We could not find any materials related to extraterrestrials or UFOs. Judging by the prevalence of television shows, movies, books, and Web pages devoted to such subjects, it might at first seem surprising that Sasquatch and aliens did not have a prominent place at such an event. Yet in our exploration of the paranormal, we have found that there are two distinct spheres within it, which we call *enlightenment* and *discovery*. These different approaches tend to align with different subjects.

Many people view the paranormal as merely a source of personal *enlightenment*. For many of those traveling in the realms of astrology, psychic powers, and similar practices, the "truth" is ephemeral and within: they seek to better themselves. So long as psychic readings of one sort or another help them to come to grips with their strengths and weaknesses, they are satisfied.

Others are interested in the paranormal because they hope to take part in, whether personally or by proxy, a major *discovery* for the world at large. People interested in Bigfoot and mysterious creatures in general, UFOs, and ghosts appear more concerned with trying to prove to themselves and others that their subject is indeed "real." They want to find the truth—a truth that anyone will accept. They study materials on Web sites and in books, and debate the best "evidence" on blogs and at conferences. They watch television shows such as *Ghost Hunters* with great interest, hoping the hosts will finally capture undisputed video of a restless spirit. They want to find out if UFOs are real, or they know UFOs are real and want to convince others of that fact. Some of the most serious Bigfoot hunters hope to drop a Sasquatch carcass on the doorstep of the Smithsonian one day.

The appeal of enlightenment is to learn about oneself. The appeal of discovery is to share in an adventure, to feel the thrill of searching for the unknown, and to perhaps be the one who finally brings in the "proof." One need only to participate in each type of activity to feel their stark contrast. We felt introspective and thoughtful (when we held back our skepticism) at the Dallas Psychic Fair. And when we chose to spend the night at a reportedly haunted house, we were ready to be frightened, to share the prospect of discovery and adventure with our group. These distinctions are useful, but also of a more general nature. And as we found out, sometimes having a psychic on a ghost hunt makes it more interesting.

Jefferson, Texas

As we noted earlier, the now defunct Big Cypress Coffee House in Jefferson, Texas, quickly became notorious for its tales of angry ghosts that push, prod, and otherwise harass those who dare to visit, and part of the building's fearsome reputation was directly due to its owner, Duane. Warlock or not, Duane proved an accommodating host,[29] as he agreed to let us, along with a group of graduate students, spend the night in the upper floor of the coffee house. Concerned that we might not have the complete "ghost-hunting experience" if left to our own devices, Duane invited three others to accompany us on our overnight stay in his ghost-infested shop. He introduced us to "Lee," a short, blond, thirty-something professional medium who lived in a smaller town nearby. On weekends Lee lingers at the coffee shop, providing psychic readings for thirty dollars. Also in attendance was "Gloria," who prefers the label "clairvoyant" to medium. Also in her thirties, Gloria is a colorful character as evidenced by her bright red hair sporting a prominent white streak. When not at her day job at a cartography company in Dallas, the recently divorced Gloria provides psychic readings and uses her skills to aid ghost hunters.

Gloria uses an EMF detector to look for ghosts.

Accompanying Gloria is her friend Victoria, a thirty-two-year-old bank employee. Making no claim to psychic powers, Victoria considers herself an amateur ghost hunter. Throughout the evening she generously allowed us to borrow her ghost-hunting equipment.

We all enjoyed a hearty dinner at a local Mexican restaurant, then we returned to the coffee house ready to begin our adventure. Immediately the psychics sensed the presence of ghosts. Lee held a brief conversation with an elderly male spirit standing behind us. The spirit was not particularly pleased by our presence, she stated in a somber voice. Victoria took us on a tour of the downstairs. A narrow hallway to the left of the coffee bar led to a bathroom and storage room at the back of the building. Only the bravest would dare set foot in the bathroom, Duane warned us, a sly grin on his face, since the spirits especially enjoy poking, prodding, and speaking to people using the facilities.

Victoria told us of a dramatic encounter she had during a previous investigation at the coffee house. Her group heard a mysterious buzzing sound coming from a storage area behind the coffee bar. There, they saw a dark red streak of light ascend through the ceiling with a loud pop. Ghost hunters believe that spirits can manifest themselves as orbs or streaks of light, which often appear in photographs and sometimes are seen with the naked eye.[30] "The color of orbs is important," Victoria told me, "because it tells you the nature of the entity involved." Unfortunately for us, Victoria continued, "red energy indicates evil."

The downstairs bathroom aside, the majority of ghostly activity is reported from a room on the second floor of the coffee house. As Victoria and our psychic guides chatted with Duane around a table, we decided to finally see the upstairs for ourselves. We cautiously ascended the staircase as it wound around two landings, wary because the ghosts have a propensity for pushing and pulling people climbing the stairs. It was with a small measure of relief that we entered the haunted upper floor without incident. The staircase ended at a hallway. To the left was a small alcove packed with a ladder, buckets of paint or plaster and assorted tools. Duane told us this was equipment left behind by workmen frightened away by the angry spirits. Turning to the right we entered the room in which we would spend the night. And what a room it was.

Dusty, wood-paneled floors creaked, groaned, and otherwise protested as we walked back and forth in a space about the size of a small café. Evidence of a "Wiccan Halloween Party" recently hosted by Duane was strewn about the room: large rubber spiders hung from the ceiling, rubber

The upper floor of the Big Cypress Coffee House

rats peered from behind furniture and between books on a shelf, a large witch doll sat on a chair, and a big, fake skull rested on an end table. Near the doorway were two thronelike chairs on a riser. According to Duane, the "thrones" remain from a time when the space was used by local Freemasons. A nearby table had been used as their altar, he said. He warned us about sitting on the thrones, as people claim to have been physically ejected from them by unseen hands.

A queen-sized bed on an iron frame was in the back half of the room. "I used to sleep there," Duane told us later, until the night he heard growling that sounded like a large dog and footsteps going around his bed. He now slept in a different part of the building, though the bed remained. "I decided they didn't want people staying in here."

More disturbing, and certainly more unexpected, was a selection of bondage equipment. Next to Duane's former bed was a large, wooden, X-shaped cross, padded with leather. It was easily large enough to hold a tall man with impressive restraints at the ends of each arm. Two large whips and a studded collar were lying across the top of a metal clothing rack that sat opposite the bed. We left well-enough alone and never asked about these particular "Halloween decorations."

A set of curtains hanging from flimsy rods blocked off the back third of the room. Behind them was another random assortment of ladders, a table saw, boxes, and more buckets of paint and plaster. As we were about to step into this area to explore further, Gloria, Lee, and Victoria entered the room, looking quite concerned. In an emotion-filled voice, Gloria told us "I don't like this room!" Gesturing at the curtains, she continued, "The evil is strongest back there. The spirits come from here." Duane later confirmed for us that most of the "activity" in the room originates from behind the curtains. He claimed that a man had been found hanged in the far left corner. Police ruled it a suicide, but the man's hands had been tied behind his back. He went on to tell us that a woman had jumped out a nearby window, and another woman had been raped in the alley outside. We did not attempt to confirm these claims.

Victoria waved an EMF meter behind the curtains. An EMF meter is a small handheld device, which detects fluctuations in electromagnetic energy. Ghost hunters frequently use these, believing that high EMF readings indicate the presence of spirits. It emitted a dramatic squeal, signaling the presence of strong energy. She then pulled out her camera and pushed her arm through the curtain to take photos and scanned the resultant pictures for red orbs.

Gloria, in the meantime, was becoming progressively more upset. She told us that she could feel the negative energies of the Ku Klux Klan. Upon questioning, however, she could not clarify what this meant. Were there ghosts of dead KKK members present in the room? Were angry victims of KKK activities looking for vengeance? As she became progressively more distraught, Gloria whispered, "I . . . just . . . don't like the KKK or what they stand for," before collapsing to the floor.

For several minutes Gloria mumbled unintelligibly as Victoria tended to her. "She is so hot!" exclaimed Victoria. Indeed, Gloria's forehead was quite warm to the touch. After some rest and a drink of water, Gloria sat up. "The spirits are angry we are here. Several rushed me at once," she said. The influx of spiritual energy had overwhelmed Gloria as if, "a hundred voices were speaking at once."

Gloria, Lee, and Victoria conferred in hushed voices. It would be impossible for us to stay the night absent some form of protection from the spirits, they decided. Springing into action, they carefully rearranged items in the room. Gloria pulled the drapes as closely together as possible. Lee pulled the strange, padded cross with restraints behind the curtains. Victoria roamed the room and removed some of the Halloween decorations.

Gloria overcome by spirits

Finally, Gloria and Lee arranged four tall candleholders in a large circle around Duane's abandoned bed.

Gloria fetched a ritual dagger from her car and began a protection spell. She murmured softly to herself as she slowly circled the candleholders, occasionally raising the dagger above her head with both hands. The ritual would create a "magic protective circle" within the area cordoned off by the candles, Victoria told us. Spirits in the room would be allowed to communicate with those within the confines of the circle if so desired, but the ritual would ensure that evil entities could cause no harm. With a final flourish, Gloria lit each candle, completing the ritual. Feeling spent by the ritual, Gloria fell back upon the bed and closed her eyes. For the next couple of hours, she would intermittently awaken, mumble, and fall back into a semi-stupor. Lee was concerned that she might have been possessed by a spirit. But other than seeming exhausted, Gloria suffered no ill effects that we could perceive.

For the next several hours we roamed the building. On occasion we would borrow an EMF meter to search for spirit energy. We shot pictures from various angles, looking for orbs. We took turns sitting in the haunted thrones. Finally tiring of the hunt, we rolled out our sleeping bags on the

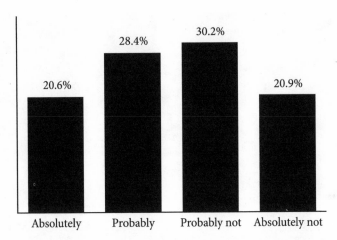

Fig. 2.8. *Do ghosts exist?* (Baylor Religion Survey, 2005, n = 1637)

floor and laid down to sleep. Christopher and Carson slept inside the "protective circle," Joseph slept outside of it, offering his services as the "control group," but the night passed without incident. We awoke in the early morning and packed up for our return home.

Naturally, family and friends who knew of our adventure wanted to know what had happened during the night. We imagine our recounting of the night's events differs substantially from the psychics.

For Gloria, Lee, and Victoria, the evening was one of continual and dramatic events. Victoria saw orbs of evil energy in her photographs. Gloria was overwhelmed by dozens of ghosts rushing her at once. They talked to ghosts that were standing behind us and conducted rituals to keep us safe. Gloria swooned, gasped, and collapsed at the behest of the pushy spirits. We were able to spend the night, in their view, only through their direct intervention to stave off evil forces.

Nearly half of Americans believe in ghosts (see fig. 2.8), and even we as researchers are not entirely dismissive. But at the same time we are skeptical. We did not see a ghost on that evening. We were never pushed or prodded. Our bathroom breaks were, thankfully, uneventful. We never heard voices nor saw dark shadows flitting about the room. The orbs that appeared in our photographs could just have easily been flashes reflecting off of dust particles.

We spent the night at the coffee house to see what it was like to engage in paranormal discovery. Yet our discovery was not as advertised. Our evening was not spent watching ghosts, it was spent watching *people who believe in ghosts*. Gloria, Lee, and Victoria needed no convincing about the reality of ghosts when they spent the night with us at Big Cypress. Everything that happened to them confirmed what they already knew.

3

The Truth Is Out There

Paranormal Beliefs and Experiences

People have seen strange objects in the sky seemingly for as long as we have had records. The Old Testament prophet Ezekiel reported the sighting of a "whirlwind from the north." UFO books and Web sites claim that Christopher Columbus reported a "light glimmering at a great distance" in his ship's log two days before first landing in the New World.[1] In the 1800s the United States experienced a rash of sightings of flying, cigar-shaped objects somewhat similar to dirigibles, which sometimes disgorged humanlike pilots.[2] During World War II some Allied pilots reported sightings of small disks or globes of light that followed their planes, and which ultimately earned them the nickname "foo fighters."[3]

What *has changed* quite a bit over time is the interpretation of such objects. Ezekiel believed his whirlwind was a sign from God. The airships of the late 1800s were widely assumed to be the work of "secret inventors." The U.S. military thought the foo fighters were weapons of the Japanese or Germans. As technology changes, so do our mysterious aerial objects, always staying one step ahead of us. Nowadays UFO enthusiasts assume Ezekiel's experience is evidence that extraterrestrials were visiting Earth in biblical times; therefore Ezekiel's interpretation is assumed to be the wrong one.[4]

The widespread interpretation of mysterious objects in the sky as extraterrestrial in origin is often traced to the June 24, 1947, sighting by Kenneth Arnold, a fire-equipment salesman. An experienced civilian pilot, Arnold was flying his private plane from Chehalis to Yakima, Washington, when he took a brief detour over Mount Rainier to search for the wreckage of a recently crashed plane. Arnold was startled by a bright flash while making a turn high over the town of Mineral. He spotted nine peculiar craft approximately one hundred miles away, soaring at a bearing that would bring them in front of his plane. At first Arnold thought the objects were

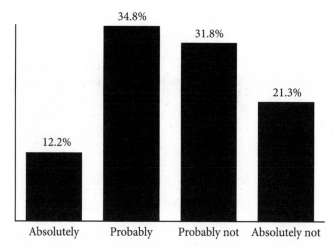

Fig. 3.1. *Do extraterrestrials exist?* (Baylor Religion Survey, 2007, n = 1577)

jets until they drew closer; he could see wings but no tails. One of the objects was almost crescent-shaped, with a small dome midway between the wingtips. The others were flat "like a pie pan," with a reflective surface. Their manner of flight was "like speed boats on rough water."[5] The craft wove around the mountaintops allowing Arnold to clock their speed at roughly 1,600 miles per hour, nearly three times faster than conventional aircraft of the 1940s.

Recounting the sighting to reporters, Arnold described the objects' flight as "like saucers skipped over water." In the flurry of news coverage that followed, writers began using terms such as "flying disks" or "flying saucers" to describe the objects, although the exact provenance of the term is unclear. Clearer was the new interpretation of strange flying objects. Arnold's report, if true, was of intelligently controlled objects clearly beyond the capabilities of the time, so the possibility that such "flying saucers" were of extraterrestrial origin became firmly cemented in popular culture.[6] In later years, the preferred term for mysterious objects of assumed extraterrestrial origin became "UFO"—unidentified flying object.[7]

Currently, more than a third of Americans believe that extraterrestrials probably exist, and another 12 percent are absolutely certain (see fig. 3.1). Of course, some might believe that life exists on other planets without thinking that those life forms have visited Earth. As any astronomer or

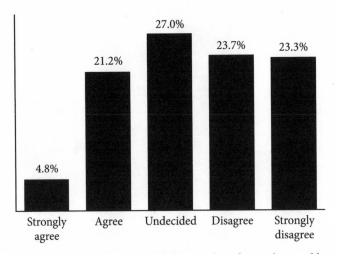

Fig. 3.2. *Some UFOs are probably spaceships from other worlds.*
(Baylor Religion Survey, 2005, n = 1628)

astrophysicist can attest, there remain vast spaces unknown to humans throughout the universe. Accordingly, we asked Americans more specifically about the possibility that extraterrestrials have flown our skies, and we found that about one-fourth of Americans (26%) think that some UFOs are "probably spaceships from another world" (see fig. 3.2). Nearly another third (27%) are uncertain about the matter, suggesting they are at least open to the possibility.

For some, the belief in extraterrestrials extends to our very origins as a species, much to the dismay of mainstream archeologists. Proponents of the so-called ancient astronauts thesis contend that aliens created mankind or at least accelerated human development via the granting of wisdom and technology. This idea dates back, in some form or another, to at least the late nineteenth-century works of the Russian mystic/theosophist Helena Petrovna Blavatsky, but the Swiss author Erich von Daniken is responsible for its most influential iteration in books such as *Chariots of the Gods* (1968), *In Search of Ancient Gods* (1973), *Miracles of the Gods* (1974), and many others.[8] His books became so popular that Daniken became a minor celebrity. His theories were the subject of countless television documentaries and the inspiration behind his own Swedish theme park, Mystery Park (unfortunately it folded in 2006). Zecharia Sitchin, who also believes that extraterrestrials played a role in human history, Daniken, and others marshal an assortment of archaeological evidence to support the theory of ancient astronauts.[9]

Followers of the former race car driver and journalist Claude Vorilhon believe that a race of aliens, Elohim, created humans in a test tube and implanted them on Earth.[10] These Raëlians, as followers of Raël (aka Claude Vorilhon) are known, believe that throughout human history the Elohim have communicated with their experiment subjects (humans) through prophets, such as Buddha, Jesus, Muhammad, and now Raël. Founded in Paris in 1975, the Raëlians, according to the sociologist Susan Palmer, fled to Quebec Province, Canada, to avoid persecution of religious sects in France. This group is a study in contrasts. They not only extol progressive values such as racial/ethnic tolerance, sexual experimentation, population control, and nonviolence but are also known for their unbridled faith in technology and science. On December 26, 2002, they claimed to have cloned a human baby, Baby Eve.[11]

Perhaps the most common claim among ancient astronaut enthusiasts is that impressive feats of ancient engineering—the pyramids of Egypt, the statues on Easter Island, the great temples of South America—were simply beyond the capacity of their associated societies. Daniken speculates openly about the builders of the great monuments of Egypt:

> How on Earth did the Ancient Egyptians build these edifices without twentieth-century technology? . . . [H]ow were the statues of Memnon near Thebes that weighed 600 tons transported, or the stone blocks of the terrace at Baalbek, some of which are over 60 feet long and weigh 2,000 tons? And now the sixty-four thousand dollar question: Who nowadays can still accept the "serious" archaeological explanation that these stone blocks were moved up inclined planes using wooden rollers? . . . I get no answers to questions like that. So could it be true that extraterrestrial space travelers helped with their highly developed technology?[12]

Daniken uses this rhetorical technique throughout his work. He outlines the incredible effort that would have been required of ancient peoples to construct a particular monument, raises concerns about their ability to do so, and finally speculates that it all would have been much easier with help from the stars. Since the entire exercise is framed in the form of questions, it allows Daniken to make astonishing allegations with the benefit of distance; he is not making unreasonable claims, simply asking reasonable questions. The ancient astronaut literature leaves the reader with the distinct impression that ancient peoples could not accomplish much on their own.

The books of Daniken and others provide a complete, alternative reading of the historical record and the meanings of religious doctrine, myth, and legend. God figures in elaborate headdresses depicted in ancient artwork become literal astronauts in their space helmets.[13] References to strange, celestial objects or godlike figures in holy texts are reinterpreted as historical accounts of visitations by extraterrestrials. Landscape features such as the admittedly mysterious Nazca Lines of Peru, a collection of lines scraped into the soil that reveal themselves to be enormous representations of birds, monkeys, and other figures when viewed from a great height are frequently mentioned by ancient astronaut theorists. Archaeologists disagree as to whether the Peruvian artists meant this amazing achievement in landscape art to function as an irrigation system, an astronomical calendar, or just maybe, simply as art. To ancient astronaut proponents the purpose is obvious—the lines are runways for ancient spacecraft, or perhaps artwork meant to be pleasing to extraterrestrials hovering high above Earth. Of course, such claims have been the focus of intense criticism,[14] but they have maintained a foothold in the paranormal subculture. These ideas are even relatively prevalent among college students taking archeology classes.[15]

Further confusing popular understanding of mankind's history is a persistent belief in ancient, advanced civilizations such as Atlantis, Lemuria, and Mu.[16] Plato's dialogues provide the first reference to Atlantis, a powerful nation that supposedly sank under the waves during a natural disaster. Ever since, those with an interest in Atlantis have fretted over whether Plato's reference is meant as a parable on hubris (even the most powerful can fall to forces beyond their control), or a recounting of historical fact. Ignatius Donnelly took up the case in his 1882 work *Atlantis: The Antediluvian World,* in which he forcefully argued that archeological data, legends, and historical records point to a real Atlantis.[17] As the legend passed through the hands of Helena P. Blavatsky, Lewis Spence, Edgar Cayce, and others, the nature of Atlantis changed. What Plato described as a society advanced for its time was transformed into an amazing civilization far beyond current understanding and with ties to extraterrestrials. Its reported destruction by natural disaster morphed into death by technological malfeasance.[18]

While we cannot assess the extent to which Americans believe in alien intervention in early history specifically, we do know how they feel about

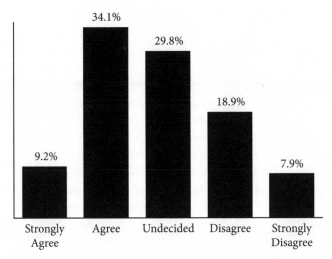

Fig. 3.3. *Ancient, advanced civilizations, such as Atlantis, once existed.* (Baylor Religion Survey, 2005, n = 1633)

Atlantis. Nearly half (43%) exhibit belief in ancient, advanced civilizations such as Atlantis. Fully another 30% are undecided about the matter (see fig. 3.3).

Aren't They Just Nuts?

Tell someone that you are writing a book on such subjects as UFOs, ancient astronauts, astrology, and the like, and you will solicit some very interesting, often colorful remarks. Carson was telling his family doctor about this book project during a routine medical appointment. The doctor listened patiently to the description of its purpose, and his first reaction was: "Why study these people? Aren't they just nuts?" Such a response has been surprisingly common. Even though a large number of people in the United States believe in UFOs and other paranormal phenomena, the popular stereotype is that those who lend credence to such topics are very strange indeed. But is this true?

A big problem in answering such questions has been a lack of good information on the believers themselves. A number of researchers have explored the social correlates of the paranormal, but have produced inconsistent findings, particularly with regard to which social factors matter the most in predicting someone's propensity for the paranormal. For example, a number of scholars have found that people with higher educations and younger people are more prone to report paranormal experiences.[19] Other studies fail to find such relationships.[20]

Data problems have played a primary role in preventing social scientists from reaching definitive conclusions about paranormal believers. Many of the surveys that have asked Americans about their paranormal beliefs and experiences are more than twenty-five years old and cannot address the contemporary situation.[21] Other surveys have been limited to a particular region of the country. Unfortunately, a study of paranormal belief in San Francisco cannot tell us conclusively what Americans, in general, think about such things. The paranormal is probably experienced differently in San Francisco than it is deep in the heart of Alabama.[22] Some studies have been limited to particular types of people. Much of the available information on paranormal beliefs has been collected from college students, as getting the captive audiences in classes to fill out surveys is quick and cost effective.[23] The problem with using such "convenience samples" is that they are unlikely to reflect what the average American thinks, and college students are *not* average Americans. It is worth exploring further the characteristics of believers in the paranormal. Using our random national sample, with its demographic, paranormal, religious, and lifestyle questions, we get a sense of the average, general paranormal believers in America.

On the Margins

Are people who believe in UFOs and other aspects of the paranormal simply nuts, as the doctor implied? Though they are more reserved in their terminology, some influential social theorists believe this to be the case for not only paranormal believers but for those who are involved in conventional religion as well. Karl Marx made one of the most famous statements in this regard. He stated that, in so many words, the rich and powerful are able to get what they need out of this world by conventional means, and the world is set up to reward them. Marx argued that religious beliefs perform the vital social function of providing comfort to the less powerful, and those who are currently suffering. Without the belief that they would be compensated for current suffering with magnificent rewards in the afterlife, the working class would revolt and undermine the capitalist system.[24] As such, he argued, belief in an unseen world is merely a coping mechanism to deal with life on the margins of society, the "sigh of the oppressed creature."

In a similar vein, many theorists wonder if the desire to experience the supernatural, whether in the organized form of religion or via the paranormal, is simply a reaction to uncertainty. Those with a higher level of social achievement such as a good education, a high-paying, "respectable" occupation, and a stable family life are apt to feel in control of their lives.[25] The decisions they have made and the actions they have taken have produced highly valued achievements. As a result they have greater confidence in their own abilities to exert influence over circumstances.[26] Those who have fewer socioeconomic resources, or who are marginalized from society, are more apt to feel as if they have lost control over their very future. They seem to be at the mercy of unseen social forces rather than in control of them because they are burdened by heavy hardships. Social scientists call the sense that one controls one's own fate an *internal locus of control* (mostly because academics love making up new terms). Women, the poor, those with low levels of education, and racial/ethnic minorities have been found to have less perceived control over their lives.[27]

Humans generally do not like uncertainty and try to reduce it.[28] We humans collect information and attempt to make the best decisions about our futures from our own current perspective. We try to find ways to take control of our lives. Some religion scholars believe that those who lack the ability to change their circumstances themselves may ultimately seek divine assistance in the task. In other words, perhaps we seek the supernatural's help when we cannot help ourselves.[29] Marx's work and the concept of a locus of control led to a widespread belief among early sociologists that all forms of religious and paranormal beliefs and expressions would be most prevalent in the poor and oppressed. Life, however, is rarely as simple as theorists would like it to be.

There are many reasons why religious beliefs should appeal to both rich and poor, those with great power and those without it. Religion's primary "products" provide answers to the big questions in life (such as whether our existence has a purpose) and usually offer a means by which to achieve life after death. These are things that cannot be bought with money or earned with a higher social status, so they should hypothetically be equally attractive to rich and poor alike, the mainstream and the marginalized. Indeed, we find that both rich and poor tend to be religious in some form in the United States. Some people are very attracted to organized religious activities and attend services at a temple, mosque, or other house of worship regularly. Other people believe very strongly in the precepts of a religion but attend services at a temple, mosque, or other house of worship rarely. Still others have an entirely personal or idiosyncratic religiosity or spirituality that is more focused on personal prayers or other contacts with the supernatural. In sum, what varies more than attraction to religion is *how* different socioeconomic groups manifest their religiosity.

In addition to promises of eternal salvation, religious congregations offer many rewards that can be obtained on Earth, such as leadership positions and access to influential financial and personal networks. The powerful (i.e., those from higher socioeconomic groups) tend to monopolize these material yet religious rewards just as they do in many other aspects of life. In the United States, religious groups are strictly voluntary associations; therefore they must depend upon the resources, both monetary and human, of their members. People who are powerful in the local community are likely to be the powerful members within conventional religious groups as well. Indeed, it is generally the more affluent members of society, not the working class, who attend church with greater frequency (see fig. 3.4).[30]

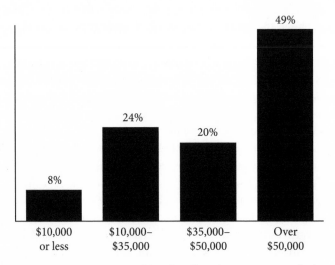

Fig. 3.4. Percentage attending church at least once a week, by yearly family income (Baylor Religion Survey 2007, n = 1525)

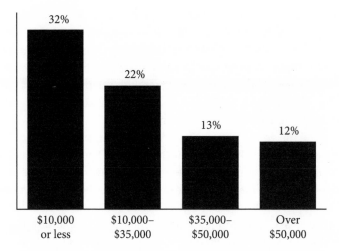

Fig. 3.5. Percentage who have "received a miraculous, physical healing," by yearly family income (Baylor Religion Survey 2007, n = 1511)

So what does this have to do with paranormal beliefs, practices, and experiences? Like most people, the socially marginal are seeking religious rewards, but they are not reaping the direct, concrete rewards from religious life usurped by the more powerful members. The failure to secure empirical rewards may lead to disappointment, alienation, and estrangement from conventional society. Such individuals may reject the beliefs of the mainstream without giving up on the desire for some sort of relationship with the supernatural realm. This can lead to experimentation with alternative beliefs or experiences. Some are able to fulfill their desires within a Christian framework. They become more open to intense and unconventional religious experiences not typically associated with upper- and middle-class religious practices, such as speaking in tongues or claiming a miraculous healing (see fig. 3.5).[31] Accordingly religious sects tend to draw heavily from those of lower socioeconomic status.[32]

Those with a weaker connection to Christian beliefs or who have grown disenchanted with the dominant religion may experiment with more esoteric beliefs such as psychic phenomena, astrology, or UFOs.[33] Finding an intense or unique supernatural experience that the upper classes do not share can be empowering to socially marginal people.[34] Unique beliefs or experiences can make one *feel* unique, worthy, and valuable. To the extent

that such a belief is an organized activity, it can even confer a certain social status among fellow seekers. In some cases alternative beliefs give the
marginalized a sense of control over their lives, which they cannot find
elsewhere. All of this suggests that groups with lesser power, however defined, may experiment to a greater extent with the paranormal.

One way to determine if there is indeed greater paranormal belief
among the marginalized is to examine patterns of belief by gender and
race. Despite the 2008 election of an African American president (and his
heated competition with Hilary Clinton for the Democratic nomination),
white males tend to hold the power in the United States. Consider that
although President Obama is African American, there remains only one
black senator: Barack Obama's replacement, Roland Burris. Additionally,
white males earn more money than women and people of color.[35] And
the glass ceiling is well known (and was commented on by Clinton during
her 2008 campaign). If marginalized people drift toward marginalized beliefs, should we then expect women to express more belief in such topics
than men, and nonwhites to show more interest than whites?

With respect to gender, we do see strong evidence that females express
higher belief in the paranormal than do men (see fig. 3.6). In general, with

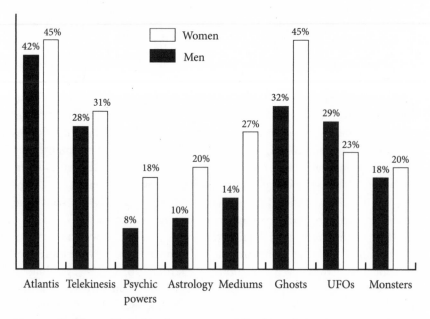

Fig. 3.6. Gender and belief in the paranormal (Baylor Religion Survey, 2005)

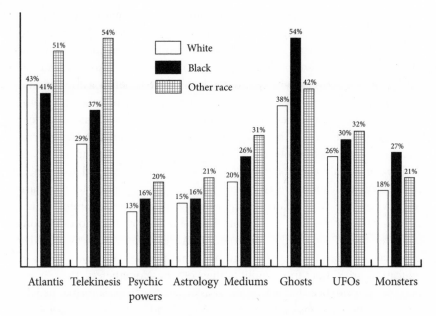

Fig. 3.7. Race and belief in the paranormal (Baylor Religion Survey, 2005)

the exception of belief in UFOs (where men show more belief) and belief in crypto-monsters (where the differences are statistically insignificant), women are more likely to believe in every paranormal topic.[36] In some cases the differences are relatively small. There is a 3 percent or smaller difference between men and women with regards to belief in Atlantis and other ancient, advanced civilizations, and the belief that objects can be moved with the mind alone (telekinesis). For other beliefs the differences are substantial. Women are twice as likely as men to believe in astrology, that people can communicate with the dead (mediums), and that at least some psychics can foresee the future.

Paranormal beliefs are also related to race (see fig. 3.7). Here we compare white respondents, African American respondents, and those of other races (Native Americans, Asians, and nonwhite Hispanics). In most cases a higher proportion of nonwhites believe in these topics than do whites. More than half of African Americans believe in ghosts, compared to around one-third of whites. There are also substantial differences between African Americans and whites in levels of belief in telekinesis and mediums. There are smaller differences between whites and African

Americans in belief in psychic powers and UFOs, although blacks are still more *likely* to believe. There are some exceptions, however. Whites are no more or less likely than African Americans to believe in the existence of ancient, advanced civilizations such as Atlantis. There is also no meaningful difference between whites and blacks in their belief in astrology, and the difference between whites and nonwhites on levels of belief in crypto-monsters disappears when we consider other factors such as education, income, and gender.[37] These findings are not uniform, but the general trend is for whites to show lesser belief in most paranormal subjects.

If paranormal believers are on society's margins, we should also expect to see large education effects: those who have less education tend to have less success in earthly affairs and may be presumed to seek comfort in the paranormal. Or perhaps, those with less education attempt to exert control over their lives via the supernatural. At least these are less offensive explanations than the popular argument that people with lower levels of education are simply more gullible than others. Nonetheless, there is indeed some evidence that education is associated with paranormal beliefs. Consider the relationship between schooling and some selected paranormal beliefs (see fig. 3.8).

Here we see how failing to complete high school impacts the likelihood that a person will believe in paranormal topics. Those who have not completed high school are nearly twice as likely to believe that psychics, astrologers, tarot readers, and the like have psychic powers. They are also more than twice as likely to believe that astrology has merit. Both of these beliefs are related to seeing the future and trying to learn about the nature and direction of one's life. So it does seem that the paranormal may occasionally serve the function of bringing "power" to the powerless, of giving people on the margins a way to exert control. Curiously, those with the lowest levels of education show greater belief in ghosts, but are no more likely than anyone else to believe that mediums can communicate with the dead.

However, other than these specific topics we find no relationship between having a lower level of education and believing in the paranormal. Those without diplomas do not gravitate to beliefs in Atlantis, are not more likely to see UFOs in the sky, and do not show a distinct propensity toward belief in monsters, mediums, or telekinesis.

Armed with this information we can provide a preliminary answer to our doctor's question. People who believe in the paranormal *are* different in some ways. We can predict someone's level of belief in the paranormal

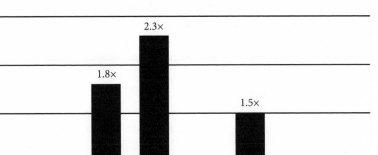

Not having a high school diploma increases likelihood of belief by . . .

Fig. 3.8. Dropping out of high school and the increased odds of paranormal beliefs (Baylor Religion Survey, 2005)

Note: Increased odds are determined using a logistic regression that controls for age, marital status, income, race, region of the country, gender, religious tradition, church attendance, and biblical literalism. See appendix for details.

if we know certain things about them. Groups with less societal power, such as females and African Americans, are indeed more paranormal in orientation. People with lower levels of education are more likely to express belief in *some* paranormal topics. Yet to characterize the paranormal as simply the province of the uneducated and less powerful would be premature and unfair. We must recognize that there are many paranormal beliefs that are not related to education.

Of course, it is one thing to be open to the possibility that UFOs exist and quite another to *know* that they exist because you have seen one (if you are lucky or unlucky depending on the scenario) or even been aboard. Perhaps these are the truly marginalized—people so distanced from society that they live within the realms of the strange and unreal. A detour into the subculture of UFO abductions allows us to consider this possibility. We also consider an alternative hypothesis—maybe belief in UFOs, Bigfoot, and other paranormal topics can be the luxury of the wealthy and well educated, as opposed to the cry of the oppressed.

The Paranormal Experience: Alien Abductions in the United States

On September 19, 1961, Betty Hill, a New Hampshire social worker, and her husband, Barney, a postal worker, were driving home from a vacation in Canada when they spotted a "white star" in the sky. At first the Hills ignored the object, until they became convinced it was tailing their car. A "chase" ensued during which they became extremely frightened. At one point Barney pulled to the side of the road to gaze at the object through binoculars. The object tilted downward in response and began a descent. Barney panicked as a row of windows came into focus, behind which stood figures in shiny black uniforms and matching caps. Fearing the creatures were going to capture him, Barney jumped back into the couple's car to escape. And then . . .

The couple was suddenly closer to home, with no memory of how they got there. Puzzled they wearily completed their journey. The next day Betty called Pease Air Force Base in Portsmouth, New Hampshire, to report the encounter.[38] Unable to forget the incident and plagued with nightmares, Betty became fascinated with UFOs. She checked out books from the library and contacted Donald Keyhoe, a well-known UFO investigator and author. Another UFO investigator, Walter Webb, interviewed the couple, who were frustrated by fragmented memories of being aboard the witnessed saucer. In reconstructing their terrifying evening with still other investigators, the Hills realized that the usual four-hour drive from Canada to New Hampshire had taken them seven hours. Where had they been during this "missing time?" The couple believed there was more about their experience to be uncovered. They tried to find the exact site of their encounter, but this did not help spur memories. Meanwhile Betty continued to dream about beings with strange faces performing medical experiments upon her.

By December 1963 the couple had contacted the Boston psychiatrist Benjamin Simon. The Hills hoped that hypnotic regression might help them to recover a more complete account of their UFO encounter, and Simon was experienced with the technique. The skeptical therapist agreed to help the Hills, though he believed their stresses had a more earthly than extraterrestrial explanation.[39] From January to June 1964 the Hills had occasional meetings with Simon, during which he hypnotized one or both. A fantastic tale emerged from these sessions, supposedly filling in the blanks of their memories.

It seems that the object that tailed the couple several years previous had landed near their car. Several strange creatures then emerged and escorted the dazed Hills into their craft. Barney described the odd creatures in a hypnosis session with Simon. At first he likened them to a "red-headed Irishman" and then a "German Nazi" before ultimately settling upon a description more familiar to modern-day UFO enthusiasts:[40]

[They] had rather odd-shaped heads, with a large cranium, diminishing in size as it got towards the chin. And the eyes continued around to the sides of the head, so it appeared that they could see several degrees beyond the lateral extent of our vision. . . . The texture of the skin . . . was grayish, almost metallic looking . . . I didn't notice any hair . . . [and] there just seemed to be two slits that represented nostrils.[41]

The beings subjected the couple to a series of medical examinations. They placed Barney on a table that was too short for his body and poked and prodded him with an assortment of tools. They expressed great curiosity about his false teeth and pulled them out, bewildered as to why Betty's teeth could not also be removed. Betty endured skin scrapings, nail clippings, a "pregnancy test" in which a long needle was inserted into her abdomen, and some type of full-body scan with a strange device. During her examination, Betty conversed with an alien who appeared to be the leader of the crew. When she asked where he was from, the leader produced a "star map" that Betty later drew from memory.[42] Eventually the creatures escorted the Hills from the ship, during which time an argument broke out between the leader and crew members. The leader had given Betty a book full of strange symbols that she planned to use as proof of the encounter. Other crew members protested. Not only did they not want Betty to have physical evidence of the encounter, they did not want the couple to remember the events at all. The leader relented, took the book, and somehow "erased" the couple's memories of the encounter. During their sessions with Simon the couple was adamant that their memories had been "immediately wiped out after they left the [UFO]" and that hypnosis had not created their memories, but *recovered* them.[43]

John G. Fuller's recounting of the Hill tale, *The Interrupted Journey: Two Lost Hours "Aboard a Flying Saucer,"* became a best-seller in 1966. It was serialized in *Look,* a popular magazine of the time and was the subject of a 1975 television movie starring James Earl Jones as Barney and Estelle Parsons as Betty. Unfortunately, Barney enjoyed little of the resultant fame; he died of a cerebral hemorrhage in 1969. Betty, on the other hand, became a celebrity in UFO circles and the subject of frequent interviews and documentaries until her death in 2004.

The publication of the Hill story arguably created the new phenomenon of UFO abductions.[44] Although abduction narratives have evolved over time, they share certain common features. The abduction is usually at the hands of diminutive, gray-skinned beings with large black eyes and oversized craniums, similar to those in the Hill story. So ubiquitous is this little creature in modern accounts that it has been nicknamed the "Grey" in the UFO subculture. Unlike the earlier contactee tales (chap. 4), abduction accounts were generally considered unpleasant and nonconsensual. Abductees often view themselves as victims, not the chosen messengers of extraterrestrials, and report various forms of mental or physical abuse on the part of the aliens, whether it be forced medical examinations or even rape and impregnation. Most abductees also report a period of "missing time" that hides the details of their encounter. Memories erased by the aliens must be recalled in some way, generally through hypnotic regression as pioneered by Benjamin Simon and the Hills. Throughout the 1970s and into the 1980s, dozens of books appeared recounting UFO abduction experiences with these key elements.

Budd Hopkins and the Abductees

In the 1980s the UFO abduction subculture blossomed. Up until this time the ranks of abductees were relatively small. Those few people who reported their tales often became minor celebrities like the Hills. For example, Travis Walton, an Arizona logger who claimed to have been zapped and kidnapped by an alien craft, only to be returned with limited memory days later, was the subject of books, tabloid reports, and ultimately, a movie called *Fire in the Sky.* But something happened wherein the count of abductees dramatically increased. We were no longer faced with a few celebrities but a mass of anonymous victims. Skeptics and believers disagree on what happened. True believers think that people have finally recognized a previously hidden problem; we are finally *aware* of alien abduction after ignoring it for years, similar to problems like child and spousal abuse. Skeptics believe that abductions are simply a new panic or mania that spread culturally with the benefit of mass media and tabloid attention. Whatever the perspective, it is clear that a New York artist named Budd Hopkins is largely responsible for the UFO abduction movement.

Born in 1931, Hopkins received an education at Oberlin College in Ohio before moving to New York City in 1953. His interest in UFOs stems from an August 1964 sighting of a large object he could not identify in the skies above Cape Cod. He began to read books about UFOs and followed the Hill case with much interest. By the mid-1970s, Hopkins was an active UFO investigator, focusing upon those cases that involved elements of "missing time." To uncover what he thought might be hidden memories of abductions, Hopkins began to hypnotize potential abductees, sometimes by himself and sometimes with the help of mental health professionals. The first book related to his investigations, *Missing Time* appeared in 1981.

A key revelation contained in Hopkins's book is that it is not necessary to have a UFO sighting to claim a potential abduction. Recall that Betty and Barney Hill claimed to have memories all along of seeing a strange object in the sky tailing their car and then watching that object speed away. They simply filled the gaps in between. One of Hopkins's first cases convinced him that a person could have been abducted by aliens without having *any* prior suspicions. It seems that a young man pseudonymed "Steve Kilburn" informed Hopkins that he was deathly afraid of a stretch of road between his home and the home of his girlfriend. Hopkins thought this "an almost ridiculously flimsy pretext for entering into the costly and time-consuming process of hypnotic regression," but ultimately relented.[45] In 1978, the therapist Girard Franklin hypnotized Kilburn, who recounted a by-then familiar narrative. While en route to his girlfriend's house on an evening, a strange force had pulled Kilburn's car to the side of the road. Beings forced him aboard a hovering craft, subjected the terrified man to physical examinations, and then released him—memory erased but with a floating, subconscious fear intact. Armed with these findings, Hopkins embraced the idea that the world might be filled with abductees who have no memories of their abuse save for a feeling of uneasiness or anxiety about a place or any piece of time that could not be accounted for. These feelings might, just might, be evidence of hidden memories of alien abduction ready to boil to the surface with proper therapy.

The second key observation in *Missing Time* concerns the reported experiences of "Virginia Horton." She underwent hypnosis with Hopkins and produced memories of encountering gray aliens as a child in the 1950s. But in a later session, she recovered a memory of a different abduction experience that occurred during a family picnic years later. To Hopkins the two distinct memories suggested that extraterrestrials had been tracking Horton throughout her life as part of an ongoing experiment of some kind. This was a virtually unheard-of notion at the time, as other early abductees (such as the Hills and Travis Walton) were assumed to be just unlucky.[46] Walton had been at the wrong place at the wrong time when the aliens appeared. Someone else could easily have gone in his stead. Horton's experience presented an entirely different scenario. Surely it was not chance alone that led this girl to have been abducted (at least) twice? The aliens must be up to something more nefarious. Horton was somehow special to the aliens.

Noting that Horton had reported suffering from a bloody nose after aliens inserted a probe into her nostril (along with other similar cases from his files), Hopkins concluded that the majority of abductees show evidence of having multiple abduction experiences going back to childhood. Aliens are using an "implant" or tracking device, usually inserted through a nostril, to keep track of these subjects over time. Clearly the "extraterrestrials need something from humans—possibly a certain kind of genetic structure," Hopkins concluded.[47] By his second book in 1987, *Intruders*, Hopkins had developed a complete cosmology, drawing upon further revelations from his clients to outline an alien breeding experiment to create half-human/half-alien beings:

> I want to describe the general pattern of these accounts. An individual, male or female, is first abducted as a child, at a time possibly as early as the third year. During that experience a small incision is made in the child's body, apparently for sample-taking purposes, and then the child is given some kind of physical examination. There will often follow a series of contacts or abductions extended through the years of puberty. In some cases sperm samples will be taken from young males . . . and ova samples taken from young females. . . . In the cases in which artificial insemination is attempted, the women are apparently re-abducted after two or three months of pregnancy, and the fetus is removed from the uterus.[48]

Hopkins's theories changed the nature of the abduction phenomenon and opened the door for UFO-related support groups to emerge—the first of which met in his New York apartment. Books such as *The Alien*

Abduction Survival Guide, Healing Shattered Reality, and *Abductions: Stop Them, Heal Them, Now!* help abductees understand their experiences while organizations such as Hopkins's own Intruder Foundation, the Program for Extraordinary Experience Research (PEER), and the International Center for Abduction Research fostered the development of support groups across the country and referred potential abductees to local therapists.[49]

Hopkins features prominently in Whitley Strieber's recollection of his alien abduction episodes from his vacation home in upstate New York. In Strieber's book, *Communion: A True Story,* he details the events of October 4, 1985, and December 26, 1985. It was Budd Hopkins who encouraged Strieber to meet with Dr. Donald Klein of the New York Psychiatric Institute. In March 1986, Dr. Klein began a series of hypnotic regression therapies through which Strieber recalled vivid details of these events.

The book was published in 1987 and quickly rose to the top of the *New York Times* best-seller list; it stayed on the list in hardback edition for fifteen weeks. In 1989 a movie with the same title, starring Christopher Walken as Strieber, was released by New Line Cinema. The book has had a major impact on the UFO abduction movement. While Strieber has his share of critics and debunkers,[50] several themes from this book recur in the 2009 Universal Studios release, *The Fourth Kind,* including the rural setting, hypnosis, loss of time, extreme lights, and the creepy appearance of a barn owl at the abduction venues.

By 1992 interest in UFO abductions was so high that a truly astonishing event took place: a dreadfully serious conference on the subject held at MIT. A discussion of UFO abductions as mass delusion would not have been surprising in such an august academic setting, but that MIT hosted dozens of talks on subjects ranging from the specific procedures reported by abductees once aboard alien spacecraft to speculation about the biological characteristics of alien/human hybrids was amazing.[51]

Alien Life Support

Aileen Bringle was in a deep sleep in the passenger seat of her car when her husband shook her awake. The couple was on their way to Stanfield, Oregon, passing through an expanse of wheat fields. She was shocked to find that, as far she could see, the land was "encompassed in a brilliant green light between kelly and chartreuse . . . everything, myself and my husband included, was green."[52] The terrified couple could never find the origin of the intense light that finally faded when they rounded a bend in the road, but it forever changed Aileen's life. She devoured books, magazines, and videos, looking for answers to her own experience, and she became fascinated with those of others. She was ultimately drawn to the tales of people who had been contacted or abducted by aliens and feared they lacked the necessary support to deal with the resultant trauma and ridicule. Determined to help, Aileen founded the UFO Contact Center International in 1981. She publicized the new group through advertisements and by leaving brochures at New Age fairs. Its mission:

> The UFOCCI (UFO Contact Center International) was started with the purpose of helping people to examine their bizarre experiences as a result of being abducted by strange beings and being taken aboard what we know of as flying discs, commonly called UFOs. After gathering the information, which has come from all parts of the globe, piecing together parts of the puzzle, the serious investigation began.
>
> Of immediate attention and concern, this organization has focused on the humanoids from our universe. We have been watched and monitored since WWII, perhaps being programmed for their use in a future take-over. Many abductees report that they have had something inserted into their nostrils, implanted into the brain at the base of their heads![53]

Although it is now defunct, the organization spread quickly during its heyday. The first UFOCCI center opened in Federal Way, Washington, a bedroom community of Seattle, and quickly expanded to sixty-five affiliate centers around the United States and into Canada. These centers were largely autonomous, holding meetings when and where they wanted, but Aileen had become a certified hypnotist in order to help the members recover abduction memories, and she encouraged affiliates to provide the same service. The UFOCCI even produced its own magazine for a time, the *Missing Link*, which contained tips on how to conduct abduction therapy and personal abduction accounts, as well as news and announcements.

Christopher observed the monthly meetings of the Federal Way UFOCCI on an intermittent basis over the course of several years, hoping to gain insight into the lives of people who claim dramatic paranormal experiences, and the group graciously allowed someone with no claimed UFO encounters to observe.[54] Meetings followed a standard format. They opened with an overview of recent news, recited by Aileen, from the UFO community. Participants would then discuss whatever UFO story or sighting had captured their interest, often followed by a guest speaker: an author of a UFO book or a self-proclaimed channeler of aliens. In a certain sense, all of this was setup for the main event—the sharing of abduction tales. Once other activities then died down, Aileen would ask those present to share any newly recalled encounters that emerged from therapy sessions she had conducted. Any member who felt that she had experienced "missing time" could contact Aileen for help recalling details of possible abduction events. Some of the memories shared at the monthly meetings were, indeed, very fresh, having been recovered in hypnosis sessions with Aileen mere days or hours before.

In his books, Budd Hopkins popularized the notion that the abducting aliens are, if not evil and selfish at least indifferent to human suffering. He has expressed outrage at the "physical rape of the abductees by a group of aliens apparently interested . . . in replenishing their own failing genetic stock."[55] Hopkins's colleague David M. Jacobs, a Temple University history professor and director of the International Center for Abduction Research, also sees UFO abduction as akin to rape or molestation:

> No matter how they handle the experience, all abductees have one thing in common: They are victims. Just as surely as women who are raped are victims of sexual abuse or soldiers can be victims of Post-Traumatic Stress Disorder, abductees are victims.

Despite this tendency toward the negative among some of the UFO subculture's leading figures, other researchers argue that such a pessimistic view of "abduction" experiences is based on fear, paranoia, and misunderstanding.[56] It is possible that the aliens have our best interests at heart and that the experiences only *seem* terrifying because we do not understand their full purpose. Positive abduction researchers such as Richard Boylan argue that "[f]or most of us, the ETs who have contacted us have become interesting acquaintances and, in some cases, friends. After getting over our initial fright and upset, we have come to share a deep respect for them."[57] As the ranks of abductees with a less negative spin on their experiences grew, they developed a new term, "experiencers," to describe themselves, devoid of the negative baggage attached to "abductee."

The personal stories of UFOCCI members definitely did not fit into tidy categorical boxes. During the same December 1996 meeting, one member recalled a harrowing account of abduction and humiliating medical experiments at the hands of aliens, while another told of a friendly invitation to board a spacecraft for a tour of the universe.

"Clay" even told of a UFO abduction in a previous life. He has hazy memories of working as a pilot in the 1930s. During a routine flight he experienced engine troubles, and while assessing his situation, a saucer-shaped object moved into position in the sky alongside him. The shock of witnessing the craft and the several "small, gray-skinned creatures" that appeared at its windows caused Clay to lose concentration and crash to the ground. Suddenly, he found himself viewing the wreckage of his plane from above, the mysterious saucer hovering above him. The ship somehow pulled his "spirit" aboard, flew away, and docked with an "enormous mothership." Once aboard the ship Clay noticed that he had a new body. His skin had become extremely white, and he was wearing a silver jumpsuit. Two small "Greys" introduced him to the crew, which featured humanlike aliens who were working in concert with the Greys. Three beings led Clay into a small room, seated him in a recliner, and showed him a movie of his just-ended life. They then ushered him into another small saucer, flew past the moon to a blue-green planet, and brought him to a room filled with glass coffins. An alien helped him into one of the coffins, and he immediately passed out. His next memory is as an infant, sitting in a crib looking up at a happy Grey alien floating near the ceiling. The aliens helped Clay to reincarnate in his current form, he believes. It is now incumbent upon Clay to discover the "higher purpose" behind these extraterrestrial manipulations.

As the end of the day's UFOCCI meeting neared, the conversation between Aileen and other members turned to scars. Alien experimentation on humans, it seemed, could leave scars on one's body. The presence of such scarring without an explanation was a sign of a hidden alien encounter. Aileen asked if I had any scars on my hands. Pointing to a long, ridge-like scar on my right pinkie finger, I admitted that I did not know how it occurred. Aileen chuckled to herself and winked at the others. "Don't worry," she said, "you'll find out."

Province of the Elites?

In spending time with people who claim to have experienced the paranormal, we have been continually struck by how poorly they seem to fit a marginal person model. For instance, while searching for Bigfoot with members of the Texas Bigfoot Research Conservancy (see chap. 5), we found ourselves sharing the woods with three men who were intelligent and capable, rather than marginalized and disenfranchised. Two of the three claim to have had visual encounters with the creature. Clearly then not all aspects of paranormal belief and experience fit most people's preconceived notions.

To find out what UFO abductees are like Chris asked the UFOCCI for permission to conduct a national survey of the organization.[58] The UFO subculture is very conspiratorial in nature, so at first some members were concerned that I might be a government agent who would pass their personal information on to intelligence agencies. But after spending time with the group and assuring them that survey information would be kept anonymous, they finally gave permission to submit surveys to UFOCCI affiliates around the country in 1989. Ultimately I was able to gather detailed demographic information on fifty-five people who claim to have been abducted or contacted by extraterrestrials, the most extensive survey of its kind. And the findings were quite interesting.

Nearly all of our UFO abductees (89%) reported their race as white, with the remaining respondents describing themselves as Native American. Despite the fact that one of the first abductees, Barney Hill, was an African American, alien abductions appear to be the province of whites.[59] More striking were the findings for income and education. In 1990 fewer than half of Americans surveyed (46%) had attended college, compared to the majority of UFO abductees (68%).[60] On the other end of the education spectrum, only about 12 percent of UFO abductees did not have a high school diploma, compared to almost a fourth of Americans (22%). More than half of the abductees held well-paying, white-collar jobs; they were electronics technicians, professors, therapists, and marketing representatives. Unless we choose to define someone as a fringe member of society simply because they claim to have been abducted by aliens or are chasing Bigfoot (which might be a reasonable definition to some), abductees are *not* marginal people. Many of the people we have met would be better described as elites.

One way to understand why elites might be attracted to the paranormal is to think of paranormal beliefs and experiences as something that is "cutting edge." Whenever a new technology enters the market there are people who immediately embrace it, people who are excited by new things and ready to take risks. Marketers call such people "early adopters." Then there are the rest of us, who want to wait until a new idea or technology is fully proven before we jump onboard. Early adopters tend to be those that have more education, more income, and expansive social networks. They are people who have been continually exposed to new ideas throughout their lives via higher education and contacts with other educated people. They also have the resources to try new things. It is hard to imagine people doubting the staying power of the television, but when TV first became available it was the more-educated, higher-income people who purchased the first sets.[61] Of course, people with higher levels of income could both afford the new sets (new technologies are always more expensive when they first appear) and could ignore the risk if TV did not take off. A $200 iPhone is a less risky purchase for someone making $100,000 a year than for someone scraping by on $10,000.

If we conceive of the totality of religion in America as a marketplace of supernatural ideas, then the paranormal represents fringe and often relatively new "products."[62] A number of religion scholars have suggested that a similar rule applies as to the consumption of other new products; early adopters of new religious ideas would be elites. Those with higher educations will have been exposed to a wider variety of new ideas and even a variety of religions they may not have experienced otherwise. In addition, rapid social and technological change can create existential crises, a deep questioning of basic beliefs about the meaning and purpose of life. Younger and better educated individuals are more likely to be acutely aware of rapid change, more likely to suffer such crises, and more open to new explanations.[63] Elites are innovators, seekers, and adapters.[64] Thus we might expect elites to be more likely to create new supernatural products and more likely to adopt those products once they appear.[65]

In fact, the histories of many religious movements have shown exactly this. For example, the early Mormons drew their first members from the more prosperous, educated areas of New York State.[66] Then there was the New Thought movement, which billed itself as a bringer of universal brotherhood, decried racism and sexism, and sought stronger links between science and religion. It was nurtured by the highly educated urban elite culture of Boston and Harvard University during the second half of the nineteenth century,[67] and counted among its practitioners and supporters Ralph Waldo Emerson and the inventor Phineas Quimby.[68] The Human Potential Movement of the 1960s developed a bohemian village (Esalen Institute) for those who were seeking to uncover the life force of the universe and use its power to transform mankind. It was co-founded by Stanford graduates Richard Price and Michael Murphy, and the noted scholar Aldous Huxley was an early advisor. Scientology has become noted for its ability to attract wealthy and powerful members such as Tom Cruise and John Travolta. Even members of witch covens tend to be in professional and white-collar occupations.[69]

But lest we think that the paranormal is a safe playground for the creative elite, we must also consider its inherent risks. To delve into unconventional beliefs and practices is to run the risk of being labeled strange or deviant.[70] For people who are already socially marginal, being labeled a deviant is of lesser importance. Those with a lot of resources are somewhat protected from the consequences of risky behaviors, but at the same time they have more to lose. Engaging in deviant behavior can have a detrimental effect on one's social standing for members of higher socioeconomic classes. Just as it is important to belong to the right clubs, drive the right cars, live in the right neighborhood, and make the right friends to maintain one's social standing, it is also important to maintain the "right" religious practices.

When it was revealed that former First Lady Nancy Reagan was consulting an astrologer about White House business, she became the object of scorn and ridicule—it was not the type of thing that someone of her standing should be doing. In fact, on November 7, 2008, President-elect Barack Obama made an off-handed remark in a news conference about Reagan's paranormal practices, for which he later apologized.[71] Interestingly, not much has been made of George W. Bush's persistent practice of opening cabinet meetings with prayer.[72] One is a conventional practice, the other is not.

A former vice-mayor of Phoenix, Arizona, by the name of Frances Emma Barwood, learned a similar lesson about the dangers of embracing the paranormal. On March 13, 1997, hundreds of persons reported lights in a flying V-shaped formation above the city of Phoenix, an incident known as "the Phoenix Lights." Those who witnessed the lights were not pleased with the government's official explanation of flares set off by the Maryland Air National Guard on special maneuvers over the Arizona desert. At a Phoenix City Council meeting, Barwood asked her colleagues to help investigate the light sightings, seeking a more convincing explanation. She was met with both silence and ridicule. Her situation was not improved by a spoof press conference called by then governor Fyfe Symington, featuring his chief of staff wearing a Grey alien costume. Ms. Barwood later described the humiliation:

I remember Mayor Rimsza handing out business cards with my name on it, saying, Frances Emma Barwood from the planet Xenon. Talk into the aluminum foil and she'll hear you. Or something like that. And he was handing them out to people like that. I wonder why they were so intent upon ridiculing me, other than to just shut me up. He was even on television, doing a speech before National Guard pilots, and he ridiculed me about trying to find out about things flying over Phoenix.[73]

Barwood's career suffered. She tried to run for secretary of state, but her opponent garnered 76 percent of the vote. Ironically, ten years after the event, the same former governor Symington admitted to having seen the Phoenix lights himself. He had refused to acknowledge this in 1997, knowing what it would mean for *his* career.

Paranormal Experiences in the United States

Do the wealthy flock to the paranormal as a creative outlet or avoid UFOs and the paranormal for fear of embarrassment and lost country club memberships? Paranormal experiences are, in fact, surprisingly common

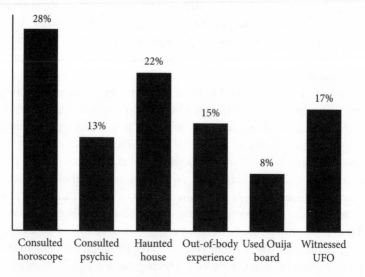

Fig. 3.9. Paranormal experiences in the United States (Baylor Religion Survey, 2005)

	Consulted horoscope	Consulted psychic	Haunted house	Out-of-body experience	Used Ouija board	Witnessed UFO
Gender	Female	Female	Female	—[a]	Female	—
Race	—	—	—	"Other" races	—	—
Age	Younger	Younger	Younger	—	Younger	—
Marital status	Not married	—	—	—	—	—
Income	Lower[b]	—	Lower	—	—	Lower, lower-middle
Education	—	Less than high school, college grad	—	College grad	—	Some college

[a] — = no statistically significant effect
[b] Lower income = < $10,000 per year. Lower-middle income = $10,000–$35,000 per year

Fig. 3.10. Profiles in the paranormal (Baylor Religion Survey, 2005)

Note: This table is based on a series of logistic regression analyses in which we predict the likelihood of claiming each experience using a model that includes gender, race, age, marital status, income, education, region of the country, religious tradition, frequency of church attendance, and biblical literalism. For more details, see full models in the appendix.

in the United States (see fig. 3.9). Nearly a third of Americans have consulted their horoscope. Given that consulting a horoscope is as easy as opening the paper or looking on Yahoo, this might be expected. However, more than 12 percent of Americans have taken the trouble to personally consult a psychic, medium, or fortune-teller for information about their future or to understand current circumstances. One-fifth have visited or lived in a home they believe to be haunted by spirits, and a smaller number (about 8%) have attempted to contact the spirit world with a Ouija board. As we found earlier, nearly one-fourth of Americans believe that some UFOs are extraterrestrial craft—and nearly one-fifth believe they have actually seen one.

Academics love to be able to tell a clear, straightforward story with their data. Unfortunately, the paranormal simply refuses to behave. When we break down paranormal experiences by key demographic characteristics, such as gender, age, race, marital status, income, and education we find a complicated tale (see fig. 3.10). By running a series of analyses we can determine which factors predict the likelihood of claiming a series of paranormal experiences. For example, age is negatively associated with consulting a horoscope, meaning that older people are less likely to do so. The likelihood of using a horoscope, likewise, decreases with income. Unmarried males and females also show an increased likelihood of consulting horoscopes as do females in general. Thus, the single most likely person to regularly consult their horoscope is a younger, unmarried female at the lower levels of income.

Gender is, in fact, related to several paranormal experiences. In addition to their use of horoscopes, women are also significantly more likely than men to consult a psychic to learn about the future, to believe that they have lived in or visited a haunted house, and to have used a Ouija board at least once. Women are not more likely than men to claim a UFO sighting or to believe they have had an out-of-body experience, but we can say that, in general, women are more paranormally oriented than men. From here the story gets more complicated, as simplistic notions of who has specific paranormal experiences are incorrect.

If paranormal experiences are the province of the marginalized, we should find a powerful relationship with education, income, and race. Income is related to three of the six experiences. People with lower levels of income are more likely to believe they have lived in or visited a haunted house, to consult their horoscopes, and to have seen a UFO. Similarly, people without high school diplomas are more likely to consult psychics. Perhaps for these people a paranormal experience is about control. Engaging psychics to learn about one's fate or hoping the stars will reveal their secrets is a way of attempting to exert control over an unkind world. Having a paranormal belief or experience is a view into another reality, a reality different from the one in which the person is marginalized and lacks control. In this sense, having a paranormal experience can be a sign of hope. And yet, those making over $100,000 a year are also attracted to haunted houses and UFO sightings, so such things are not merely the opiate of the masses.

People who join and form new religious movements tend to be from the upper classes, but we do not find conclusive evidence that paranormal experiences are primarily a creative outlet for the privileged few. Those at the highest levels of income and education are more prone to some paranormal experiences, but not others. People who have a college degree are more likely to consult psychics, and have out-of-body experiences than those at mid-levels of education. Those who attended college but did not finish are the most likely to claim UFO sightings. But education does not impact the use of horoscopes, living in a haunted house, or the use of Ouija boards.

Perhaps our most important finding is that we can not use simplistic, broad-brushed explanations to understand the paranormal. Nevertheless, we can answer our family doctor conclusively: people who believe in and experience the paranormal are not simply "nuts." We find no evidence that paranormal beliefs or experiences are the exclusive realm of hypermarginalized people, as we should expect if they have mental problems.[74] More than two-thirds (69%) of Americans believe in the reality of at least one of the topics we discuss in this book (psychic powers, fortune-telling, astrology, talking to the dead, haunted houses, ghosts, UFOs, and monsters). More than half of Americans (51%) claim at least one of the paranormal experiences listed above (consulting a horoscope or psychic, visiting or living in a haunted house, an out of body experience, using a Ouija board, or witnessing a UFO). To attribute these beliefs and experiences to being "crazy," we would have to believe that more than half of the adult population of the United States is "crazy," a frightening prospect to be sure.

Oftentimes we search for simple answers to phenomena we do not understand. For example, "brainwashing" is frequently trotted out to explain why people join strange religious groups even though sociologists have been outlining the complicated reasons people do so for years.[75] In a similar vein, it is much easier to flippantly label someone as nuts if they have seen a UFO than it is to delve into the complex sociological, psychological, and idiosyncratic reasons why someone might interpret a light in the sky as extraterrestrial in origin. The media relies on such demonization and simplicity far too often. Complex stories make poor copy.

Over the next several chapters we buck the trend toward labeling and oversimplification by exploring several additional types of interaction with the paranormal. This approach enables to us find out if there are clearer patterns of participation. We begin, in the next chapter by examining how the paranormal interacts with "conventional" religion. Does going to church lead a person to avoid the enticements of the paranormal?

4

Round Trip to Hell in a
Flying Saucer?

But the cowardly, the unbelieving, the vile, the murderers, the sexually immoral, *those who practice magic arts,* the idolaters and all liars—their place will be in the fiery lake of burning sulfur. (NIV)[1]
—Revelation 21:8

Americans are a remarkably religious people. More than 80 percent fall within the Judeo-Christian lineage, while just over 5 percent claim a faith outside this heritage. Half attend church or temple at least once a month. Nearly another third maintain *some* contact with a religious group by attending at least once a year.[2] Whether they attend church services or not the great majority of Americans (82%) identify as a Christian of some form or another,[3] and most hold relatively traditional beliefs. Almost three-fourths of Americans (73%) believe that Jesus is the one and only son of God.[4] Even more (81%) believe in an anthropomorphic God.

Given the ubiquitous faith of Americans, the popularity of the paranormal in the United States may be tied to the fate of conventional religion. To the extent that the paranormal is in direct conflict with conventional religion, its growth may remain limited to the minority of Americans outside of conventional religion but still open to the supernatural. On the other hand, should conventional religion decline in popularity, its decline could open the door to a revival of interest in alternative spiritualities and paranormal topics.

There is an alternative to tying the fate of the paranormal to the growth, stability, or decline of conventional religion—the possibility that religious Americans will accept paranormal beliefs as a *complement* to their existing religious beliefs. Clearly, at least some Christians must be interested in the paranormal judging by the ubiquity and popularity of related television shows, books, and movies. Perhaps religious individuals simply do not see a conflict between believing in angels and ghosts at the same time, or simultaneously reading the Bible and UFO literature. Is there any harm in a Catholic visiting an astrologer?

Throughout American history there have been sporadic movements that directly tested the boundaries of Christianity by attempting to fuse Christian ideas with paranormal concepts. One of the most audacious of these was George Adamski's endeavor to bring Jesus to the flying saucers.

Jesus on a Flying Saucer

A colorful character by all accounts, George Adamski founded the Royal Order of Tibet in the 1930s to espouse his "cosmic philosophy," and attracted a small following. He had little formal schooling but enjoyed being called "professor" by eager students. By the 1940s, Adamski was living near the Mount Palomar observatory in California, working as a short-order cook. Fortuitously (his critics would say by design), Adamski began to claim UFO sightings just as interest in the subject was reaching new heights in the late 1940s. In October 1946 while peering at a meteor shower through his telescope, Adamski claimed that he spotted an object "similar in shape to a giant dirigible."[5] Adamski began to make frequent trips to the desert near his home, believing that "spaceships" might choose to land in less populated areas.

On November 20, 1952, Adamski and six associates traveled to a barren area near Desert Center, California, spent the morning exploring, and sat down to eat lunch at about noon. At that time a plane passed low over their heads, drawing the group's attention to a "gigantic cigar-shaped silvery ship without wings or appendages of any kind" hovering nearby.[6] According to his later recounting of the events, Adamski experienced a strange "feeling" that he must move to a location close to the area. He asked his friends to drop him off there, and he then moved to a position about a mile away. Once safely alone, Adamski claims to have seen a flash in the sky, followed by the appearance of a "beautiful small craft," which descended into a nearby cove. As he took pictures of the vicinity, he noticed a man standing near the entrance of a ravine. Upon approach, Adamski realized that he was face-to-face with an extraterrestrial:

Now for the first time I fully realized that I was in the presence of a man from space—A HUMAN BEING FROM ANOTHER WORLD! . . . The beauty of his form surpassed anything I had ever seen. And the pleasantness of his face freed me of all thought of my personal self. . . . He was about five feet, six inches in height and weighed—according to our standard —about 135 pounds. . . . He was round faced with an extremely high fore-head . . . and average size mouth with beautiful white teeth that shone when he smiled or spoke. As nearly as I can describe his skin the colour-ing would be an even, medium-colored suntan. And it did not look to me as though he had ever had to shave, for there was no more hair on his face than on a child's. His hair was sandy in colour and hung in beautiful waves to his shoulders, glistening more beautifully than any woman's I have ever seen.[7]

Adamski asked the being where he came from, but the long-haired spaceman apologetically shook his head to indicate that he did not speak English. Thankfully, he and the alien managed to communicate through a combination of "feelings, signs, and above all . . . telepathy."[8] The being indicated that he was part of a friendly landing party from Venus visiting Earth out of concern for recent nuclear testing. If humans do not change their ways, he warned, they will destroy themselves and surrounding plan-ets. Having delivered this dire warning, the alien indicated that he had to leave and returned to his craft, which ascended out of sight.

Far tamer than modern day UFO abduction tales, Adamski's story was revelatory at the time. A ghost-written account of the event was tacked onto a recently completed compendium of UFO reports written by Des-mond Leslie and published under the title *Flying Saucers Have Landed* in 1953.[9] The book was a great success and went through several printings. Adamski became a minor celebrity, appearing on radio shows, lecturing to large groups, and even meeting Queen Julianna of Holland in 1959, who had shown an interest in UFOs.[10] Adamski followed up with two sequels, *Inside the Spaceships* and *Flying Saucers Farewell*, that recounted continued adventures with his "space brothers" including trips to outer space and a visit to a giant mothership.

Whether by accident or design, Adamski's tales represented an attempt to merge the paranormal with conventional religion. Adamski's books fre-quently utilized Christian symbolism. Jesus, it seems, was an alien incar-nated on Earth to help humans learn to be peaceful. In *Flying Saucers Farewell*, Adamski devotes considerable space to demonstrating biblical support for his claims, including the argument that the space people are the biblical angels:

> The idea of angels having wings growing out of their shoulders and wearing long robes, was instilled in the minds of present-day people by the great artists who pictured them as such. The Bible has always described them as ordinary men from other worlds.[11]

He is even more direct, later in the same book: "Many people want to know if the space people are Christians. I would say they are better Christians than we are."

Adamski's attempt to merge Christianity with flying saucers did not succeed as his personal fortunes faded in the early 1960s. Some of his most ardent fans became disenchanted after his 1962 claim that the space brothers took him to Saturn to attend a conference.[12] Photos of spaceships included in his books were viewed with suspicion and proved easy to fake. Moreover, his eyewitness descriptions of outer space did not match the experiences of astronauts. Critics also noticed the astonishing similarities between Adamski's "non-fiction" works and *Pioneers of Space: A Trip to the Moon, Mars and Venus,* a science fiction novel he had published in 1949. Nevertheless, Adamski proved to be the template for the UFO "contactee" movement.[13]

Contactee tales frequently include Christian symbols and themes.[14] The late George King (1919–97) claimed to receive channeled messages from "cosmic masters" such as Mars Sector 6, Mars Sector 8, and Jesus himself (a Venusian according to King, echoing Adamski).[15] The audacious King even claimed that Jesus personally endorsed his book *The Twelve Blessings.*[16] It seems that King's mother, Mary, was invited by the aliens to take a trip to space on January 19, 1959. Ever the proud mother, she brought a copy of her son's book to a rendezvous point where she was picked up by "a Space Craft Commanded by a Being known as MARS SECTOR 8." The craft traveled deep into space and entered a mothership wherein Mary King met "The Great Master Jesus Himself." Jesus thumbed through the book, blessed it and kept the copy for himself.

Laura and the Chair of Knowledge

Although the movement certainly had its heyday in the 1950s and 1960s, there remains the occasional contactee representing this curious merger of Christianity and the space age, as we learned by visiting Laura Cyr, a formal postal worker who lives in Washington State.

Late one spring evening in 1984, Laura was driving home after visiting a friend in Auburn, Washington. Her favorite route was a calm road that wound past Lake Tapps. Back then the area was rural with scattered farms and ranches and the occasional herd of elk. Nowadays upscale developments and apartment complexes have scattered the animals, and the few remaining farms are surrounded on all sides by suburban minimansions. As Laura rounded a bend near a marshy area, she saw what she thought were orange headlights in a field. She immediately felt very tired and pulled her car to the side of the road. As she approached the lights in a daze she realized that they were attached to a strange, landed craft shaped like a piece of Skittles candy.

Next to the strange craft were two odd-looking creatures beckoning to Laura. Standing between five and six feet tall, they had bronze skin,

Laura at the location of her encounter with a UFO

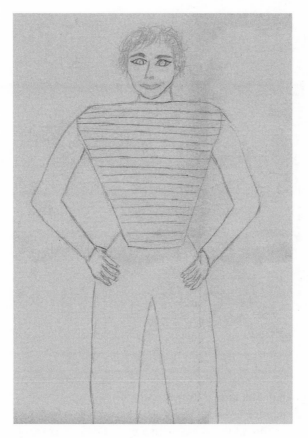

The captain

lightbulb shaped heads, and large black eyes. She agreed to enter the saucer, which then ascended into the heavens and docked with a "mile-long" craft in Earth's upper atmosphere. The aliens somehow erased or hid Laura's memories every time she left the ship, Laura told us, but upon boarding she immediately realized that she had been there many times. The aliens onboard knew her as "Saleetha," and in preparation for boarding she had shed her earthly body, exchanging brown hair for blonde, her earthly clothes for a silver jumpsuit.

By now it was almost midnight, and the commander of the vessel's night shift anxiously greeted her. Laura recognized the handsome being as an old friend and beamed when talking about him. "He was like a big puppy," she said, "so happy to see me again!" Unlike the creatures that had

The bridge

transported her to space, the commander was humanoid with white skin and blonde hair. She kindly drew him for us.

The commander brought Laura to a balcony overlooking the "well" a multistory opening in the vessel with a gigantic black computer taking up part of the vessel's curved walls. Other humanlike aliens sat in chairs that floated in midair, in front of an array of monitors and controls. Laura/Saleetha was awestruck by the simplicity of the obviously advanced computer system.

After a short elevator ride, Laura's friend led her to the commissary for a meal. She was stunned by the vibrant colors in the room: the rose-colored walls, draperies and valances, even the tables and chairs. Sitting among a group of friendly humanoids, Laura ate a delicious meal consisting of some sort of vegetable protein formed and shaped to look like a chicken patty, and a drink, which looked and felt like green shampoo but tasted of delicious sugar water.

Once Laura was refreshed and reacquainted with the ship, the commander finally told her the purpose of this visit. The aliens were training Laura for some obscure future purpose, at which point she would be needed to help the Earth in a crisis. On each of her trips to the mother-ship Laura received a related lesson of her choosing. The commander directed her to a room occupied by a computer and a large chair, similar to what one might find in a dentist's office.

As Laura sat in the chair, the commander adjusted a strange, cone-like device attached to a metal arm, until it rested on her temple. Following instructions she selected the subject about which she wanted to learn and the "intensity" at which she wished to learn it. Laura decided to learn about holistic medicine. Fearing that "maximum intensity" learning would be overwhelming, she chose medium intensity, sat back, relaxed, and allowed information to be relayed into her brain.

The commander was pleased with Laura's efforts. "What you need to know is now in your mind," he told her, "and there will come a time when you need this information to help others." With a sad look on his face the commander told Laura that this concluded their visit. He gave her a necklace, "a gift given to you because you have come to this point" but had to tell her that it could not leave the ship. The two hugged warmly before he led her to the two bronze-skinned escorts. The beings dropped Laura off at her truck, her memories somehow erased. They could not erase, however, a nagging sense in her mind that she had had a "spiritually

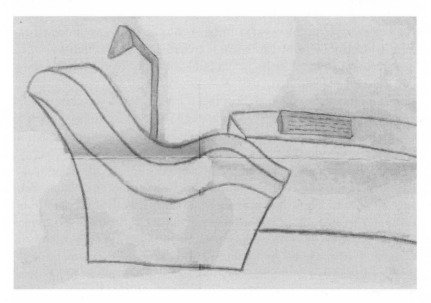

The chair of knowledge

transforming experience." Eventually Laura sought out a hypnotist to help recover her memories of the events.

A Small Step from Jesus to UFOs?

Like many of the contactees of the 1950s, Laura sees no conflict between her UFO encounters and Christianity. At various times she has attended a Roman Catholic church, and is very attracted to the teachings of the Unity Church. She told us that her flying saucer experiences complement that faith. After all, Laura's experiences are teaching her to be a healer and to help others when they really need it, an inherently Christian message. Besides, she said, Jesus is also an enlightened being and probably a space person as well.

The contactee movement did what many other new religious movements have tried to do—promote their new ideas while drawing heavily upon the beliefs and practices of the existing culture.[17] Religion scholars recognize that new religions have an easier time selling their ideas if they can somehow couch them in concepts with which potential converts are already familiar.[18] In a largely Christian culture, this means that new religious groups would be wise to include elements of Christianity in their belief systems. The Church of Jesus Christ of Latter-day Saints (Mormon) is a key example in this regard. The early Mormons were considered extremely deviant by many Christians,[19] chased across the country for their new revelations about visits by Jesus to the New World, beliefs about plural marriage (since redacted), and doctrine regarding personal ascension to godhood. Yet the mere fact that the LDS church includes the Old and New Testament among its holy books certainly aids in its outreach to Christians as attested to by the phenomenal growth rate of the church in the past few decades.[20]

Susan Palmer's research with the Raëlians documents the many parallels in their theology and the Judeo-Christian version of creation. Yahweh is the name of the leader of a team of alien scientists who landed on earth and created the first humans (i.e., Adam and Eve); there is even a Noah's Ark equivalent. Yahweh, convinced of the evil nature of humans by Satan, the head of an Elohim organization opposed to human creation, destroyed the earth with a nuclear holocaust. Lucifer (bearer of light), an opponent of Satan and stranded on earth, managed to save two of each animal in a spaceship that orbited earth until the radiation levels returned to normal. Yahweh and Satan are in a perpetual struggle over the state of humans on earth: Yahweh sees humans as good and redeemable, while Satan sees humans as a failed experiment that must be destroyed.

The Raëlians are awaiting the advent of Elohim in the year 2035. Raël is the current Elohim prophet who is tasked with instructing the humans how to prepare for the coming of the Elohim: unite in world peace and build an embassy for them in Israel. Why Israel? The Jews are chosen people in Raëlian theology. They were created by the cross-breeding of the aliens and the daughters of the humans created by the Elohim. The Raëlians spend considerable effort to convert Jews to the cause and to convince them that Raël is the Messiah. It is imperative that Israel provide the Raëlians land to build the embassy. Upon returning to earth, and provided the prophecies have been fulfilled, the Elohim will share with humans all of their knowledge and technology. If we fail to heed this prophecy, the Elohim will allow us to destroy ourselves in a nuclear holocaust.

The Raëlians have also incorporated a number of Judeo-Christian practices, rituals, and symbols into their belief system. Members are expected to give 11 percent of their incomes, and like Christians, only a small percentage actually gives the full tax. There is a baptism, or transmission ceremony, in which Raël dips his hands in a bowl of water and then holds the head of the recipient, linking her/him with the Elohim in telepathic communication. They have a "holy ground"—UFOland in Valcourt, Quebec—which will be replaced by the embassy in Israel, once it is constructed.[21]

All of this implies that attempts to merge Christianity and the paranormal just might work. After all, there are many similarities between these two spheres. Christian beliefs and paranormal beliefs frequently share a spiritual orientation: a belief that the entirety of the world cannot be fully explained by conventional science and materialism.[22] Many of those same beliefs are non-falsifiable and cannot be directly challenged (or supported) by scientific research. Of course certain religious beliefs have a distinct advantage over paranormal beliefs in that they enjoy widespread acceptance in our culture. Given that the United States is predominantly Christian, belief in God, heaven, hell, the resurrection of Jesus, and the virgin birth are more culturally acceptable supernatural beliefs. Belief in psychic powers, ghosts, and UFOs, however, lack the benefit of association with the majority belief system.

Nevertheless, both Christians and paranormal believers devote themselves to things that require a measure of faith and a willingness to accept

Percentage of respondents who claim to have had a paranormal experience

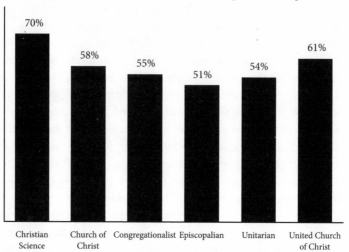

Fig. 4.1. Paranormal experiences in selected denominations (Baylor Religion Survey, Wave 1, 2005)

Note: Respondents were counted as having had a paranormal experience if they checked yes to any of the following possible experiences/activities: consulted a horoscope, visited a medium or psychic, lived or visited a haunted house, consulted a Ouija board, witnessed a UFO, or had an out-of-body experience.

the ephemeral.[23] Perhaps, as the political scientist Tom W. Rice put it, "It is a small step to move from believing in the devil and angels to believing in ghosts and aliens." Indeed, a look at the religious beliefs of the members of seven selected Christian groups might suggest little discord between Christianity and the paranormal (see fig. 4.1).

If you happen to be a Christian Scientist, Congregationalist, Episcopalian, Unitarian, or a member of the Church of Christ (United Church of Christ), on any Sunday morning you have a 50/50 chance of sitting near someone who has interfaced with the paranormal in some way. Half or more of the members of each of these denominations have consulted a horoscope, visited a psychic or medium, seen a UFO, lived in or visited a haunted house, had an out-of-body experience, or used a Ouija Board to contact spirits.[24] Does this mean that Christianity and the paranormal have learned to get along? Not so fast.

Readers familiar with U.S. denominations will have caught the bit of trickery in the table in figure 4.1. All of the selected groups are mainline Protestants. Christianity is not monolithic, and individual denominations vary widely in their beliefs and practices. For ease of comparison, American religion scholars often group specific denominations into larger religious traditions. There are obvious distinctions between Roman Catholics and Protestants, but Protestantism itself can be further subdivided into two religious traditions, mainline and evangelical Protestants.[25] Some of the largest mainline denominations in the United States include the Episcopal Church, the Presbyterian Church (USA), the United Methodist Church, and the Evangelical Lutheran Church in America. The Southern Baptist Convention is the largest evangelical denomination, with nearly twenty million adherents as of 2000. Other large evangelical denominations include the Assemblies of God, Lutheran Church–Missouri Synod, Pentecostals, and the Seventh-Day Adventist Church, among many others.

Evangelicals and mainline Protestants share the belief that Jesus is the son of God and that the Bible is a holy book, but they differ on other key issues. In a nutshell, evangelicals have a much more conservative perspective on doctrinal issues: they are more likely to believe in the complete inerrancy of the Bible, while mainline Protestants are more apt to see the Bible as a historical document, informed by the word of God yet grounded by its historical context and not to be taken literally on all topics. Evangelical Protestants also believe that individuals must knowingly accept salvation through Jesus and have a personal relationship with God. Thus, evangelicals stress the importance of informed baptism and believe that Jesus is the only route to Heaven. Mainline Protestants, on the other hand, are more likely to accept infant and childhood baptisms, and place greater emphasis on an individual's spiritual journey instead of on their conversion or born-again experience. Evangelical Protestants take very seriously the responsibility to proselytize others. Mainline Protestants are not *as* concerned about converting others to the faith, but see proselytizing as one form of living their faith, along with community service and other forms of social ministry.[26]

Put another way, religious groups and traditions vary in their level of strictness—how much they expect from members and how literally they interpret doctrine. Evangelical Protestant groups are much stricter in this regard than the average mainline Protestant group, and this difference in strictness impacts experimentation with the paranormal. To understand why, we must take a diversion into the world of economics.

The Economics of Paranormal Exploration

Economics is a complicated discipline with many schools and subareas. In the simplest terms, classic economic theory attempts to understand the workings of the marketplace by analyzing the movement (production, consumption, and distribution) of scarce "goods" and the motivations of the key actors involved. Economics typically focuses upon scarce items, for there is little to study when a particular entity is available to everyone. If oil were as plentiful as the soil it is found in, then the modern history of mankind would not have been partially determined by attempts to control its discovery, manufacture, pricing, and distribution.

The most creative economists apply the concept of goods and scarcity far beyond the marketplace. Love is a scarce commodity, as is happiness, career satisfaction, personal freedom, health, and well-being. People greatly value such nonmaterial rewards and are willing to exchange other material and nonmaterial goods to get them. Seeking love will usually require some money, but it will take an even greater investment of time and emotional energy. We have all experienced the give-and-take of everyday life, even if we do not view it through the lens of the market. Economists focus upon the human desire to avoid risk in such exchanges. Just as good investors try to find the right combination of risk and reward in their business dealings, we all try to do the same in other spheres of life. Put another way, humans do their best to secure the outcomes that they want in the most certain way possible.

The economist Laurence Iannaccone argues that such economic principles can also be applied to such seemingly personal and ephemeral subjects as faith and personal religiosity.[27] Religion claims to offer some of the greatest rewards imaginable such as salvation and eternal life, satisfactions not available through other alternative means. People will be highly motivated to seek such rewards and desire as much certainty as possible that they will get them. Religious acts, argues Iannaccone, "have the character of risky investments," for those engaging in religious activity cannot know for certain if their faith will be rewarded in the manner that they desire.[28] As would any sensible investor, religious consumers will attempt to reduce their risks by holding "diversified portfolios of competing religious assets."[29] In other words, Iannaccone argues that it is human nature to hedge our bets with regards to religion: given the option, people will naturally explore many different religious and spiritual alternatives. A particular religious "consumer" may attend services at one church, while consulting psychics and reading about alternative spiritualities. Should one religious investment strategy "fail," then at least there is another possibility for salvation to fall back upon.[30]

Holding a "portfolio" of competing religious goods may be good for the believer, but it is not particularly healthy for the religious groups involved. People have only a limited amount of time, effort, and resources, so the more they spread those resources around, the less they have to give any one of them. Religious groups that do not actively curtail outside spiritual exploration will become plagued with lackadaisical members who attend rarely and give little of their time and money to further the group goals.

Economists often refer to the concept of a free rider to explain a key problem that some groups encounter. A person who manages to sneak onto a bus without paying the toll has gotten a free ride. The bus will reach its destination with or without his money, an amazing bargain to be sure. The problem is, that if everyone acts like our free rider, then the bus will no longer have the money to operate and nobody will get a ride. Religious organizations are also forced to deal with the "free rider" problem: many people would prefer to reap the benefits of belonging to a religious organization without having to offer anything in return. The stereotypical "Christmas Catholic" is the ultimate free rider, enjoying Mass once a year but avoiding services for the rest. People who want to get married in their church but have little interest in it otherwise are another example of free-riderdom.

One way in which a religious group can reduce the number of free riders is to make strict demands of its members.[31] If a congregation makes it clear to potential members that weekly attendance is expected, and if they enforce that rule either through peer pressure or by more official means such as dismissal, those free riders will leave to find a less demanding home. In the same vein, requiring members to dress or act in a certain way or placing prohibitions upon behavior makes the cost of minimal participation outweigh the potential benefits for the marginally religious. Groups that have strict rules, regulations, and expectations serve to limit the religious portfolios of their members. In strict religious groups, Iannaccone states that "[p]otential members are forced to choose: participate fully or not at all."[32]

Iannaccone's creative work suggests that those religious groups with conservative theologies and high expectations of members will be strongly motivated to restrict members from involving themselves with other religious or spiritual activities. Following his line of reasoning, we would expect that evangelical Protestants would develop a strong resistance to the paranormal. Indeed, as our UFO contactee friend Laura learned, evangelicals do not simply believe the paranormal to be an "economic" threat, but a threat to the soul.

That "Flying Saucer Religion"

Laura may not see a conflict between her flying saucer experiences and Christianity, but her father was not in agreement. Laura's relationship with her father was most certainly troubled—at times he had physically abused her and even spent some time in prison. While incarcerated, Laura's father "found God" and became a devout Pentecostal who "believed in the Bible word for word." When Laura told her father of her UFO experiences, he was dismayed. "I don't like this spaceship religion," he told her. UFOs are not spoken of in the Bible and therefore they must be Satanic in nature, he argued.[33] When Laura reiterated that the aliens she encountered seemed friendly and peaceful, her father was unimpressed. "If a spaceship lands and an alien comes out, I know what that alien really is . . . a demon or devil." Laura's father is not alone in his beliefs.

Many evangelicals and other conservative Christians generally have a negative view of the paranormal. Christian supernatural beliefs, however, are normally accepted, and expected; supernatural beliefs outside of the Christian purview are discouraged, challenged, and avoided, not embraced.[34]

A visit to a Christian bookstore will reveal a slew of books warning of the dangers of the New Age and paranormal,[35] including the vastly popular series by Frank Peretti, wherein the New Age movement plays a central, villainous role. In these novels the New Age is not seen as a loosely organized collection of paranormal beliefs, but as a threat to organized religion with realistic power. While the novels are considered fiction, the message has been taken seriously by some Christian groups; some even distributing copies of the novels to their congregations.[36] Perhaps more informally and more humorously, there is the case of Marguerite Perrin, who appeared on the reality TV show *Trading Spouses*. She unleashed a torrent of objection to the New Age practices of her briefly adopted family, labeling herself the "God Warrior" and proclaiming that practices such as tarot cards, psychics, and astrology were "dark-sided," among other things.

As the reaction of Laura's father to her UFO tales illustrates, Christian concern about the paranormal is not limited to divination and psychic phenomena. A number of evangelical authors have warned of the dangers of UFOs. Ron Rhodes's *Alien Obsession* warns that public fascination with UFOs and other "occult" topics is drawing attention away from Christian messages. Among the pieces of evidence Rhodes uses to prove that extra-terrestrials are merely demons and devils in disguise are:

- The "aliens" never say anything that *affirms* the Bible as being God's Word.
- The "aliens" never say anything about man's sin problem and need for redemption.
- "Revelations" from these so-called "space brothers" not only consistently contradict the Scriptures but consistently promote a New Age worldview.
- It is typically people who are already involved in the occult who have [UFO] abduction experiences.[37]

The theme of UFOs as a manifestation of Satan has been echoed in many other Christian books,[38] films, and documentaries. The Christian Broadcasting Network's *Newswatch* analysis of UFO lore concludes that alien abductions are the outward and visible expressions of Satan, in which people are put into trancelike states so that it is nearly impossible to distinguish truth from reality.[39]

In addition, one might think that the possible existence of an undiscovered ape or hominid would be unthreatening to Christians, but even Bigfoot has not been spared from the ire of some evangelicals. The authors of a recent paranormal handbook for Christians warn that Bigfoot might be a demon:

> It would appear to us that the question of the existence of these "ape men" hinges upon whether or not they are demons inhabiting the bodies of animals. . . . The fact that (as in the case of UFOs) all, or almost all, of the encounters involved non-Christians may suggest either that there aren't that many Christians roaming the wildest reaches of the earth . . . or that there are demonic forces manifesting themselves on planet earth.[40]

To hear for ourselves about the potential conflict between Christianity and the paranormal, we interviewed a forty-year-old youth minister at a suburban, conservative Baptist church in central Texas. "Sam" is a mild-mannered, friendly, intelligent person who worked as a science teacher before moving into the ministry. He is also quite opinionated with regard to the paranormal and the "threat" it poses. In Sam's words, "paranormalists are a greater threat to the Kingdom of God than are atheists." Sam was distressed to hear about our visit to a psychic fair (see chap. 2). It did not matter to him that the psychics we met were kind, quite spiritual in character, and did not make negative statements about the Christian faith. When people engage in paranormal activities, or attempt to mix together Christianity and the paranormal, Sam explained, they are "working for the Devil . . . whether they realize it or not." God will only protect Christians from harm, he warns, so long as they avoid such activities.

Sam is concerned about the paranormal's prevalence in American entertainment. "Young people have the paranormal coming at them from all angles today. What popular culture is teaching our kids is that it is okay to believe in anything. The paranormal, all these shows on television, make it hard to teach young people a pure biblical doctrine because they want to mix and match beliefs. It scares me about the future of Christianity in America."

UFOs in the Pews

Those evangelical authors who fear that the paranormal is "corrupting" conventional religion may have a valid concern, depending upon how you look at it (see fig. 4.2). As mentioned earlier, the mainline Protestant tradition includes non-Catholic Christian groups that tend to have more liberal views on social issues and less restrictive views of doctrine and salvation, while denominations in the evangelical tradition tend to have more literal interpretations of the Bible and be more conservative on social issues. In addition to these two traditions and Roman Catholics, scholars frequently consider four other traditions in the United States: Protestant groups with an explicitly African American heritage, Jews, other traditional, organized religions (Hindu, Buddhist, Muslim), and claiming no religious affiliation (none).[41]

It is immediately clear that religion does not entirely "protect" against belief in the paranormal. Despite the warnings of some Christian authors regarding the dangers of New Age, occult, and paranormal, the majority of people in each religious tradition hold at least one paranormal belief. One Catholic might believe in the reality of UFOs but discount the

Percentage of respondents who believe in at least one paranormal topic

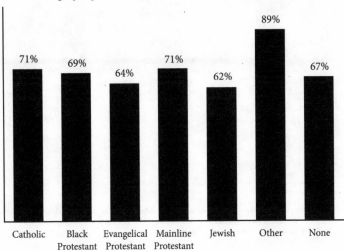

Fig. 4.2. Religious tradition and paranormal belief (Baylor Religion Survey, Wave 1, 2005)

Note: Percentage of respondents who believe in the reality of at least one of the following subjects: Atlantis and other advanced civilizations, haunted houses, the power to influence the world with the mind (telekinesis), UFOs, the ability to contact the dead (mediums), Bigfoot and other monsters, psychic powers, and astrology.

possibilities of astrology. Another Catholic may be convinced that civilizations such as Atlantis demonstrated advanced technology in ancient times but find tales of Bigfoot silly. But most Catholics (71 percent) believe in *something* paranormal. The same goes for those in black Protestant traditions, evangelicals, mainline Protestants, Jews, those of other religions and even those who claim no religion. The majority of those in black Protestant traditions are attracted to some paranormal idea. People who belong to religious groups that are already outside of the religious mainstream in the United States appear more comfortable with the paranormal than those in other religious traditions; almost all (89%) of those in other religious traditions have some paranormal belief. It is also clear that claiming no religion does not mean that one entirely rejects the possibility of the supernatural since most "nones" embrace the paranormal in some way.

If Sam and other alarmist evangelical commentators can take any comfort, it might be in the fact that evangelicals are among the least interested

Atlantis (47%)	Hauntings (53%)	Atlantis (39%)	Atlantis (47%)	Atlantis (51%)	Hauntings (65%)	Hauntings (41%)
Hauntings (42%)	Atlantis (38%)	Hauntings (33%)	Hauntings (36%)	Hauntings (30%)	Atlantis (52%)	Atlantis (41%)
Telekinesis (29%)	Monsters (29%)	Telekinesis (27%)	UFOs (30%)	UFOs (18%)	Telekinesis (47%)	Telekinesis (34%)
UFOs (29%)	Telekinesis (28%)	UFOs (19%)	Telekinesis (30%)	Astrology (17%)	UFOs (45%)	UFOs) (26%)
Mediums (25%)	Mediums (25%)	Mediums (16%)	Mediums (20%)	Monsters (14%)	Mediums (36%)	Mediums (21%)
Monsters (24%)	Psychics (21%)	Monsters (16%)	Monsters (18%)	Telekinesis (12%)	Astrology (18%)	Astrology (17%)
Psychics (14%)	UFOs (18%)	Astrology (14%)	Astrology (16%)	Mediums (12%)	Psychics (17%)	Psychics (15%)
Astrology (14%)	Astrology (13%)	Psychics (9%)	Psychics (14%)	Psychics (6%)	Monsters (15%)	Monsters (15%)
Catholic	Black Protestant	Evangelical Protestant	Mainline Protestant	Jewish	Other religion	No religion

Fig. 4.3. The paranormal thermometer: interest in the paranormal by religious tradition (Baylor Religion Survey, Wave 1, 2005)

in the paranormal. Jewish respondents are the least accepting of paranormal beliefs (62%), but evangelicals follow close behind.

The relative distaste that evangelicals and Jews have for the paranormal is even more apparent when looking at individual beliefs (see fig. 4.3). Religious traditions vary in which paranormal subjects are found to be the most attractive and in what percentage of members believes in those topics. The most popular paranormal belief among black Protestants is that houses can be haunted by ghosts (more than half believe in that). Hauntings are also the most popular topic for those of other religions and those with no religion, but those outside Judeo-Christian religious traditions find Atlantis to be of greater interest. Black Protestants have relatively little use for UFO tales, but extraterrestrials rank near the top of the list for Catholics, mainline Protestants, and Jews. The belief in Atlantis is the most popular paranormal subject for evangelicals, yet only by a percentage of a little more than one-third. By comparison, the most popular paranormal beliefs in non-evangelical religious traditions net nearly half or more of members. Indeed, of the Christian religious traditions, evangelicals show lower levels of belief in hauntings, telekinesis, Mediums, monsters, and psychics than do Roman Catholics, black Protestants, and mainline Protestants.

Belief

A key distinction and area of great contention between religious traditions and individual Christians is their view of the Bible. Some Christians believe that the Bible is God's literal word. Everything in the Bible is exactly as God meant it to be and everything within should be taken to mean exactly what it says. In practice, taking the Bible literally is quite difficult if not impossible. For example, two devoted Christians might disagree as to the literal meaning of more opaque passages. Nevertheless, literalists clearly have a different view of the Bible's meaning than those who believe it reflects the will of God, but not as a literal document. Such people imagine a Bible that must be interpreted in light of current events, but it is still a holy work and the word of God. Those that are more skeptical of the Bible's veracity may simply conceive of it as a book of fables and stories. Others believe that the Bible may in some way reflect God's message, but it has been significantly tampered with by human hands and interests. Americans clearly disagree as to the meaning of the Bible (see fig. 4.4).

An individual's conception of the Bible impacts his view on controversial moral or social issues upon which biblical verses are thought to pass judgment. For example, conservative Christians who decry gay marriage often reference biblical prohibitions on homosexuality (such as

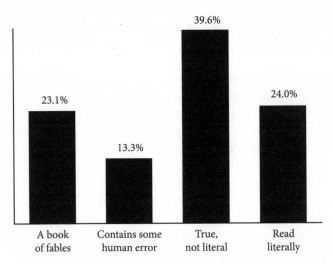

Fig. 4.4. American opinions about the Bible (Baylor Religion Survey, Wave 1, 2005)

Leviticus 18:22, ASV) which states: "Do not lie with a man as one lies with a woman; that is detestable." Christian supporters of gay marriage argue that such passages should not be taken literally as they are either reflections of the historical circumstances in which the Bible was recorded, or do not mean exactly what they say—perhaps this passage simply means that men should not engage in casual sexual relationships with other men outside of committed relationships.

Views of the Bible will also impact how people view the paranormal. Consider the instructions that Moses presented to the Israelites in the Old Testament:

> When you enter the land the LORD your God is giving you, do not learn to imitate the detestable ways of the nations there. Let no one be found among you who sacrifices son or daughter in the fire, who practices divination or sorcery, interprets omens, engages in witchcraft, or casts spells, or who is a medium or spiritist or who consults the dead. Anyone who does these things is detestable to the LORD, and because of these detestable practices the LORD your God will drive out those nations before you. You must be blameless before the LORD your God. The nations you dispossess listen to those who practice sorcery or divination. But as for you, the LORD your God has not permitted you to do so. (Deuteronomy 18:9–14, NIV)

Not to be outdone, the New Testament provides its own anti-paranormal sentiment:

> The acts of the sinful nature are obvious: sexual immorality, impurity and debauchery; idolatry and witchcraft; hatred, discord, jealousy, fits of rage, selfish ambition, dissensions, factions and envy; drunkenness, orgies, and the like. I warn you, as I did before, that those who live like this will not inherit the kingdom of God (Galatians 5:19–21, NIV).

For Christians with a literal understanding of such verses, paranormal phenomena are not simply silly or misguided, but a possible route to damnation. So an important part of understanding when a religious person will experiment with the paranormal is how that person views the Bible (see fig. 4.5).

People who do believe the Bible contains human error are the most likely to believe in the paranormal. They even show higher levels of para-

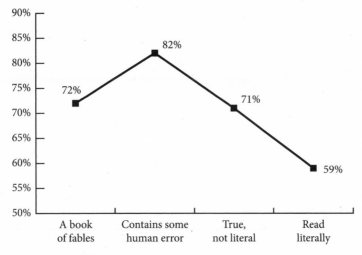

Fig. 4.5. Holding a paranormal belief and views of the Bible (Baylor Religion Survey, Wave 1, 2005; Chi-square = 49.35, p < .001)

normal belief than those who entirely dismiss the Bible. This implies that a certain level of religiosity indeed opens up a person to the paranormal. For someone who believes that the Bible is a holy book but is open to interpretation, it can be a small step from Jesus to flying saucers.

If we were to look only at people with liberal interpretations of the Bible, we could conclude that the contactees of old might find great success merging Christianity and UFOs. However, while we found a surprising amount of paranormal belief even among biblical literalists, it would no doubt be of great concern to evangelical critics of the paranormal. Interest in UFOs, ghosts, and other paranormal topics falls off precipitously with more literal interpretations of the Bible. For many of these literalists, the paranormal and Christianity occupy separate and distinct spheres of belief.[42]

Behavior

We find a similar pattern at work when we examine religious behaviors, such as attendance at religious services (see fig. 4.6). The highest levels of paranormal belief are among marginal attenders. A person that never attends church is much *less* likely to believe in paranormal topics than

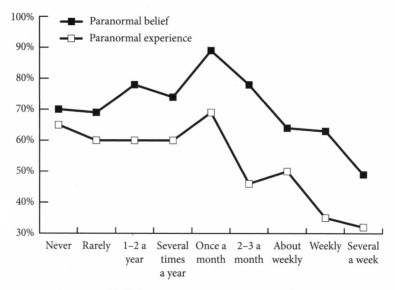

Fig. 4.6. Paranormal belief, paranormal experience and church attendance

Note: Chart shows percentage of respondents who claim belief in at least one paranormal belief (Chi-square = 69.04, p < .001) and percentage of respondents who claim at least one paranormal experience (Chi-square = 183.5, p < .001), by levels of church attendance.

someone who attends once in awhile (once a month). Again, it appears that simple exposure to the supernatural in the form of church attendance can open one up to other forms of the supernatural.

Looking only at the left half of the chart, one might become convinced that religion and the paranormal walk hand in hand. Once attendance is greater than once a month, however, paranormal belief drops dramatically. People who attend church two to three times a month are much less interested in the paranormal than monthly attenders, and those who fill the pews every week less interested still.

Some congregations offer additional activities beyond the Sunday service like Bible studies, and midweek and evening services. The most devoted members of these congregations may attend services at their church several times a week, and their frequent involvement deters paranormal interest. It is only among the most dedicated church members that we find minority belief in psychic phenomena, UFOs, haunted houses, and other aspects of the paranormal. Less than half (49%) believe in one or more paranormal phenomena.

The same pattern manifests for paranormal experiences. People who attend about once a month are the most likely to report having a para-normal experience such as witnessing a UFO—these marginal attenders are even more likely to report such experiences than people who never at-tend church. As church attendance becomes more frequent, claimed para-normal experiences drop dramatically. Over two-thirds of once-a-month church attendees report a paranormal experience, compared to less than one-third of those who attend several times a week. Announcing one's ex-perimentation with a Ouija will not garner favor at a Wednesday night church service.

Selling Saucers

What does all of this mean for the troubled relationship between Christi-anity and the paranormal? To whom should an up-and-coming psychic try to sell her services? Should the next budding contactee call the local Bap-tist church to advertise his lecture about meeting Jesus on a flying saucer?

Putting all of the pieces together, it is clear that the type of religious person least likely to report paranormal beliefs or to have paranormal ex-periences is a devout evangelical, a biblical literalist, and frequently at-tends church services. This is due in part to the anti-paranormal rhetoric of some Christian pundits, which certainly has its origins in a literal in-terpretation of certain Bible passages. But as economists such as Laurence Iannaccone argue, such rhetoric also serves to drive away members who are not willing to commit fully to the church and a single belief system, leaving a committed core behind.

While evangelicals have had some success in curtailing paranormal interest, no group is entirely immune. The majority of people believe in something paranormal, no matter what religious tradition they belong to (see fig. 4.2). It is also clear that a measure of faith opens people up to the paranormal. Rationalists who entirely reject the idea of faith in "conven-tional" supernatural subjects will not be as attracted to unconventional supernatural topics either. It is people with midlevels of interest and com-mitment to conventional religions who have the greatest interest in the paranormal. Someone who attends church *sometimes* and believes that there is *something* supernatural about the Bible is the most likely to de-velop an interest in or already believe in paranormal topics. It appears that religion can have a conditioning effect that, unless actively curtailed, indeed makes the paranormal but a small step away.

5

Paranormal Subcultures

In their pioneering research, the sociologists Charles Y. Glock and Rodney Stark noticed that two people can identify themselves as "very religious," yet mean very different things by it.[1] There are five primary ways that people manifest their personal religiosity, they argue. For some, (1) being religious is most importantly about *belief*; one must believe without doubt in the tenets of one's faith. Or perhaps (2) being religious means that one has religious *experiences*, such as feeling born again or receiving answers to prayers. For others, (3) one's *knowledge* of the doctrines and documents of the faith are proof of devotion. Still others feel religious because (4) they frequently engage in religious *practices* such as attending church services and praying. Finally, religiosity can be gauged by (5) proving that one's faith requires accepting *consequences* such as restrictions on behavior. An individual's involvement with a religious organization could be adequately summarized by knowing one's levels of belief, knowledge, practice, experience, and consequences.

While Glock and Stark focus their attentions upon religion, their ideas have much wider applicability. What they labeled as five dimensions of religiosity could easily be considered five dimensions of involvement in any belief system, hobby, or interest group. For example, consider members of People for the Ethical Treatment of Animals (PETA). Some members will have a strong faith in the cause but do little else. There will be other members for whom belief is simply not enough. They will participate in PETA activities and may even be willing to engage in risky behaviors for the group. As with any group there will be PETA members who have no real sense of group history or a deep understanding of its mission or methods. Perhaps they have joined for social reasons, or they simply have a deep belief in animal rights that does not necessitate an understanding of PETA itself. This raises the possibility that even within the same organization or area of interest, different types of people will be involved in different ways.

The same ideas apply to levels of involvement with the paranormal. Any given person's involvement with the paranormal could be considered to be composed of Glock and Stark's combination of five elements:

Belief: The extent to which an individual believes in a paranormal topic or topics

Experiences: The extent to which an individual has experienced the paranormal topic in question (has seen a ghost, sighted a UFO, etc.)

Knowledge: The extent to which an individual is aware of the history, details and specifics of a paranormal topic

Practices: The extent to which a person engages in activities related to a paranormal subject (attends conferences, joins organizations, joins group activities)

Consequences: The extent to which a person has suffered negative outcomes, such as ridicule, as a result of their interest in a paranormal subject

With the exception of skeptics,[2] people interested in the paranormal as a cultural phenomenon, and the occasional curious onlooker, engagement with the paranormal typically involves some level of belief. That does not mean that belief always comes first. In some cases a person will develop a paranormal belief as the result of having a paranormal experience. We have met many people during our research who claim they never believed in UFOs, Bigfoot, psychic phenomena, and the like until "it" happened to them.

Chapter 3 examined those who hold paranormal beliefs and have paranormal experiences. For many, involvement with the paranormal will end with belief or an experience. For example, a person may have a strong belief in ghosts because of an uncle's encounter with a restless spirit, but have no interest in pursuing the subject further. Indeed, it is quite possible to have belief in a paranormal subject with very little knowledge of its particulars. Many people who follow their horoscopes religiously probably have no idea exactly *how* one is supposed to be influenced by the stars. And just because a person has seen a UFO does not mean that he or she has an awareness of UFO history. Judging by the ubiquity of paranormal beliefs in American society, only a handful of those who believe in UFOs, ghosts, and other paranormal subjects ultimately engage in paranormal practices such as attending UFO conferences or joining a ghost hunt.

This chapter examines those who move beyond paranormal belief and experience into a deeper involvement in a paranormal subculture. We explore the world of people who expand their knowledge of the paranormal by purchasing paranormal books, visiting paranormal Web sites and attending conferences and get-togethers. Finally we take a close look at the most dedicated members of a subculture—those who actively engage in the pursuit of their quarry. To do so, we enter one particular paranormal subculture, people who research and hunt Bigfoot.

Bigfoot: Wild Man of the Woods

By many accounts, a mysterious ape-man known variously as Bigfoot or Sasquatch has long inhabited the United States. Native American myths and legends include a rich body of tales of hairy, manlike beasts that roam the forests.[3] Depending on the tribe, such creatures are known as *Wendigo, Tornit, Strendu, Chenoo, Oh-Mah, Sookum,* and a host of other names.[4] "Sasquatch" is merely an anglicized version of *Sokqueatl* (or *Ssosq'tal*), used by Salish-speaking tribes.[5]

As far back as 1818, the *Exeter Watchman* reported the sighting of an "animal resembling the Wild Man of the Woods" near Ellisburgh, New York.[6] In his 1893 memoir, *The Wilderness Hunter,* Theodore Roosevelt recounted a harrowing tale told to him by a hunter/trapper known only as "Bauman."[7] The story goes that Bauman was trapping with a friend in the Bitterroot Mountains of Idaho and Montana. The men noticed that something was raiding their camp whenever they went out to check their traps. Bauman awoke one evening to see a large, dark shape standing outside his lean-to; he fired his weapon at the shape. Over the next few days, the men felt watched and felt that they were being followed by something that stayed hidden just within the trees. The men ultimately became unnerved and decided to leave the mountains. To expedite their departure, Bauman went to collect traps, and his partner remained to pack up camp. Upon returning to camp, the frightened trapper found the mutilated body of his friend. Bauman fled the scene as quickly as possible.[8]

The creatures continued such aggressive behavior in fantastic accounts from the early twentieth century. For example, Fred Beck claimed that he and three other miners were attacked by "mountain devils" while working their claim near Mount Saint Helens. The men had been hearing strange whoops and hollers from unseen animals for several days when Beck spotted a strange creature staring at him from across a small canyon; immediately Beck opened fire:

> The creature I judged to have been about seven feet tall with blackish-brown hair. It disappeared from our view for a short time, but then we saw it, running fast and upright, about two hundred yards down the little canyon. I shot three times before it disappeared from view.[9]

That evening the miner's cabin was attacked, perhaps in response to Beck's aggression. At least three large, hairy creatures circled the cabin, pounded on the walls, tossed rocks, and jumped on the roof. At one point a hairy arm reached through a chink in the wall and grabbed one of the men's axes. Beck turned the head of the axe before the creature could pull it outside. During the assault, the men alternated between huddling in fear and firing their guns at the roof and through the walls.

Just before daylight the attack ended. Beck and his friends fled the scene, but not before he fired parting shots at another creature he saw standing at the edge of the canyon: "I shot three times, and it toppled over the cliff, down into the gorge, some four hundred feet below."[10] The area where the incident purportedly occurred was nicknamed "Ape Canyon" after the story appeared and still bears that name today.[11]

An equally harrowing encounter also stems from 1924, although it was not discovered until 1957.[12] Albert Ostman, a Canadian lumberjack, claimed to have been kidnapped by a Sasquatch while camping in British Columbia. The creature simply picked the frightened man up, sleeping bag and all, as he lay asleep one evening. Slung uncomfortably across the beast's shoulder, Ostman endured a long hike until they arrived at a canyon. There he was held captive by four Sasquatch. His kidnapper was a large male Ostman called the "old man." Also present were an older female and a younger male and female, perhaps children of the older couple. A small cache of supplies that Ostman had stashed in the bottom of his sleeping bag provided his avenue of escape. Each morning Ostman boiled coffee and took a pinch of snuff as the apelike family watched with curiosity, resulting in a scene seemingly straight out of a slapstick film. After about a week of watching, the old man grabbed Ostman's can of snuff and swallowed it whole. It did not sit well. The beast tried to soothe his stomach by emptying Ostman's can of cold coffee, grounds and all, into its mouth. As the old man doubled-over in pain with his frightened family attending him, Ostman quickly gathered his gear and fled.[13]

Despite such dramatic reports, Bigfoot proved merely an occasional curiosity until August 1958. A construction crew was preparing a roadbed outside of Klamath, California. On August 27, a worker named Gerald Crew discovered large humanlike tracks (sixteen inches long and seven inches wide in places) around his bulldozer. Although the tracks were destroyed once roadwork resumed, they reappeared every few days. The foreman, Wilbur Wallace, later reported that something tossed an enormous, seven-hundred-pound spare tire into a gulley near the work site, further disturbing the crew. Finally, a wife of one of the crewmen wrote to the *Humboldt Times* about the worksite's visits from "Big Foot," and a series of stories in local newspapers followed. There is good reason to suspect that the entire incident was a prank played by the contractor,[14] but the societal impact was undeterred. When wire services transmitted the local newspaper story countrywide, Bigfoot finally had a name.[15]

The creature's popularity soared from this point on, and it has become an indelible part of American popular culture.[16] Among other things, Bigfoot has starred in movies such as *Harry and the Hendersons* (1987), along with a spinoff television show of the same name, and in a children's film titled *Little Bigfoot* (1997). *Bigfoot and Wildboy* aired as a segment on the Krofft Supershow in the 1970s. The Six-Million Dollar Man battled and then befriended Sasquatch. As of this writing, Bigfoot appears in a series of "Messin' with Sasquatch" commercials for Jack Link's Beef Jerky. In the comical bits, humans find various ways to torment Bigfoot (such as offering him a ride, only to pull away) and receive payback (such as being pulled from the car). A young Sasquatch ("Quatchi") is one of the mascots for the 2010 Winter Olympics in Vancouver, Canada. The now defunct Seattle Supersonics also had a Bigfoot mascot, Squatch.[17] Pizza Hut even offered a Bigfoot pizza for a brief period in the 1990s. Indeed, Bigfoot has crossed all media, appearing in countless books, television documentaries, comic books, and video games.

The popular media often depicts Bigfoot/Sasquatch as a solitary creature roaming the Pacific Northwest. Most believers think of Bigfoot as a separate *species*. Witnesses have claimed sightings of males and females, adults, juveniles, and children. Books, Web sites, and documentaries outline migration routes, speculate on dietary habits, and even provide population estimates. One source estimates that between 1,500 and 2,000 adult Sasquatch inhabit the Pacific Northwest alone.[18]

Unlike the murderous, kidnapping creatures reported by Bauman, Beck, Ostman, and others, the modern Bigfoot is shy and retiring. The typical encounter involves a hairy beast, at least six feet tall, seen only briefly as it flees from the witness on two legs. Many sightings occur when the furtive creature quickly crosses the road in front of a startled driver. When sufficiently close to observe, witnesses report a hairy, apelike face with a heavy brow and large nostrils.[19] In some famous cases large, pendulous breasts are reported, but most appear to involve adult males.[20]

That Bigfoot is a creature of the Northwest only is also a popular misnomer. Washington, Oregon, and California have the highest number of incident reports, but Bigfoot sightings have been reported from every state except Hawaii. The Bigfoot Field Researchers Organization (BFRO) provides a popular Web site that collects sighting reports.[21] It lists 102 encounters in Michigan and 198 in Ohio; even little Rhode Island claims four. Residents of states across the union have collected local reports and their own encounters into an abundance of self-published, vanity, and small press books, such as *The Mogollon Monster: Arizona's Bigfoot*; *Bigfoot Encounters in Ohio*; *The Maryland Bigfoot Digest*; *Swamp Bigfoot: Tales of the Louisiana Honey Island Swamp Monster*; *Bigfoot in Mississippi*; *Sasquatch: Alabama Bigfoot Sightings*; and *50 Years with Bigfoot: Tennessee Chronicles of Co-Existence*.[22]

Ubiquity does not guarantee acceptance, however. With a few exceptions, scientists have dismissed the possibility of Bigfoot.[23] The American public is equally skeptical about the creature's existence. Only a handful is convinced that Bigfoot is real, although a larger percentage is willing to entertain the possibility that Bigfoot "probably" exists (see fig. 5.1).

Frustrated Bigfooters point to a mountain of evidence. Thousands of supposed Bigfoot footprints have been cast in plaster by researchers. There are an abundance of photographs and enough purported films to warrant their own book-length listing.[24] Bigfoot hunters have even collected samples of hair and feces. Most scientists, however, are simply not convinced of the *quality* of this evidence. The films, photos, and foot-castings are obvious hoaxes, they argue. The feces and hair samples must be from known animals; the many sightings are simply misidentifications of bears, if not outright hoaxes themselves.

How the different types of Bigfoot believers respond to public skepticism about their quarry is a key distinction between them. Less than half (41%) of those who believe in creatures such as Bigfoot have ever read a book about the subject, consulted a Web site, or otherwise researched the subject.[25] The interest of *casual believers* is limited to watching the occasional Bigfoot documentary or turning up the TV when a sighting

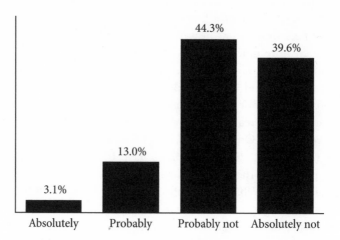

Fig. 5.1. Does Bigfoot exist? (Baylor Religion Survey, 2007, n = 1572)

Note: A series of questions on the Baylor Religion Survey, Wave 2 (2007) asks respondents "In your opinion do each of the following exist?" We asked about Bigfoot, extraterrestrials, ghosts, and a host of other subjects covered in later chapters.

is reported on the local news. The casual believers we have talked to are relatively uninterested in and unaffected by the skepticism of the scientific community. For them Bigfoot is simply one more item added to a paranormal shopping cart that includes UFOs, ghosts, and psychic phenomena. It is something that is believed in but rarely inspected. Both scholars and the press have too frequently painted all those who believe in a particular paranormal subject with the same brush. We have found most dedicated pursuers of paranormal subjects to be different from what we call casual believers.

Paranormal Research

As we found with paranormal beliefs and experiences, there is a surprising amount of paranormal research going on in the United States (see fig. 5.2); many Americans are taking their interest in the paranormal beyond causal, unconsidered belief. Some subjects are more popular than others, but more than half (53%) of Americans have researched at least one paranormal topic.

We asked Americans if they have ever read a book on the paranormal, consulted Web sites, or otherwise researched six different paranormal subjects. The most popular of these subjects was the prophecies of Nostradamus. Nearly one-third of Americans were sufficiently intrigued by the French seer's claims of a fiery end to the world to delve into the subject. Unfortunately, we can only speculate as to whether much of this interest occurred at the turn of the millennium in 1999, as we did not ask about dates. Four topics closely follow Nostradamus in popularity. Close to one-fourth (25%) of Americans have read about or researched the world of ghosts, apparitions, haunted houses, and/or electronic voice phenomena. Twenty-four percent of us have delved into astrology. Nearly the same number is fascinated by UFO sightings, abductions, or tales of government UFO conspiracies. Bigfoot, the Loch Ness Monster, and similar beasts are not quite as popular, but have, at least at one point, attracted the attention of one-fifth of Americans (21%).

Given that psychics, mediums, and fortune-tellers are one of the most heavily advertised aspects of the paranormal, we were surprised to find it to be one of the least popular subjects for Americans to research; only about 13 percent of Americans show a deeper interest in the subject; even fewer (12%) have researched the New Age as a movement, which suggests that the term is of little meaning to most Americans.

It is possible, however, to predict with fair accuracy the specific subjects that will interest a particular type of person. Overall, the paranormal is popular, but certain subjects are more popular among some segments of the population than others. One of the most consistent and powerful predictors of enthusiasm for paranormal subjects is gender.[26] Men and women are, quite simply, attracted to different paranormal topics (see fig. 5.3). Even when taking into account differences in marital status, education, income, personal religiosity, and age, men are still more likely than

Have you ever read a book, consulted a Web site, or researched the following topics?	% answering yes
The prophecies of Nostradamus	28
Ghosts, apparitions, haunted houses, or electronic voice phenomena	25
Astrology	24
UFO sightings, abductions, or conspiracies	23
Mysterious animals, such as Bigfoot or the Loch Ness Monster	21
Mediums, fortune-tellers, or psychics	13
The New Age movement in general	12

Fig. 5.2. American paranormal research (Baylor Religion Survey, 2005, n = 1721)

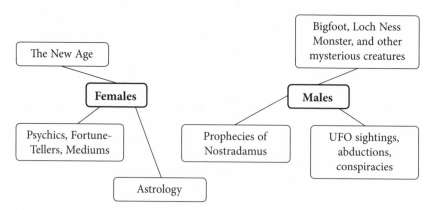

Fig. 5.3. Gender and paranormal research (Baylor Religion Survey, 2005, n = 1721)

females to develop an interest in "cryptozoology" (the study of Bigfoot, the Loch Ness Monster, and other mysterious creatures), UFO sightings, abductions and conspiracies, and the prophecies of Nostradamus. Women are more interested in astrology, psychics, fortune-tellers and mediums, and the New Age in general. If there is a trend here, it appears that men are somewhat more interested in "concrete" paranormal subjects. In theory at least, it *would* be possible to capture, kill, or find concrete physical evidence for the existence of Bigfoot, lake monsters, or extraterrestrials—and men seem to enjoy the hunt.[27] Women have greater interest in more ephemeral topics related to personal destiny and self-improvement.

Given the wide diversity of topics that fall under the rubric of the paranormal, it is not surprising that the enthusiasts themselves vary quite widely. For example, unmarried people are, on average, significantly more interested in the New Age and UFO sightings, abductions, and conspiracies than are married people. Yet marital status is not predictive of whether one will become invested in the subject of psychics and fortune-tellers, Nostradamus, or Bigfoot and other monsters. Married people are just as likely as unmarried people to chase Sasquatch.

Using a statistical technique, we can simultaneously consider the relationship between different demographic characteristics and enthusiasm, and research toward Bigfoot, UFOs, or other subjects. This allows us to paint a profile of the "average" person as will delve into each paranormal subculture (see fig. 5.4). Different types of people more likely to move beyond simple belief and into deeper involvement with each paranormal subject.

For each topic of interest, we have sorted demographic factors in order of importance. For example, the most powerful demographic determinant of becoming interested in monsters is being male: *gender* is a stronger predictor of interest in researching cryptozoology (monsters) than is *age*. Gender is related to interest in psychics, but is less important than income, age, and other factors. Each listed factor simply increases the probability of researching a particular subject, but it is not determinative.

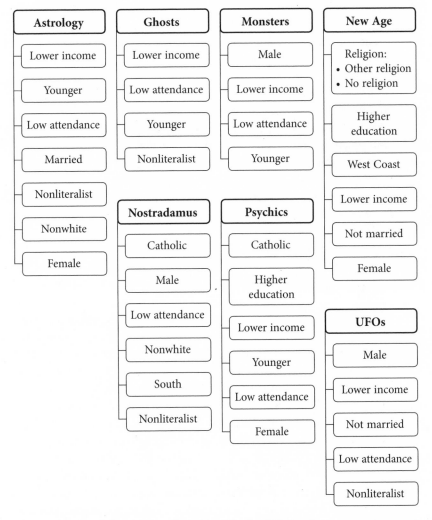

Fig. 5.4. Paranormal researchers by subject (Baylor Religion Survey, 2005, n = 1721)

Women also research Bigfoot; they are just less likely to do so than males. Being male does not, however, *make* one study Bigfoot.

Taken together these factors paint a picture of what people who delve into paranormal topics are like. The person most likely to read about ghosts, research them on the Web, or perhaps purchase related projects is a younger, lower-income male or female who rarely attends church and does not view the Bible in literal terms. The average monster enthusiast tends to be a younger male who rarely attends church services.

Several interesting factors are important in predicting who will research paranormal topics. As we found in chapter 4, religion plays an important role in determining interest in the paranormal because the paranormal often operates as an alternative belief system to conventional religion. Consequently, those who are heavily invested in conventional religion may be less attracted to the paranormal. Indeed, the sole factor that consistently impacts all of the paranormal topics under consideration is church attendance. With exceptions of researching the New Age, people who infrequently attend church are the most likely to express an interest in the paranormal. Those who frequently attend a traditional church service are simply less likely to examine alternatives. If we know that a person is a frequent churchgoer it is unlikely that that person is researching the paranormal when they get home from church on Sunday. Further, holding a nonliteral view of the Bible also helps to further interest in ghosts, Nostradamus, and astrology.

While it can be difficult to pinpoint from demographics who will attempt to gain knowledge about paranormal subjects, there are some very consistent predictors. One of the strongest is belief in a subject. People who believe in a supernatural subject are *much* more likely to investigate it further than those who do not believe. Certainly there are skeptics who research paranormal subjects, but they are far outnumbered by believers (see fig. 5.5). Of those people who do not believe in Bigfoot, the Loch Ness Monster, or other monsters, less than one-fifth (18%) could be bothered to investigate further, but true believers are highly motivated to do so. Someone who believes in Bigfoot and other creatures is more than twice as likely to acquire knowledge about the subject as someone who does not believe.

Having a paranormal experience is an even more powerful entry point to researching paranormal subjects. Of those Americans who claim to have seen a UFO, nearly half (48%) have researched the subject (see fig. 5.6). Only a handful of those who have not seen a UFO have any interest

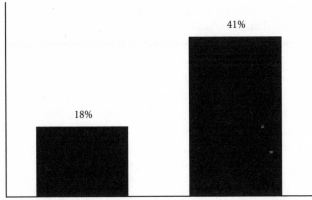

Percentage of respondents who have read a book, consulted a Web site, or researched Bigfoot, the Loch Ness Monster, and other mysterious creatures

Fig. 5.5. Paranormal belief prompts paranormal research (Baylor Religion Survey, 2005, n = 1721)

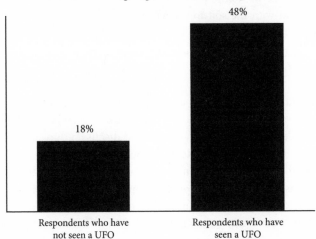

Percentage of respondents who have read a book, consulted a Web site, or researched UFO sightings, abductions, or conspiracies

Fig. 5.6. Paranormal experience prompts paranormal research (Baylor Religion Survey, 2005, n = 1721)

in researching the subject. Of course, chicken-and-egg arguments necessarily arise with such data. It is possible that people come to believe in Bigfoot or other paranormal topics because they have studied them. It is also quite likely that some people have paranormal experiences only *after* they have researched a subject at length, what could be formulated as the "social construction of reality factor." After all, there are many books available that tell one where to go to find ghosts or to have the best chance to see Bigfoot, or that provide instruction on how to develop psychic powers. Nevertheless, in our time spent with people who have had paranormal experiences, it is clear that those experiences marked major turning points in their lives. Such was the case with Craig Woolheater of Texas.

An affable forty-eight-year-old with graying hair, Woolheater owns a plumbing business in Dallas, Texas. On May 30, 1994, Craig and his then-fiancée were driving a dark, two-lane highway between New Orleans and Alexandria, Louisiana, when their lives changed forever:

> It was about twenty-five to thirty feet to the wood line from the road. About halfway to the wood line, a figure was visible in the illumination of my headlights. It appeared to be about seven foot tall, hairy and looked to be gray. Its back was toward us and it was walking in the direction we were traveling, parallel to the road. My wife, then girlfriend, and I looked at each other and simultaneously said "Did you just see what I saw?" I wanted to stop and go back, but she did not. I was driving an Isuzu Amigo with the soft top rolled up, so I could see why she wasn't in favor of this. It did become a topic of long discussion for the remainder of the trip. It was something that we talked among ourselves, but not with others.[28]

The encounter reignited a dormant childhood interest in Bigfoot. Craig began reading all of the Bigfoot books he could find and rummaged the Web for information. He joined discussion groups and posted his thoughts on blogs. Ultimately, Craig reached the conclusion that a solution to the Bigfoot question would require concentrated effort. Bigfoot enthusiasts cannot rely upon the hope that a hunter or hiker would someday accidentally stumble upon a body, or that vacationers might finally capture a close-up, indisputable video of a Bigfoot sunning itself by a creek. Craig decided to focus his efforts upon Texas. Readers who have not visited Texas (or only its western portions) may be under the impression that the state provides no cover for a large, hairy beast. In fact, much of Texas consists of rolling hills and trees, and east Texas is covered with mile upon mile of dense, swampy forests.

Woolheater has a great sense of humor and frequently makes jokes at his own expense, but he is serious in purpose. In 1999 he founded the Texas Bigfoot Research Center (TBRC) to organize the quest for evidence of Bigfoot's existence. By 2007 the center officially changed its name to the Texas Bigfoot Research Conservancy and reorganized itself as a non-profit organization., which now claims about fifty volunteer members. The TBRC has worked hard to develop a reputation for serious research in the Bigfoot subculture.

One of the most common ways to delve deeply into a paranormal subject is to attend a related conference or fair. Frequent psychic and New Age fairs are easily found in most major cities. UFO enthusiasts appear to benefit from the greatest choice of regular conferences from which to choose. Those who are fascinated with claims of crashed flying saucers can attend the annual UFO Crash Retrieval Conference or visit annual festivals in Roswell, New Mexico. One of the largest UFO research organizations, the Mutual UFO Network (MUFON), has held its annual conference for more than forty years. The International UFO Congress conference offers its own film festival in addition to well-known UFO speakers. The Bay Area UFO Expo draws UFO enthusiasts to the West Coast.

Since 2001, the TBRC has held the "preeminent Bigfoot conference in the United States" in the east Texas towns of Jefferson[29] and Tyler. With the exception of curious locals, the occasional skeptical onlooker, and the press, people who attend a Bigfoot conference are passionate. These are people who are not content with mere belief and nor satisfied with the research they can do on their own. They want to meet Bigfoot celebrities face-to-face, purchase the latest Bigfoot products, trade stories from the field, and hear tips from veteran hunters. Some of them have taken it upon themselves to answer skeptics. They hope to learn tips and tricks that will help them find proof of Bigfoot that scientists cannot ignore. To visit such a Bigfoot conference is to meet some of the beast's most dedicated enthusiasts.

Bigfoot Knowledge

On a recent Saturday morning we arrived at an auditorium in downtown Tyler, Texas. We had agreed to speak to the nearly four hundred Bigfoot enthusiasts assembled for the TBRC's annual conference. Our topic was the subject of this chapter—the differences between casual believers in Bigfoot and those who express a deeper interest in the subject. In return for our talk, the TBRC agreed to encourage the audience to complete a detailed questionnaire, allowing us to present a rare glimpse into the characteristics of those deeply interested in Sasquatch. We found out their views on key controversies in the Bigfoot subculture, learning their opinions on purported pieces of Bigfoot evidence, determined the extent to which attendees have interacted with the creature itself, and perhaps most important, learned about the type of person who attends a major Bigfoot conference.

As hundreds of the Bigfoot faithful streamed through the doors, anxious to hear from the day's speakers, about a dozen vendors set up tables of Bigfoot-related books and DVDs, a line of Bigfoot watches called Sasq-Watches, Bigfoot cookies, and original art.

One of the first things we noticed as we milled about waiting for our afternoon presentation was how serious those in attendance were about their subject. These were not people new to the study of Bigfoot, nor were they only curious locals just hoping to have a laugh at the Bigfooter's expense. This was a distinctive and hardcore Bigfoot subculture. We saw much joking around, lighthearted banter, and hugs between old friends. But most of the people who showed up had been deep into the subject for years. Nearly two-thirds had been interested in Bigfoot for at least a decade, and about half (49%) had been studying Bigfoot for more than twenty years.

Gathered knowledge of Bigfoot was on display throughout the day. In attendance were Bigfoot "celebrities" that elicited gasps of recognition and excitement from the assembled faithful but who probably would not be recognized by anyone outside of the auditorium. Loren Coleman, the author of numerous books about Bigfoot and related phenomena, shook hands and autographed books. Smokey Crabtree, whose Bigfoot experiences around Fouke, Arkansas, inspired the popular 1970s docudrama *The Legend of Boggy Creek*, held court at his booth, where he sold T-shirts, posters, and an assortment of autobiographies such as *Smokey and the Fouke Monster* and *Too Close to the Mirror: The Continuing Story of the Life of Smokey Crabtree*. Our lead researcher recognized Loren Coleman without the need for an introduction, earning the admiration of one TBRC member. My inability to recognize Smokey Crabtree (he was away from his booth at the time) led to gentle chastisement from another conference attendee.

Remove the element of Bigfoot, and there is nothing particularly unique about this. Most Americans belong to one or more subcultures, sometimes without even realizing it. A subculture is simply any group that possesses characteristics that distinguish it from the wider culture. Mutual hobbies and interests or any other shared characteristic such as age, race, social class, or geographical location can become the basis of a distinctive group with shared values and behaviors. Youth can be described as a subculture, having shared interests, lingo, styles of dress, and habits that differ from the rest of the population. The youth subculture itself can be further subdivided based on favorite music styles, particular hobbies, region of the country, relative age (adolescents vs. tweens vs. teens), and in any number of other ways. A shared passion or characteristics can spawn a subculture that baffles outsiders. There are biker subcultures and Goth subcultures. There is a NASCAR subculture and a Twilight subculture; subcultures for hunters and for comic book collectors. NASCAR has its own celebrities that are completely unknown to those who do not like watching people drive in circles. Stan Lee, a godlike figure to many comic book enthusiasts, would engender little excitement at the Indy 500. Members inside any subculture demonstrate their devotion to their subject by being familiar with its key personalities and history.

The TBRC conference was most abuzz about a recent addition to the lineup, a thin, spry, seventy-eight-year-old cowboy from Yakima, Washington, by the name of Bob Gimlin. Bob is such a celebrity in the world of Bigfoot that he had been brought to the event without even the requirement of giving a presentation: his mere presence was enough to electrify the crowd. Bob wandered the vendor area and auditorium, taking pictures with thrilled attendees. We were handed cameras on a number of occasions to snap a photo of an excited fan with his or her arm around the perpetually grinning Gimlin. In a certain sense, he unwittingly served as a method of distinguishing the few casual believers in attendance from the serious Bigfoot enthusiasts. As Melissa Hovey, a Bigfoot blogger, commented in a post about Gimlin's appearance at the conference:

> If you don't know who Bob Gimlin is, please hang your head in shame and stop reading. Not knowing the name Bob Gimlin is like not knowing who John Green is. Your [sic] not a researcher, or you should really pay more attention.[30]

Gimlin's claim to fame is in being the Gimlin part of the famous Patterson-Gimlin film, a purported film of a Sasquatch.[31] In October 1967

Bob and his friend, the former rodeo rider Roger Patterson, visited Bluff Creek, California, in hopes of capturing a Bigfoot on film for a planned documentary. Patterson had previously written a book on Bigfoot and believed that the Bluff Creek area was a good spot to search for the creature.

As luck would have it, the duo was rounding a fallen tree in a creek bed on their horses in the early afternoon of October 20 when they spotted a large, dark creature about six or seven feet tall, which that rose up from a crouched position and walked across a gravel sandbar.[32] The strange, stocky figure was covered in black hair with the exception of small parts of its face. It had arms that hung below its knees and pendulous breasts. For fifty-three seconds of shaky 16mm footage, the figure shambled across the sandbar toward the tree line. At frame 352 it turned its head to look at Patterson, one arm swung in front of its body, the other to its back. This frame of film has been reproduced countless times and its subject, often nicknamed "Patty," became the face of the Bigfoot movement.[33]

In our time with the Bigfoot subculture we have learned of other famous pieces of evidence. We heard attendees debate the merits of Albert Ostman's claim that he was held captive by a Bigfoot family in 1924 along with other tales about a family making friends with Bigfoot in Kentucky. Of more recent provenance is the *Skookum Cast,* taken in the Gifford Pinchot National Forest in Washington State. In September 2000, a team from the Bigfoot Field Researchers Organization (BFRO) tried to entice any nearby Bigfoot into leaving clear footprints by dropping a piece of fruit into the center of a soft and muddy patch of ground. When the investigators returned to the area they found the large impression of an animal at the edge of the mud wallow. Supporters see the imprints of Bigfoot's arm, thighs, buttocks, and heel. They theorize that a clever Bigfoot tried to avoid leaving footprints by reclining on the harder ground and reaching its arms toward to the fruit. Other Bigfoot enthusiasts have discounted the cast, believing it to be the impressions of a reclining elk. The BFRO took an enormous (3.5 × 5 ft.) cast of the impression, copies of which occasionally surface at Bigfoot exhibitions.

Also of fairly recent vintage are the *Memorial Day Bigfoot Film,* taken by Lori Pate during a family fishing trip at Chopaka Lake, Washington, on May 26, 1996, which purports to show a Bigfoot running across a meadow, and a 1994 recording of a Bigfoot moaning "the *Ohio Howl,*" recorded by Matt Moneymaker and Jamie Watson (which can be heard on www.bfro.net).

Despite such alternatives, the Patterson-Gimlin (PG) film remains the

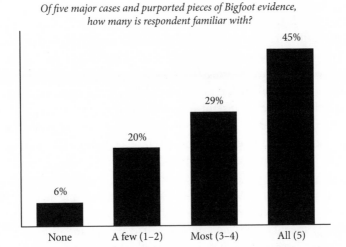

Fig. 5.7. Bigfoot knowledge among attendees of a major Bigfoot conference

current highlight of Bigfoot evidence. Entire books have been written about the film,[34] new analyses are the subject of conference presentations, podcasts, and radio shows. More than 80 percent of the people in attendance at this conference believed that the PG film constitutes a somewhat or very credible piece of Bigfoot evidence.[35] No other piece of purported evidence for the creature's existence even approaches this level of acceptance. Around half of the attendees find the Skookum Cast to be credible evidence (58%) or think the Ohio Howl is really a moaning Sasquatch (46%). Less than a third believe that the Memorial Day Footage really depicts a Bigfoot.

Perhaps the greatest sign that one has entered a distinct subculture, however, is the level of knowledge on display. When we asked attendees if they were familiar with the Skookum Cast, PG Film, Memorial Day Footage, Ohio Howl, and Albert Ostman case, nearly half in attendance were familiar with all of them (see fig. 5.7), and two-thirds were familiar with most of the presented evidence.[36] Many of the attendees were Bigfoot experts when they entered the conference.

A defining characteristic of a subculture is the development of a specialized vocabulary, known as *argot*. Shared interest in a subject naturally leads people to make distinctions that are of no interest to outsiders. For those involved in the world of role-playing video games, it is useful and necessary to distinguish *MMORPGS* from single-player games and to know the difference between *turn-based* and *real-time* combat.[37] Those with no patience for battling goblins and dragons on their computers find this to be so much boring trivia—they are all just video games. Explore any hobby or interest group and you will find similar categorization systems, which serve the useful function of distinguishing insiders from outsiders. One becomes a valued member of a subculture by learning its lingo, often at the tutelage of more senior members. Put another way, knowledge is a key marker of membership in a subculture.

As researchers in this arena, we have had to become fluent in the argots of a number of different subcultures in researching this book. We learned the difference between UFO contactees and abductees and what an abductee meant when she said aliens had placed an "implant" (tracking device) in her brain or that she had birthed a "hybrid" (a half-human/half-alien child). To navigate the world of ghost hunters we learned the workings of EMF detectors, the differences between residual and intelligent hauntings, and human and inhuman entities, and how to spot "orbs" in our photography and listen for EVPs in our tape recordings.[38]

We also had to learn the argot of Bigfoot enthusiasts to navigate their conference. For example, we overhead several attendees talking about a "shoot/don't shoot" controversy. Some Bigfoot hunters advocate the killing of a Bigfoot specimen, since it seems that only a body will attract the attention of mainstream science? To those on the "don't shoot" side of the fence, it could be potentially deadly to an obviously endangered species to take even one specimen. If Bigfoot is close relative to humans, it may even be considered murder. The shooters were slightly outnumbered in the so-called "shoot/don't shoot" controversy (54% disagree with shooting a Bigfoot to prove its existence to the world).

Each type of Bigfoot experience has its own specialized term. They talked of "vocalizations," purported Bigfoot screams and howls heard in the woods, such as the Ohio Howl. Nearly one-fourth (24%) of those in attendance claimed to have heard the screams, howls, or chatter of a Bigfoot. Around the same number have used a technique known as "call blasting" to entice Bigfoot to speak. Call blasting involves playing at high volume the Ohio Howl, other purported Bigfoot screams, sounds of animals in distress, recordings of a baby crying, or any other noise believed to be a possible attractant to a curious Sasquatch. Usually the sounds are played on a boombox/CD player attached to large speakers.

Twenty-six percent of the Bigfoot hunters at the conference have heard a different kind of suspicious noise in the forest, the sound of wood knocking on wood. This so-called wood knocking is believed to be a form of nonvocal Sasquatch communication wherein a Bigfoot bangs sticks on the trunks of trees to communicate with other nearby Bigfeet. On occasion the Bigfoot hunters will pick up a branch and try wood knocking themselves in the hopes of hearing an answer from the deep woods.

A more concrete form of evidence comes in lines of alleged Bigfoot tracks, or "trackways," which about 20 percent of the people at the conference claim to have found. Even better, as the wildlife biologist John Bindernagel discussed during his presentation, is when tracks include dermal ridges, or swirls equivalent to those found in fingerprints.

Of course, the holy grail of a Bigfoot researcher would be to see the beast itself, known as a "visual" among the Bigfoot hunters. Only twenty-three people at the conference had been lucky enough to actually see a Bigfoot, although another ten people think they may have seen one but are not absolutely certain. The epitome would be to capture that visual on camera, the modern equivalent of the PG film. Presenters discussed a number of methods by which they might accomplish this goal, often in quite technical terms. Jerry Hestand discussed the TBRC's "Operation Forest Vigil" in which dozens of motion-activated cameras have been attached to trees in areas of Texas and Oklahoma known for Bigfoot sightings. Bill Draginis, an engineer, discussed the "Eye-Gotcha" photographic system that could be placed in an area known for Bigfoot sightings.

"More Boring Than You Think": Profile of a Bigfoot Hunter

At the end of the long day of presentations we joined a group of Bigfoot luminaries on the auditorium stage for a question-and-answer session. The audience's questions were serious and mostly about the speculative biology of Bigfoot. Does the creature migrate? Does it sometimes walk on all fours or only on two legs? Are the creatures nocturnal, diurnal, or crepuscular?

We were well acquainted with the TBRC by the time we spoke at their annual conference. We already knew that its members did not fit the stereotype of paranormal believers. Nevertheless, we were still surprised by the staid nature of the conference and the conventionality of most of those in attendance. We can now consider conference attendees to be

	Average Americans	All conference attendees	Bigfoot hunters
Percentage male	53	67	88
Average education	some college	four-year degree	four-year degree
Average income	$35k–$50k	$50k–$100k	$50k–$100k
Married?	57	63	77
Protestant?	61	43	70
Church attendance	once a month	several times a year	once a month

Fig. 5.8. Profile of Bigfoot researchers and hunters: attendees at the Texas Bigfoot Research Conservancy's annual conference, compared to national averages

of two broad types. Some of those in attendance we might call Bigfoot hunters—members of the Texas Bigfoot Research Conservancy, Bigfoot Field Researchers Organization, or other organization devoted to entering the field to find evidence for the existence of Sasquatch. Nearly one-fifth (20%) of those in attendance had taken the step of joining such an organization. The remaining attendees were simply Bigfoot enthusiasts with an interest in the subject and which has not yet moved to the level of organizational membership. Comparing these two groups of people to the general population provides some interesting findings (see fig. 5.8).

Unless one defines a person as "strange" simply *because* they express an interest in Bigfoot (and we realize that some people would use that definition), the Bigfoot enthusiasts at the all-day Sasquatch event were remarkably normal, everyday people. The average Bigfoot enthusiast was married, and above average in education and income (a four-year degree from a college or university and $50,000 a year or more). If conference attendees were slightly unconventional, it was in terms of religion. While the majority of Americans (61%) are Protestant in some form or another, less than half of the Bigfoot enthusiasts claimed affiliation with a Protestant denomination. They also attend religious services several times a year, which is less frequent than the national average of once a month.

If we separate out those in attendance that are members of Bigfoot hunting groups, however, we find a very conventional group of people. One might even call them hyperconventional. The average Bigfoot hunter had a higher level of education than the average American, a higher yearly income, was more likely to be married, more likely to claim a Protestant affiliation, and in line with the average American in frequency of church attendance. There was the occasional obvious eccentric, such as an angry truck driver from Dallas who pinned the lead researcher in a corner to discuss theories of Atlantis, but these types were the exception, not the rule. For the most part we were among very normal people talking about a very strange subject.

Some of the reporters in attendance were clearly stymied by the lack of colorful characters or bizarre Bigfoot witnesses at the proceedings —strange people make for better headlines. Mike Leggett of the *Austin American-Statesman* was downright irritated as he recounted in his bitter review of the event, "Texas Conference more boring than you would think":

> I went to the 2009 Texas Bigfoot Conference expecting people in gorilla suits milling about among semi-crazed gangs of gonzo, tattooed, barrel-chested beandips. I found instead only a polite, older crowd of mildly sleepy true believers who only came alive at the mention of the TV show *MonsterQuest* or the movie *The Legend of Boggy Creek*. I thought surely someone would be selling BLT—Bigfoot, lettuce and tomato—sandwiches and Abominable Snowman cones during the lunch break, but there were only Cokes and Subway sandwiches.
>
> Trying not to sound breathlessly moronic and relentlessly off kilter must be hard work. The stream of people calling themselves Bigfoot researchers—an astounding number of them PhDs, college professors, and scientists from any number of fields—droned on all day, talking about satellite imagery, global rainfall patterns, Bigfoot territorial behaviors, and specialty fieldwork searching for Bigfoot signs. Even the crowd of believers was nodding off by the afternoon. I was asleep and drooling down the front of my shirt.
>
> The discussion was arcane, jargon-laden, and focused often on something they call cryptozoology.[39]

Practice: Hunting Bigfoot

If people who seek paranormal *knowledge* by reading books, scanning Web sites, or attending conferences can be characterized as more involved in a paranormal subculture than those who simply hold a belief or have had singular experiences, then *practice* may truly separate the dabblers from the serious enthusiasts. There are a number of ways that someone with an interest in a paranormal subject can put their interest into practice. Someone with an interest in ghosts can join a ghost-hunting club. Budding astrologers and psychics can attempt to use their powers.

Monster enthusiasts, on the other hand, must enter the field to search for their quarry.

When we joined some TBRC members on a hunt for Bigfoot, we witnessed something much different than the lighthearted, casual experimentation of the Dallas Psychic Fair. These men were single-minded, focused, and serious in their quest to bring Bigfoot into the light of day. "Bigfoot ain't no unicorn," one member told us, "and we will prove it."

December: Big Creek Scenic Area, Sam Houston National Forest, Texas

"David" is a forty-something ex-air force intelligence officer and now manager of a bank in a central Texas. In 2004 he caught a brief glimpse of a five- to six-foot, manlike creature, covered in reddish brown hair jump across a trail in the woods of Liberty County, Texas. "Mitch," also in his forties, played basketball in college and now works with computers near Temple, Texas. He has been interested in Bigfoot since he was a child. After seeing David give a lecture about Bigfoot, Mitch began driving into the woods on ad hoc Bigfoot hunts. While driving down a country road with his brother, he spotted a Bigfoot run across the road in front of his truck. A friendly, quiet man, Mitch's "beginner's luck" led him to formalize his quest for Bigfoot with the TBRC. "Keith," a surgeon, is also in his forties. Over six feet tall with salt-and-peppered brown hair, Keith has not yet seen Bigfoot but believes he has been close. On a recent excursion he heard "something" knocking on trees and pounding rocks together in the forest. Although serious in his interest in Bigfoot, Keith also joked continually about the benefits of the hunt. "I get to spend my weekends chewin' tobacco and eatin' what I want." Indeed, we were astonished at the volume of meat Keith was able to cook and consume from a portable oven in the back of his pickup.[40]

The three men graciously allowed us to accompany them on a field investigation to the Big Creek Scenic Area in the Sam Houston National Forest, outside of Cold Spring, Texas. Per David's instructions, we wore camo clothing (newly purchased from Wal-Mart) and brought enough food to make it through the evening. Early in the afternoon, we met at David's home and helped him pile five large plastic tubs of equipment into the back of his truck. After about three hours of driving, we pulled into a hunter's camp: a clearing in the woods with a dumpster and several pads on which we could pitch our tents.

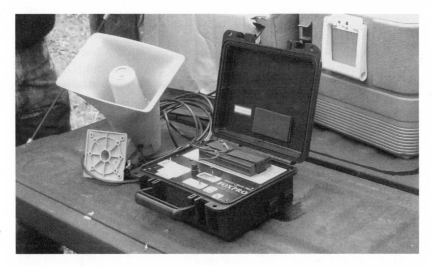

A "call blaster"

As we set up camp David informed us of the evening's plan. Our goal was to attempt to attract any Sasquatch that might be in the area via call blasting. David pulled a cooler from the back of his truck and opened it for us. Inside was his call blaster—a small device with dials and knobs attached to a loudspeaker. Throughout the night the call blaster played the Ohio Howl, the sounds of animals in distress, and the whoops of gibbons.

Shortly after 10 p.m. we hopped in their car and followed David and the other investigators to a series of trails a short distance from our camp where Keith had experienced wood knocking. We parked at the trailhead and gathered around David's truck to receive instructions. By this point the temperature had dropped below thirty degrees, leaving the authors feeling ill prepared.[41] We shivered uncomfortably and hopped from foot to foot to keep warm.

David was dressed from head to toe in camo clothing,. He stored cameras, flashlights, water, and other supplies in the multiple pockets on the camo outfit. An imposing .357 Magnum was strapped to his hip. The gun was there only to protect us against "indigenous wildlife," David informed us. He falls on the "don't shoot" side of the shoot/don't shoot Bigfoot debate. David could see "no good reason" for shooting at a Sasquatch, even though a real body would provide indisputable evidence of the creature's existence. He would use his gun only if a Sasquatch attacked or if we were threatened by other dangerous animals, such as wild boars. As David showed us his gun, Keith fiddled with his "new toy," a bizarre headlamp with two glowing lights attached to its top. By pressing a button he could switch between white and red lights that sputtered and died when he moved too quickly. The red light was supposed to keep it from being visible to creatures without the capability to pick up the different coloration of the light. We avoided talking directly to Keith lest we had to look directly into the painfully bright lights.

The TBRC's newest call blaster featured a remote control. It is possible that Bigfoot is deterred from investigating sounds produced by a call blaster because it hears or smells the humans operating the device, David told us. Therefore, we placed the unit and its speakers in the crook of a tree deep in the woods and retreated. The team then spread out. Each of us was paired with a TBRC investigator and followed his partner to a location in the woods. Keith would activate the blaster via remote. Ideally, a curious Bigfoot would walk right past us on its way to investigate the sounds coming from the call blaster.

It is an eerie experience to crouch by the side of a path, deep in unfamiliar woods on a bitterly cold evening, waiting for a terrifying howl to erupt from the call blaster. Between each blast, Keith would wait for responses from the local wildlife and then try again. For those of us who had no idea when the next blast would come, these waits were nerve-wracking. The sudden sound of chattering monkeys echoing off the trees caused one researcher to fall to the ground from his crouching position. The creepy Ohio Howl briefly produced chills to rival the temperature. Unfortunately, the experiment did not seem to produce an immediate response from resident Sasquatch. An irritated cow responded to one call blast, and we greatly annoyed the local dog population. We shudder to think of how we must have terrorized any unsuspecting campers in the area.

After an hour of call blasting, David yelled for the team to gather. We quietly marched single file back into the woods to retrieve the blaster and speakers. Several events occurred during the walk that intrigued the TBRC investigators as outlined in the group's written report of this excursion:

[A]t approximately 11:30 p.m., the investigators . . . heard several sounds like extremely loud knocks on trees. Also noteworthy: investigators . . . were overwhelmed with a very obnoxious odor smelling very much like an animal that had been immersed in garbage. The knocks seemed to be in response to [our] broadcasting playbacks of gibbon and gorilla vocalizations.

The authors indeed heard what sounded like something knocking on a tree and briefly noticed a foul odor, akin to an animal carcass. We could not locate the origin of the smell, as it came and went. Perhaps the source of the smell was moving or the wind was shifting the smell of a fixed object. Unfortunately, we are not sufficiently familiar with the Texas woods, or its wildlife, to know potential sources for such phenomena. Nevertheless, David, Mitch and Keith were excited by the possibility of having attracted a Sasquatch to the area. "We'll come back in the morning and look for more evidence," David told us.

A Trackway

A fitful night's sleep and a hot breakfast at a local diner later, the TBRC returned to the call blasting location. We split into two teams. Keith and Mitch asked Joseph to follow them in one direction; Carson and Christopher followed David in another.

David slowly walked along a creek, hopping from side to side, scanning the ground carefully, most of which was hard-packed and covered with leaves. Our best chance of finding the tracks of any Bigfoot drawn to the area by our call blasting was in the soft, wet sand around the creek, he reasoned. After searching for about twenty minutes, David said "I think we've got something here fellas!" He knelt next to the creek and brushed leaves away from an impression in the sand.

David's cautious optimism transformed into excitement as he examined the "potential hominid track." He pointed at the indentation in the ground and pointed to what appeared to be toe prints. It certainly looked like the track of a person, but we are not experts on animal tracks and so cannot speculate on what animals could make these tracks. "It's not a raccoon," he said. "It's not a fox or a horse or a hog either. There are only two things it could be—a human or a Sasquatch." As he scanned the area, David found what he likened to a heel print to the left of the full print. Across the small creek were what he thought might be knuckle prints. He speculated that a Bigfoot might have knelt beside the creek, resting on one hand and scooping a drink of water with the other.[42] The TBRC made plaster casts of the tracks, which now reside in their evidence collection.

David spots a potential Bigfoot track on the banks of a small creek.

Recently the findings from this excursion were reported on an episode of the History Channel series *MonsterQuest* titled "Swamp Stalker."

Paranormal Complications and Consequences

In our research we have found that the paranormal is difficult to predict. As social scientists we hope to answer questions when possible, not simply raise new ones. But we are compelled to note that attempts to predict who will engage the paranormal often ignore the multitude of different ways that a person might interface with a paranormal subculture or belief. Some people will simply hold an unexamined, uncritical belief in one or more paranormal subjects and their interest will go no farther. Some of those who are inclined to believe in UFOs, ghosts, or psychic powers probably think about those subjects rarely unless asked. Other people have indeed had what they perceive to be a paranormal experience. Sometimes this event, whether it be a psychic experience, Bigfoot sighting, or other encounter, will have a dramatic impact upon a person's life, upending paradigms and upsetting established ideas about the cosmic order. For others a personal ghost sighting is merely a fun story to tell one's children around the campfire, no more, no less. Still others will be compelled by a belief or experience to explore a paranormal subject further by studying the topic through reading books, visiting Internet sites, and watching documentaries. A small subset of these casual researchers will be funneled into deeper levels of a paranormal subculture and will start attending psychic fairs, UFO conferences, or ghost fairs. A select few will become psychics, ghost hunters, and UFO watchers themselves.

The point being, not only do different types of people become attracted to different paranormal beliefs and have different types of paranormal experiences, it is quite possible that different types of people will be more attracted to different levels of involvement in a paranormal subculture. For example, those who have spent time researching the subject of Bigfoot online, through books, and documentaries tend to be younger males who infrequently attend church and who live on the West Coast. Yet a different type of person is attracted to the highest, most serious levels of

Purported Bigfoot tracks from Cold Spring, Texas

the Bigfoot subculture and joins the hunt for Bigfoot. We cannot speak to other paranormal subcultures, but at least within the Bigfoot hunting subculture, the people at its most involved levels are quite conventional in other aspects of their lives, contrary to public expectations.

In the time we spent with Bigfoot hunters, we found them to be well aware of the way they are perceived by outsiders. David, Mitch, and Keith all have much to lose by "being branded as nutcases," David told us. Mitch's uncle and brother continually poke fun of his fascination with Bigfoot. David is careful who he tells at work, concerned that people will not trust a Bigfoot hunter to manage their banking. Keith would not dream of telling his fellow surgeons about his quest for the beast. The men's devotion to their quest allows them to press on in the face of public scorn, not that the men would not change how others perceive them if they could. Their willingness to accept the consequences of their quest for Bigfoot evidence separates them from casual Bigfoot believers and from those who read the occasional magazine story and watch *MonsterQuest* once in awhile. Their focus on proving Bigfoot's existence appears largely motivated by vindication, and they dream of the day that the scientific community is forced by the weight of evidence to announce to the world that Bigfoot is indeed real. They think of themselves as normal people who just happen to have seen or believe in Bigfoot. They appear to be correct in this regard.

The willingness to be unconventional is a key distinction that separates people who are involved in the paranormal. Some people are willing to face the consequences of exploring the full range of the paranormal. Others try their best to maintain conventional lives in the face of limited paranormal interests. As we explore in the next chapter, those who are unconcerned about the consequences of paranormal belief are truly different from the rest of us. For once the paranormal will become less complicated.

6

Paranormal People

As we have discussed throughout this book, there are several popular and academic ideas regarding people who believe in the paranormal. Sociologists and social commentators such as Karl Marx have argued that religious and paranormal beliefs will be the province of the downtrodden, searching for supernatural solutions to earthly troubles. Other religion scholars have theorized that paranormal beliefs represent comparatively new and fringe elements of the American religious marketplace. New ideas tend to be adopted first by elites, and therefore, some argue, the paranormal will be the province of those with higher educations and incomes.

Outside the halls of the academy a broader stereotype is often applied to paranormal believers—people who believe in or have experienced the paranormal are "different." People who do not believe in the paranormal are perceived to be normal; those who believe in paranormal topics are considered weird, unconventional, strange, or deviant.

There is a big problem with this simplistic assessment—believing in something paranormal has become the norm in our society. When asked if they believe in the reality of nine different paranormal subjects including telekinesis, fortune-telling, astrology, communication with the dead, haunted houses, ghosts, Atlantis, UFOs and monsters, over two-thirds of Americans (68%) believe in at least one (see fig. 6.1).[1] In a strictly numerical sense, people who do not believe in anything paranormal are now the "odd men out" in American society. Less than a third of Americans (32%) are dismissive of all of nine subjects. What this means is that distinguishing between people who do and do not believe or experience the paranormal is becoming increasingly less useful. Rather, people may be more readily distinguishing by *how much* of the paranormal they find credible.

Very few Americans (2%) believe in all nine of these paranormal subjects. Only about 11% believe in six or more paranormal topics. What this

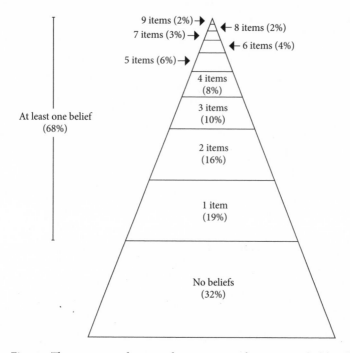

Fig. 6.1. The paranormal pyramid: percentage of Americans holding simultaneous paranormal beliefs (Baylor Religion Survey, 2005)

Note: We examined the responses of each respondent to determine how many of nine paranormal beliefs items they believed. A respondent who believed in any of the nine items (Atlantis, ghosts, psychic powers, fortune-telling, astrology, talking to the dead, haunted houses, UFOS, and/or monsters) received a 1. A respondent who reported belief in any two of the items received a 2, and so on. Relatively few respondents (about 2%) indicated belief in all nine. Percentages are rounded.

means is that most Americans are not entirely dismissive of the paranormal but display a form of particularistic skepticism. Some people believe strongly in UFOs and Bigfoot, but find the claims of astrologers and psychics incredible. Some believe wholeheartedly in ghosts and the ability to communicate with the dead, yet have little patience for claims that ancient, advanced civilizations (such as Atlantis) once existed.

To put it quite simply, people who believe in the paranormal could be placed along a continuum ranging from *paranormal particularists,* who believe strongly in one aspect of the paranormal or have had a single type of paranormal experience, to *paranormal generalists,* who hold multiple different types of paranormal beliefs and may claim multiple different types of paranormal experiences.

Throughout this book we hope to have dispelled many stereotypes about the paranormal, but in this chapter we will see that popular notions about the paranormal do indeed fit. In our fieldwork and in our data we have noticed that there are strong demographic differences between *paranormal particularists* and *paranormal generalists*. Sometimes paranormal generalists are quite unconventional and do indeed inhabit the fringes of society—you just have to know where and how to look.

To understand the important differences between these *paranormal generalists* and *paranormal particularists* we will first revisit two people we met earlier in the book.

Laura: Paranormal Generalist

In chapter 4 we introduced Laura. In 1984 she claims to have been taken to a large UFO hovering above Earth. Once aboard the ship she met a group of friendly, humanlike extraterrestrials and their commanding officer. Laura was connected to an advanced computer system to receive lessons about holistic health and medicine. This was information she would need someday to help the planet, the aliens told her. Following her lessons and an amazing meal, Laura was returned to Earth unharmed. Laura's story is not particularly unusual within the UFO subculture. It fits in rather nicely alongside George Adamski, Billy Meier, and other UFO contactees who have received wisdom from their humanlike space brothers.

But Laura is not like other people we have met who have had a singular UFO experience. She does not obsess over UFO tales and does not seem to dwell on this particular experience unless asked about it. The reason? She lives a life filled with paranormal beliefs and experiences, and her visit to space was but one of many.

On a recent rainy weekend, I visited Laura at her home in Federal Way, Washington, to chat about her varied interests. Laura lives in a mobile home in what she cheerfully described over the phone as a "trailer park that has seen better days." Having retired from a job with the post office several years previous, Laura now lives on a fixed income but is "busier than ever" with her reading, hobbies, and interests.

One of her strongest interests is Native American spirituality, which I noticed immediately upon entering her well-kept home. As her new puppy jumped at my legs and an older cat stared petulantly from behind a chair, I looked around the room. Nearly every surface had a popular representation of Native Americans on it. To my left was a small bookshelf. Covering the wall above it was a series of small collectors plates, each emblazoned with reverent paintings of Native Americans. In one, a chief in full headdress sits on the back of his horse, his arms outreached to his sides. In another, a medicine man communes with a wolf in the forest. On top of the bookshelf was a resin statue of three wolf heads, howling at the sky. Across the room and on top of another bookshelf was a two-foot-tall teepee made of cloth. A large ceramic maiden doll with feathers in her hair was standing inside the teepee. A dream catcher hung from the ceiling in a corner. Paintings of saintly Native Americans filled the open wall space. They sat near streams, danced in fields, and gazed at totemic animals in the sky.

I asked Laura about her obvious interest in Native Americans. She is one-eighth Native American and finds this group to be the "most in touch with nature and most in touch with their inner spirituality." Indeed, she believes Native American tribes to be the descendants of star ancestors as "they have legends about coming from the sky." To explore this interest Laura recently joined a "Medicine Wheel" formed by a local shaman. The creation of medicine wheels or sacred hoops is a rather common practice among Native American tribes who used them as calendars and for various healing rituals and rites of passage. Most often the wheels were physically laid upon the landscape using stones. Lines of rocks radiated outward in a circular pattern from a center point of stones.

Recently, the symbol of the sacred circle has been adopted in paranormal circles, and it is this blending of the old and the new that Laura practices. She describes her Medicine Wheel as "basically Northwest Indian astrology" and symbolic in nature. Sometimes when the group meets, they do not bother to lay out a wheel on a ground. Each member is given an animal representation based on their birth dates. Laura is a bear, a natural leader. In the group's irregular meetings, they stand in a circle and meditate, often focusing upon their animal representations.

Laura also told me with pride of her membership in a "Grandmother's Meeting." Although Laura has several grandchildren, this group is not only for grandmothers in the literal sense. Rather the grandmother is a "symbol that represents an aspect of the divine that has come to heal the Earth." Grandmothers represent the "yin," Laura said. She continued:

> Yin energy finds the divine in the world as it is. People flooded with yin
> energy look at the forest and marvel in its beauty. Yang energy looks at a

forest and sees the profit that can be made from its woods or from building on it. Yang represents movement and change. Yin is peace. When the two are in balance, the world works as it should. When they are out of balance there are problems. The world has too much yang now. That is why we have wars.

The grandmothers believe that by coming together and meditating they can raise the level of yin in the world thereby bringing renewed peace, prosperity, and balance to the planet. When not meditating with her Medicine Wheel or Grandmother's Meeting, Laura pursues a dizzying array of other paranormal interests. She once signed up for astrology courses at a New Age school, but soon realized that she would have to invest considerable time, energy, and money to become a truly proficient astrologer and withdrew her enrollment. Laura still occasionally reads a book on astrology, but she now has more interest in numerology, which "just makes sense to [her]."

She has attempted automatic writing at times, wherein the "writer" holds a pen or pencil over a pad of paper and enters a trancelike state during which the writer's hand scribbles out messages and drawings. Some think these messages are from the writer's subconscious, others believe that aliens, ghosts, angels, or other entities enter the writer's body and use this opportunity to communicate. Laura has a strong interest in Bigfoot and believes the creatures come in more humanlike and more beastlike varieties. Both versions of Bigfoot escape detection via the ability to become invisible, even though several of her friends claim to have seen one.

Laura has not been lucky enough to spot Bigfoot herself, but she has had other paranormal experiences. For example, she believes that a guardian angel once saved her from great harm. It seems that as a young girl Laura was duck hunting with her father near a swamp in southern California. She was crouched next to her father behind some tall grass waiting for ducks to fly overhead when she heard a male voice in her head yelling at her. "Laura! Move your head! Now!" it said. She ducked down and at that very moment heard a gunshot. It seems that duck hunters on the other side of the swamp had fired at a duck crossing in front of Laura's position. If Laura had not ducked, she claims, she would have been shot directly in the face. She believes that the voice she heard was that of a guardian angel sent to protect her. Her father was not so warned, however, and *was* hit in the face. He lived the remainder of his life with bullet fragments embedded in his forehead.

More recently, Laura's son became interested in Scientology and loaned her some of his books. Scientology has a complex belief system that involves the improvement of the current life by reliving traumas that occurred in previous lives. The church claims to provide tools that will help the initiate learn about their previous lives. Through reading her son's books, Laura says she became aware of a number of past lives she has experienced.

She now believes that she was sent to Earth eighty thousand years ago by a consortium of extraterrestrial "higher beings" called the Goodly Company. Members of the Goodly Company share an agenda of helping to format peaceful intelligence throughout the universe. Laura herself was involved in the creation of the human species. She has memories of observing Neanderthal man with a team of other higher beings. They would look for the selfless Neanderthals—the ones who helped others and did not seem to think only of themselves. They selected the noblest Neanderthals as breeding stock and used them to create the human race.

As part of her life journey, Laura occasionally lived among the early humans. In a recent correspondence, she told us of her experience with wooly mammoths:

I was [once] a young unmarried woman of a small band of cave dwellers. Our people were starving. Our medicine man went into the between worlds and talked to the leader of the Mammoths. He pleaded for a sacrifice from one of them so our people would not die. The old Mammoth agreed ONLY if one of our children was sacrificed as well. Their children were as precious to them as ours were to us. The shaman agreed.

On a certain day my parents came and were so excited. I was massaged with grease and my hair was straightened and flowers were put on me and in my hair. I was excited too. I thought that a mate had been found for me and I was to be married. I was brought out to a jumble of rocks that overlooked a narrow strip of plain between two cliffs. All the people were there and the shaman was telling us how this was a good day. The Mammoth were coming and we would eat. The day was beautiful and sunny and the rocks were warm. It seemed like fall because the grasses in the valley were golden. The Mammoths started walking through the valley but too far away for our hunters to reach them. The shaman had me sit on the rock and lay back. He told my parents to hold my arms. They looked bewildered but did it. Quickly the shaman took a knife and stabbed me in the heart. Everyone was horrified because this sort of thing had NEVER been done before. My parents were devastated because they had not been told. I was startled and then I was out of my body watching.

A young female Mammoth with a beautiful shining golden coat turned away from the herd and walked close to the wall where our people were. She looked me straight in the eye and I was dumbfounded by the intelligence and beauty I saw there. Our hunters pushed down boulders and killed her. She knowingly sacrificed herself because I was sacrificed. And the people lived.[2]

Once the human race was firmly established, Laura says, extraterrestrials sent Jesus to Earth to teach us further. Laura was also around to help with his mission. During Jesus's time she lived as an old widow named Rachel. She became extremely close friends with Jesus after traveling with him and the apostles. Jesus was crucified, says Laura, because he was so good at changing people's mind. "He brought out the best in everyone and the powerful people couldn't stand it." Laura/Rachel could not bear to witness the crucifixion of Jesus but afterwards became a vocal advocate of his message. Eventually she also became an irritant and was stoned to death for "talking to [*sic*] much about Jesus."[3]

Learning so much about her own past lives has opened Laura up to new revelations. She believes that we are all connected to a big "Oversoul," and that each individual person is merely an extension of it. Those who tap into the Oversoul can tap into the lives and experiences of others, something that Laura has learned to do. She experiences not only her own past lives but can relive and re-experience the past lives of people she has never even met.

Were a UFO author to interview Laura, he would probably ask her only about adventures aboard a spaceship and label her a "contactee." A professional astrologer or numerologist would find a budding initiate in Laura. Someone producing a documentary on guardian angels might have interest in her story. She would be the perfect call-in guest for a talk show about past lives. But she is not any one of these things. She is all of them, simultaneously. She lives in a paranormal world where each day can bring a new paranormal experience or interest in a new paranormal topic. She knows that she is not like most people and takes pride in her unconventionality.

In chapter 5 we met David, a Bigfoot hunter from Texas. He has devoted himself to finding conclusive evidence for Bigfoot's existence since he sighted the creature in 2004. Nearly all of David's free time is spent in the woods searching for Bigfoot or helping with the operations of the Texas Bigfoot Research Conservancy. Someone who had not met David and Laura might lump them together—they both claim to have had an experience that we have labeled paranormal in this book. But in almost every other way, they could not be more different. To understand this difference we must first visit a controversy within the Bigfoot community regarding the nature of their quarry.

Bigfoot and the Star People

A key challenge that has faced Bigfoot believers over the years has been the subject's frequent association with other aspects of the paranormal.[4] To those outside Bigfoot circles, the subject is akin to ghosts and astrology. Sasquatch is something for the tabloids or a silly story with which to end the local evening news. The anthropologist Jeff Meldrum, one of the few academics to openly express an interest in Bigfoot, ruminated on this issue in his recent book *Sasquatch: Legend Meets Science*:

> Unfortunately, the legitimate search for elusive animals had become embroiled in the mix of the mystical and the pseudoscientific. Accounts of lake monsters and wildmen continue to be the stuff of sensational supermarket tabloids. Walk into a bookstore in search of reading material on Bigfoot and you will most often be directed to the occult section, somewhere between Bermuda triangle and crop circles.[5]

Meldrum has only stated part of the problem faced by the Bigfoot subculture; the community itself is divided as to the nature of their quarry. Some people, whom we might call the Bigfoot naturalists, believe that Bigfoot is an undiscovered species of primate. It is an animal waiting to be discovered, an elusive one to be sure, but still an animal. Just as mankind discovered the mountain gorilla and orangutan, we can, with proper funding, one day kill a Bigfoot, capture one, or discover indisputable evidence of its existence. But there are others within Bigfoot circles, whom we might label Bigfoot paranormalists, who argue that Bigfoot has magical powers or is associated with other paranormal phenomena.

Bigfoot's most frequent paranormal crossover is with the subject of UFOs. In the 1970s a number of witnesses claim to have seen a Sasquatch emerging from or at least nearby a UFO. In other cases, Bigfoot creatures were simply seen in areas where UFO sightings had recently been reported, implying a connection between the two phenomena.

For example, at about 9 p.m. on October 25, 1973, several witnesses near Uniontown, Pennsylvania, claimed to have seen a large, red, spherical object hovering in the sky and then descending into a pasture. A younger man and twin boys walked to the field to investigate and claimed to have discovered a white, dome-shaped object that was about one hundred feet in diameter resting on the ground. The object was making a loud whirring sound, and light from it illuminated the surrounding area. The witnesses were approaching the object when they noticed two strange figures with glowing green eyes walking along a nearby fence line. Each was between seven and nine feet tall and covered in hair. The creatures' arms hung down past their knees in a gorilla-like fashion.

The group fired upon the creatures. The larger of the two beasts then turned toward the other, and at that instant the white object in the field disappeared, and the whirring noise stopped. The witnesses fled the scene and called the state police. A trooper arrived at the scene, purportedly witnessing a glowing circle in the grass 150 feet in diameter. Upon returning to his station the trooper called the UFO hotline of Pennsylvania UFO investigator Stan Gordon, who sent a team to investigate.

Later that night the group arrived at the location and reported several strange incidents. The glowing area observed by the trooper earlier was gone, but a farmhouse nearby suddenly lit up "like daylight" for several seconds.[6] In his recounting of the events, Stan Gordon continues:

> Strange events began to occur . . . in this dark secluded location. . . . The main witness, a rather large individual, while being questioned suddenly begins to growl, throwing his father and my assistant George Lutz toward the ground. The man ran into the field growling like an animal and emitting screams, one which was near inhuman. His own dog approaches him as to attack, then runs off whimpering. The man suddenly collapses onto the ground. Then two of my team members begin to complain that they are having trouble breathing. Suddenly the air is filled with a strong odor that can best be described as rotten eggs. . . . The man as he came out of what appeared to be an almost trancelike state, began talking about visions he saw about the end of the world.

Gordon has kept in touch with the principals involved in this bizarre combination of Bigfoot, UFOs, possession, and end-time prophecies. According to Gordon, the primary witness continues to report the occasional paranormal experience, including an encounter with the Men in Black from UFO lore, but we have not attempted to confirm any aspect of this case. We do not know the names of the witnesses, nor have we attempted to track down the state trooper in question. To do so would be missing the point. What is important for the current purposes is not whether the Uniontown incident happened as reported, but the effect it and cases like it had upon the Bigfoot subculture.

The Uniontown incident and similar cases convinced some that Bigfoot creatures were extraterrestrial beings. From the 1970s on, speculation about Bigfoot's paranormal associations became a popular area of interest in some Bigfoot books and later in online forums and blogs.[7] The 1976 book *Bigfoot* captures the Bigfoot paranormalist genre well. In successive chapters, the authors B. Ann Slate and Al Berry recount cases in which Bigfoot has communicated telepathically with humans, disappeared into thin air, or been seen in the presence of UFOs. They variously speculate that the creature is a Native American that has developed the ability to shape-shift, that it might live in caves laced with advanced technology, and that Bigfoot might be used by extraterrestrials as a research animal. This final theme was strikingly similar to the storyline of a 1976 episode of popular television show *The Six Million Dollar Man* in which hero Steve Austin battles Bigfoot, only to discover that the creature is an android bodyguard created by alien beings.

As such theories about Bigfoot's origins spread in the subculture and in popular media, several unique personalities emerged to vex the Bigfoot naturalists. For example, since 1983 the former logger Stan Johnson has claimed telepathic communication with "The Big Foot Peoples," peaceful forest beings who worship the Christian God. "The first time I met Sasquatch he got up and prayed . . . to God, and to Jesus Christ," Johnson claimed.[8] Through Bigfoot Allone of the Rrowe family of Bigfeet, Johnson has learned that the Bigfeet are visitors from the fifth dimension who travel in UFOs. Originally from the planet Centuris, the Bigfoot Peoples were rescued by the inhabitants of nearby Arice when their planet was about to be destroyed. The Bigfeet lived happily with the humanlike people of Arice until an evil ruler came to power, forcing many to find another home. Some of the Bigfeet made their way to Earth sometime before the last Ice Age where they were forced to contend with rampaging dinosaurs and aggressive cavemen. Compounding their problems was a troop of evil Bigfeet sent to Earth by the evil conqueror. After many bloody skirmishes the good Bigfeet fled to various corners of the earth. Allone warned Johnson that the bad Bigfeet remain especially numerous in Russia, China, the mountains of Oregon, and parts of Washington and Canada.[9]

Perhaps the greatest thorn in the sides of more staid Bigfooters was the late Jon-Erik Beckjord, who died in 2008. Beckjord regularly appeared on radio talk shows and on TV programs such as the *Today Show* and *Late Night with David Letterman* to espouse his unique theories about Bigfoot. We were able to speak to Beckjord by phone shortly before his death to hear his unique perspective.

"We should have captured Bigfoot by now if it was flesh and blood," he told us. He went on to explain that a hunter should have shot one of them. Would it not be possible to follow the footprints of such a large beast until we found one? Why hasn't a Bigfoot been struck and killed by a car? Those who favor a simple, naturalistic origin for Bigfoot have provided their own responses to such criticisms.[10] Beckjord believed he had a more reasonable answer. Bigfoot "cannot be caught or shot" because it is a shape-shifter that can "manipulate the light spectrum they're in so that people can't seem them" and use its telepathic powers to sense the presence of humans. Further, Bigfoot creatures share a "space-time origin and connection with UFOs and come from an alternate universe by a wormhole."[11]

"That UFO Nonsense"

In our time with members of the Texas Bigfoot Research Conservancy we have observed how little patience David and most other members have for connecting Bigfoot to other aspects of the paranormal. A summary statement on the group's Web site attempts to frame their highly ridiculed subject matter in serious terms:

> The Texas Bigfoot Research Conservancy is a 501(c)(3) tax-exempt non-profit scientific-research organization, as recognized by the Internal Revenue Service, comprised of volunteer investigators, scientists and naturalists.

With a diverse, dedicated, professional, and talented roster of approximately fifty members, including biologists, and other professionals, the TBRC pursues education and research activities pertaining to the centuries-old "wildman" or "hairy man" phenomenon in North America. The TBRC proposes that the source of the phenomenon is a biological entity, probably an unlisted large primate. The organization is actively engaged in activities designed to test that hypothesis.

The TBRC desires to enhance the credibility of bigfoot/sasquatch research and facilitate a greater degree of acceptance by the scientific community and other segments of society of the likelihood of a biological basis behind the sasquatch phenomenon.

The TBRC is steadfast in its belief that Bigfoot is simply an undiscovered animal that science will one day recognize. Its members dream of Bigfoot moving out of the tabloids and into the academy. Bigfoot paranormalists threaten these ambitions. With their outlandish theories and colorful personalities, Beckjord, Stan Johnson, and others further convince already wary academics and government agencies that Bigfoot is a fringe topic from which serious people should stay away. "We have lots of scientists that quietly support us, " David told us, "but they don't say it publicly because they are worried about their reputations." To date most have not taken the time to truly examine their evidence, David told us, but merely dismiss it out of hand.

David and other TBRC members make a point of talking about their level of skepticism to try to counteract the perception that Bigfoot is a silly subject. "Just because I hunt Bigfoot doesn't mean I believe everything I hear. I'm a skeptic," one told us. At TBRC meetings we have heard speakers who spent as much time debunking potential cases as they did presenting exciting new pieces of evidence.[12] More importantly, David told us, the group is very careful to avoid being caught up in "that UFO nonsense."[13] Potential members who wonder if Bigfoot might be a visiting extraterrestrial or who attribute psychic powers to the beast are discouraged from joining, lest they further muddy the waters. Those with a more paranormalist bent on Bigfoot are unlikely to agree with the clear biological stance outlined in the group's materials, and if they were to join they would find little hearing for their theories. This is not to suggest that the TBRC is rude or close-minded, they just have a clear perspective on the nature of their enterprise.

Popular and academic discussions often treat the paranormal as an either/or proposition. Either you are "normal" and do not believe in topics such as Bigfoot, UFOs, and psychic phenomena, or you are deviant and believe in the paranormal. The reality is much more complicated. Among paranormal believers we find a strong distinction between people like Laura, who see their involvement with the paranormal as a lifelong exploration of the unknown in many forms, and people like David, who are seeking credibility and focus upon only one subject. David tries very hard to make sure that his topic of interest is not associated with other paranormal topics. Laura sees the paranormal as an interconnected, holistic web of beliefs and experiences, waiting to be explored. She is a paranormal person. David has almost reluctantly found himself involved in the study of Bigfoot and will not cross the line into other topics.

The differences between David and Laura may seem idiosyncratic and unique to their biographies. In fact, we can predict with some accuracy what type of person will become involved in one or many aspects of the paranormal.

The Paranormal as Deviant Behavior

To explain and predict why someone might become a paranormal particularist like David and many other members of the TBRC versus a paranormal generalist like Laura, we turn to research by scholars of deviant and criminal behavior. We want to be clear about several points though. The reader might ask why we would apply theories of deviant and criminal behavior to people who believe or participate in the paranormal. Does this mean that we think that people who visit astrologers are potential criminals or that UFO believers are weird and dangerous?

Typically, it is the bizarre examples of a phenomenon that are the most heavily publicized. Consider homicide in the United States. Judging by news coverage, popular police dramas, and reality series, one might be left with the impression that most murders are committed by strangers and that serial killings are on the rise. The opposite is true. Most homicide victims are killed by someone they know, usually in the heat of passion, as in cases of domestic violence.[14] Law enforcement is well aware of this fact. Most detectives start their murder investigations by interviewing spouses and other in-home family members before moving to extended family members, close friends, and finally acquaintances and co-workers. Only when such leads fail to produce a viable suspect do police seriously consider the possibility that a complete stranger was involved in the crime. There is also no evidence that serial killings are on the increase. Serial killings rise and fall with the overall homicide rate. Serial murders constitute a very small percentage of all murders; during times of increased violent crime we will see more serial killings and fewer in less violent times.[15] The reason we have such a skewed sense of what murder is like is that shocking and atypical murders are considered bigger news than "routine" domestic violence incidents.[16]

The same problem applies to coverage of the paranormal. The most eccentric personalities receive the most airplay. Those very rare instances (such as the mass suicide of the Heaven's Gate UFO cult) wherein paranormal believers have been a danger to themselves or others receive so much media attention that they often come to typify the paranormal in the minds of the public. We have run into our share of eccentric personalities while researching this book along with those who are indistinguishable from the average man on the street. We find that people who believe in the paranormal are not to be feared. Therefore, we do not want the reader to think that our application of ideas from criminology and deviance studies means that we have bought into stereotypes about paranormal believers.

To call something "deviant" is not the same as calling it bad, evil, or crazy. Deviance simply refers to beliefs or behaviors that diverge from the norms of society. A more appropriate synonym for deviant would be "unconventional." Unconventional beliefs and behaviors *can* be bad for society: for example, criminal acts are a form of deviance, as would be the holding of white supremacist beliefs. At other times, unconventional behaviors and beliefs are beneficial. Rosa Parks engaged in an act of deviance that helped to spawn the civil rights movement. Inventors, entrepreneurs, and scientists often have to think in unconventional ways and break with norms to make advances in their fields. Something is defined as paranormal because it has not yet been recognized by conventional science and conventional society. Therefore, the paranormal is, by definition, deviant, and theories of deviance can sometimes help us understand involvement with the paranormal.

We also must be very clear about another point. Many theories that attempt to explain deviance focus upon criminality, particularly gang violence and juvenile delinquency. This is not surprising as the reduction of crime is of much greater interest to public officials and granting agencies than is the understanding of noncriminal deviant or unconventional behaviors and beliefs. Our reference to this research does not mean that we believe the paranormal to be akin to criminal behavior.

Stakes in Conformity

Criminologists and deviance researchers have proposed a wide variety of different theories to explain what causes unconventional beliefs and behaviors. Much of this work has assumed that people naturally desire to conform and that it takes a negative event or circumstance to push someone into deviant behavior. In other words, much criminological theory rests on the implicit assumption that people are inherently "good" until something makes them "bad."

The criminologist Travis Hirschi pushed for a different approach to understanding deviance in his landmark book *Causes of Delinquency.*[17] Although he focused his theory upon the explanation of juvenile delinquency and crime, its core ideas have wider applicability and can also be applied to unconventional beliefs and behaviors. Drawing upon the work of earlier criminologists, Hirsch argued that conformity is not a given for humans.[18] Crime and deviance can provide an easy, quick, and often thrilling means to desired ends. For example, one way to buy a car is to work long hours at a job, slowly saving up the necessary funds to finally purchase a sensible vehicle. It is much quicker to simply steal the expensive sports car that one actually wants. If a person is angered or humiliated by another person, the sensible thing to do is walk away and cool down, when the most gratifying thing to do would be to instantly retaliate. Hirschi's point was simple, most people know the conventional routes they are expected to use to reach desired goals, but unconventional or deviant routes to those same goals are often quicker and more appealing on a base level. So why do people conform at all?

The answer is reasonable, but insightful. Most people do not act on their base instincts or take the quickest route to desired goals because to do so would be too risky. Consider two men, one of whom has a high-paying job with opportunities for advancement, a higher education, a wife he loves, and children that he dotes on. The other man has had less luck in life. He was never able to go to college and has briefly held a series of low-paying jobs. Recently divorced, he is entirely estranged from his ex-wife and children. Following Hirschi's line of reasoning, the first man should be much less likely to engage in a deviant act, such as visiting a prostitute. Were he to be caught soliciting by police, his name might reach the papers. His wife and children would be humiliated and angry and might never forgive him. His boss and co-workers may find out about the arrest, costing him future promotions or even his job. The other man is not concerned about losing his high-paying job or future opportunities for advancement in his chosen career. With no current desire to reconcile with his wife and kids, he is not concerned about them finding out that he consorted with a prostitute. The temptations of deviance should be less attractive to the first man because he has more at risk, more to lose if he gets caught.

We must be clear about certain matters. Hirschi and related theorists do not argue that people who do not have a job or who are lonely are inherently criminal. Nor do they argue that people who have much to lose will never deviate, as evidenced by high-profile scandals involving politicians and public figures. They simply claim that people who are more tied to the conventional order will be more concerned with conventionality. People who have significant investments in conventional lines of action will be loathe to risk those investments. Someone who has spent years acquiring the advanced education for a high-paying engineering career would be less likely to engage in risky behaviors than another earning low, hourly wages at a dead-end job. On average, people who have a high "stake in conformity" have more to lose by engaging in deviant or unconventional behavior and should be less likely to be engaged in deviance than people with lesser stakes in conformity (see chap. 4).[19] Those with low stakes in conformity are comparatively free to indulge in deviance.

For Hirschi, deviance is the result of a weak or broken bond to society or stake in conformity, and thus the task of theorists is to determine the elements that make up a stake in conformity. Hirschi attempted to quantify a stake in conformity, arguing that there are four primary ways in which an individual is bonded to conventional society: *attachments, involvements, commitments,* and *beliefs.* Attachment refers to the extent to which an individual has strong relationships with people that he desires to maintain. An individual who has strong attachments will, theoretically, not want to risk the disapproval of these significant others by engaging in deviant behavior. Involvement refers to the extent to which individuals engage in conventional activities. Hirschi argues that an individual who is frequently involved in social clubs, charities, or other such activities will be too busy doing those things to find time to engage in deviant behavior. Commitments of money, energy, or time made by a person in order to obtain a certain lifestyle, compose another part of the stake in conformity. Someone who has worked hard and achieved material success will, theoretically, avoid unconventional behavior since it might threaten the investments they have made in a certain lifestyle. The final element of the social bond, belief, assumes that an individual will be less likely to accept unconventional beliefs if she already has conventional beliefs.

People with high levels of attachment, involvement, commitment, and belief will be conformists, while people with extremely low levels of each will be deviant, unconventional, or nonconformist. People can range between these two extremes. For example, Hirschi would expect a youth with an average number of strong attachments to be more deviant than a youth with a high number of attachments, but less deviant than a youth with no valued relationships.

Hirschi's ideas help us to predict how involved someone will become in the paranormal, both in the specific examples of David and Laura, and in the trends we find in our national surveys. There is strong evidence that a person's stake in conformity helps to predict her level of involvement in the paranormal. People who are wedded to conventional society are less attracted to paranormal beliefs. They will tend to have no paranormal beliefs or to be paranormal particularists like David. People with lower stakes in conformity lean toward the more unconventional in general. They are more likely to be paranormal generalists, like Laura, who are interested in multiple paranormal subjects at once. To demonstrate this trend we examine each element of a stake in conformity in turn and then return to David and Laura.

Attachment

The attachment element of a stake in conformity refers to the extent to which an individual has strong relationships that she desires to maintain. It is risky to engage in deviant or unconventional behaviors if to do so will result in ridicule or shame from family members, friends, and co-workers. Depending upon the behavior in question, one may end up losing those relationships if the deviance is discovered. Someone who lacks such relationships is comparatively free to deviate—they do not have to factor the opinions of others into their decisions.

Although we did not ask respondents to our national surveys how many friends they currently have, we can examine one measure of attachment—marital status. Marriage is a marker of conventionality in American society. A number of studies have found that people who are married tend to be more conventional in a variety of ways.[20] They take fewer risks, have fewer social problems such as addiction to drugs and alcohol, and are likely to have greater levels of physical and mental health.

To see if marital status relates to the paranormal, we first created a paranormal beliefs scale and a paranormal experiences scale. The paranormal beliefs scale is composed of nine questions that ask respondents their level of belief in ghosts, fortune-telling, Atlantis and other ancient, advanced civilizations, telekinesis (the power to move objects with the mind), psychic powers, astrology, UFOs, haunted houses, and monsters such as Bigfoot. Someone who scores a zero on this scale does not believe in the reality of any of these items. A person who scores a nine believes in the reality of all of them—a true paranormal person. Of those people above zero, lower scores are indicative of paranormal particularists, people who are convinced of the reality of one or a few paranormal topics but are skeptical of others. Our scale of paranormal experiences is composed of five items that determine if the respondent has consulted a horoscope, consulted a medium, fortune-teller or psychic, visited or lived in a haunted house, used a Ouija board, and/or witnessed a UFO. Again, people may have experienced none of these things or all five.

The number of paranormal beliefs a person holds and the number of paranormal experiences claimed are both significantly related to marital status (see fig. 6.2). People who are married hold fewer paranormal beliefs on average than those who are unmarried. Specifically, married Americans tend to believe in two of the nine paranormal beliefs, while unmarried Americans believed in three on average. The same trend holds for paranormal experiences. The average married person has had no paranormal experiences, the typical unmarried person claims closer to two.

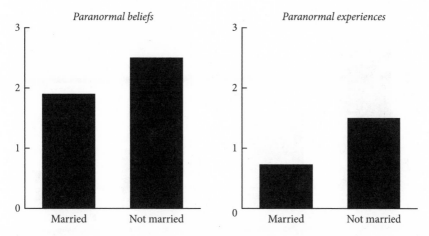

Fig. 6.2. Attachment: number of paranormal beliefs and experiences by marital status (Baylor Religion Survey, 2005)

Note: Paranormal experience scale ranges from 0 to 5 and indicates how many of the following paranormal experiences are claimed by the respondent: consulting a horoscope; consulting a medium, fortune-teller, or psychic; visited or lived in a place believed to be haunted; used a Ouija board to contact a spirit; witnessed a UFO. Married respondents hold 1.9 paranormal beliefs on average, compared to 2.4 for respondents who are not married. Difference in means is significant at $p < .001$. Married respondents on average have had less than one paranormal experience (.73), compared to respondents who are not married, who report more than one (1.5).

Belief

Travis Hirschi's argument that conventional beliefs will tie a person to conformity is straightforward. Someone who is conventional or traditional in the way that they think or in what they believe is going to be less attracted to ideas or beliefs that are outside of convention. In our surveys we have found strong evidence that conventional belief is a deterrent to the paranormal. People who have more conventional beliefs in other spheres are simply less likely to hold paranormal beliefs or to have paranormal experiences.

We examined the relationship between being married and having paranormal beliefs and experiences in the previous section. The relationship between paranormal beliefs and experiences and marital status is even more striking if we consider people who are cohabitating. 39 percent of Americans think that living together before marriage is immoral. Another 18 percent believe that cohabitating can be reasonable in some circumstances but wrong in others. The remaining 43 percent, think that

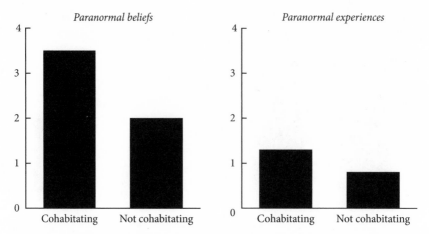

Fig. 6.3. Belief: number of paranormal beliefs and experiences and cohabitation (Baylor Religion Survey, 2005; all differences are statistically significant)

cohabitation is not wrong at all.[21] Although it is much less controversial than it used to be, living with a partner is still considered unconventional by the majority of Americans. The choice to cohabitate with another person is a sign that a person is willing to buck convention, at least in certain spheres of life. Indeed, cohabitation is strongly associated with paranormal beliefs and experiences (see fig. 6.3).

People who are currently cohabitating report nearly twice as many paranormal beliefs as those who are not cohabitating. Further, on average, a person who is cohabitating has had at least one paranormal experience. For a person who is not cohabitating the average is less than one.

Political preference provides another means of determining the types of beliefs a person holds. Americans are fairly evenly split between Democrat (38%) and Republican (41%) with the remainder identifying as independents. It would be incorrect to claim that identifying as either Democrat or Republican is unconventional or deviant in the United States, but clearly Republicans have more traditional and conservative attitudes on most social issues.[22] Thus, we might expect the claiming of a Republican identity to tie a person more tightly to conventionality and deter experimentation with the paranormal. Indeed, we find such a trend (see fig. 6.4).

Republicans are significantly less interested in the paranormal than

Democrats and Independents. The typical Republican believes in fewer than two of the paranormal subjects we asked about on our survey (ghosts, fortune-telling, Atlantis/ancient, advanced civilizations, telekinesis, psychic powers, astrology, UFOs, haunted houses, and monsters). Democrats and Independents believe in two of these subjects, on average. A similar relationship holds for paranormal experiences. Republicans are the least likely to have a paranormal experience, and self-described Independents are the most likely.

Chapter 4 explored the complicated relationship between conventional religion and the paranormal. In particular, we discussed how conventional religion often acts as a competing paradigm to the paranormal. Some religious groups will allow their members the freedom to investigate alternative beliefs while stricter groups will discourage or forbid such behavior.

Religion can also be thought of in a different way—as a sign of conventionality. Certain religious beliefs are held by the majority of Americans. For example, the majority (82%) report affiliation with a Christian denomination of some type (Catholic, Evangelical Protestant, Mainline Protestant, Black Protestant), and most attend services at their chosen denomination at least once a month. Differing from majority religious beliefs is, in certain cases, a sign that a person is unconventional in his or her worldview.

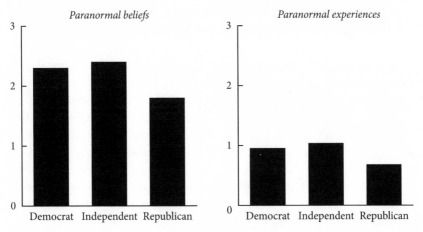

Fig. 6.4. Belief: number of paranormal beliefs and experiences by political preference (Baylor Religion Survey, 2005; all differences are statistically significant)

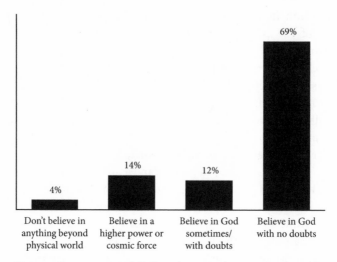

Fig. 6.5. Conceptions of God in the United States (Baylor Religion Survey, 2005)

A succinct means by which to gauge the conventionality of an individual's religious views is his conception of God. Sociologists have found that conceptions of God impact a variety of other beliefs and attitudes.[23] More than two-thirds of Americans believe in God without doubts and another 12 percent believe in God, even if they sometimes have doubts (see fig. 6.5). Of greatest interest for the current purposes are the remaining two views of God. A small percentage (4%) of Americans do not believe in anything beyond the physical world, including God. Since such people exhibit skepticism toward the supernatural in general, they should be unlikely to hold paranormal beliefs.

Another 14 percent of Americans refer to God as a "cosmic force" or higher power. These people eschew phrases such as "God" that imply a singular figure or a man in the sky. This is too abstract for many Americans, who tend to ascribe feelings, emotions, and judgment to God. In other words, imaging God as a "force" is a relatively unconventional belief in our society. Holding this belief about God may indicate that an individual is open to unconventional supernatural beliefs as a whole. Indeed, this appears to be the case (see fig. 6.6).

People who do not believe in God reported the fewest paranormal beliefs. People who believe in God with or without doubts were not significantly different from one another in terms of paranormal beliefs. Those who hold an unconventional view of the supernatural, seeing God as a cosmic force or higher power, are significantly more likely to believe in the paranormal and to believe in a greater breadth of paranormal subjects. The same pattern holds true with paranormal experiences. People who believe in a cosmic force report nearly twice as many paranormal experiences than those with more conventional/traditional conceptions of God.

Involvement

Although a rather large body of research generally supports Hirschi's ideas, the concept of involvement is problematic.[24] Hirschi argued that people should be less deviant to the extent that their time is filled with conventional activities such as youth groups, clubs, and volunteering. Similar to the popular idea that "idle hands are the devil's playthings," he argued that youth who have unsupervised free time are more likely to get into trouble because they are bored or because they simply have more time to do so. There is, in fact, little evidence from studies of juvenile delinquency or crime that involvement in conventional activities has an independent effect upon levels of deviance.

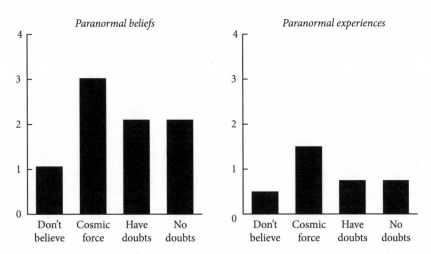

Fig. 6.6. Belief: number of paranormal beliefs and experiences by conceptions of God (Baylor Religion Survey, 2005; all differences are statistically significant)

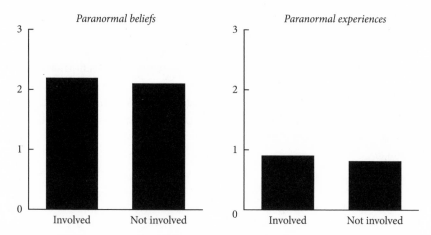

Fig. 6.7. Involvement: number of paranormal beliefs and experiences by involvement in community groups (Baylor Religion Survey, 2005)

Note: Respondents were asked if they belong to any of the following organizations/community groups: an arts or cultural organization; a charitable organization or group; a civic or service group; an ethnic or racial organization; a neighborhood group or association; a political party, club, or association; school fraternities, sororities, or alumni association; sports, hobby, or leisure group; therapeutic/counseling group; trade union or youth groups/organizations. The differences in paranormal beliefs and paranormal experiences were not statistically significant.

Similarly there is no evidence that involvement in conventional activities deters belief in the paranormal (see fig. 6.7). We asked respondents to our national survey to indicate if they are involved with any of twelve different community groups or associations such as an arts or cultural organization, a civic or service group, a political party, a sports, hobby or leisure group, and several others. People who belong to one or more such groups report about the same number of paranormal beliefs and experiences as those who are entirely uninvolved in the community. The minor differences between the involved and uninvolved are statistically insignificant. Put another way, one cannot assume anything about another person's propensity toward the paranormal if all that is known is how much he or she volunteers. The local cub scout leader may have seen a UFO.

Commitment

Commitments of money, energy, or time made by a person in order to obtain a certain lifestyle make up another part of the stake in conformity.

Someone who has worked hard and achieved material success will, theoretically, avoid deviant behavior since it might threaten the investments they have made in a certain lifestyle. Following this line of reasoning, those who are in high-paying careers with possibilities for advancement and those who have worked hard to obtain a higher education should be more wedded to the conventional system.

While we did not find a straightforward relationship between education and individual paranormal beliefs, education is a strong predictor of whether a person will believe in many paranormal subjects. People who have achieved at least a high school diploma believe in fewer paranormal topics and have fewer paranormal experiences than those who have not achieved a high school diploma (see fig. 6.8).

The same relationship holds for income. People who have achieved a higher level of income have theoretically invested their lives in the furtherance of a high-paying career or job and have more to lose by engaging in deviant or unconventional behavior. Paranormal beliefs do, in fact, steadily decline as income increases. People who have lower levels of income have a strong tendency to believe in a wider variety of paranormal subjects than those at higher levels of income. Those at the lowest levels of income ($10,000 or less a year) believed in an average three (of nine)

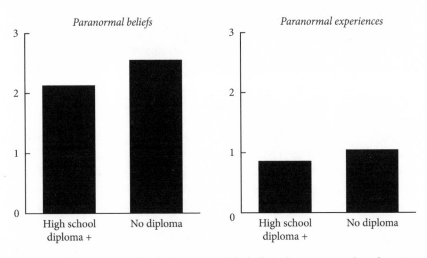

Fig. 6.8. Investment: number of paranormal beliefs and experiences by education (Baylor Religion Survey, 2005)

Note: Analysis compares respondents who did not receive a high school diploma with those who have a diploma or have achieved further education, such as some college or a college diploma.

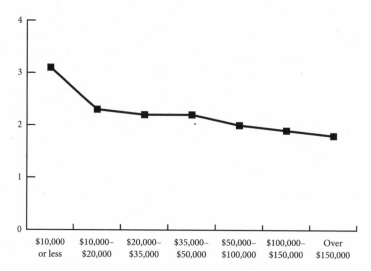

Fig. 6.9. Investment: number of paranormal beliefs by income (Baylor Religion Survey, 2005)

Note: The same pattern exists when examining the number of paranormal experiences reported by respondents: as income increases, number of paranormal experiences decreases.

paranormal subjects, while those making $150,000 a year or more believe in two on average (see fig. 6.9). Importantly while income level matters, people at all levels of social standing still average at least some paranormal beliefs.

Conventionality and the Paranormal

With the exception of involvement in community activities, there are relationships between aspects of an individual's stake in conformity and how much of the paranormal they find credible. Attachments to others appears to limit engagement with the paranormal, as do traditional beliefs and investments one has made in a conventional life such as a higher education. The relationship between conventionality and the paranormal becomes even clearer when all of these factors are considered together. We assigned each respondent to our survey with an overall stake in conformity score ranging from zero to five based on their marital status, political leanings, beliefs about God, income, and education. A respondent with a five has a very conventional/traditional life; they are married, Republican, prefer to think of a personified God rather than a cosmic force, have a higher income and a college education. Someone with a zero is unmarried, non-Republican, did not acquire a college degree, prefers to think of God as an impersonal essence or force, and earns a lower family income. People with a mixture of these characteristics, e.g. unmarried but Republican, high income but lower education and so on, would score somewhere near the middle of the index.

The relationship is clear for both paranormal beliefs and paranormal experiences. As stakes in conformity increase, paranormal beliefs and experience steadily and markedly decrease (see fig. 6.10). A person with

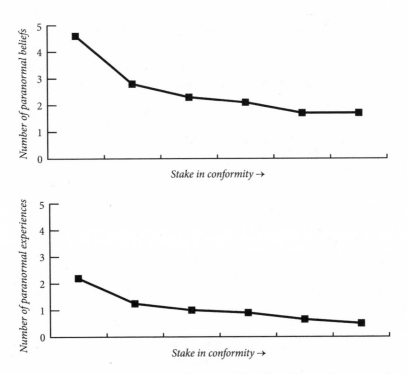

Fig. 6.10. Conventionality and the paranormal (Baylor Religion Survey, 2005)

Note: Conventionality scale ranges from 0 to 5, indicating whether a respondent is married, a Republican, has a high income ($50k and above), has a college education, and/or believes in a cosmic force/higher power. A person who scores 5 on the scale is married, Republican, college-educated, believes in God (not a cosmic force/higher power), and has a higher income. Difference in means in paranormal beliefs and experiences are significant across levels of conventionality.

the highest stakes in conformity accepts on average only two paranormal beliefs. This is less than half the level of belief exhibited by those with the lowest stakes in conformity. With regard to paranormal experiences, people at the lowest stake in conformity have had two paranormal experiences, on average. The likelihood of having a paranormal experience declines steadily with the typical person at the highest stakes in conformity having no such experiences.

In our time with David and Laura it became clear that they had distinctly different ways of living their lives and distinctly different views about the paranormal. David knows that some people think he is strange and told us of occasions when people have ridiculed his interest in Bigfoot. He is cautious about who he talks to about Bigfoot and is occasionally reticent to discuss his personal sighting of the creature. Now David faces a quandary. Slowly but surely, he is becoming a player in the Bigfoot world. His leadership skills and passion have turned him into a key spokesman for the Texas Bigfoot Research Conservancy. At first, he appeared only on local newscasts, often as the "silly story" to end the show. Recent appearances on the Discovery Channel and Travel Channel are moving him into the big leagues. Soon his celebrity as a Bigfoot hunter will negate his ability to pick and choose his confidants.

David has reason to be concerned with being branded as strange. With the exception of Bigfoot, he leads a conventional life. A veteran of the Air Force, he shares a tidy house with his wife, Margo, on the outskirts of a small Texas town. During the week he manages a bank and makes a good living. On the weekends he faithfully attends a small, conservative Baptist church. He is a born-again Christian holding very traditional views of God as a father and the Bible as the word of God. Traditional religious views are coupled with conservative political views. He is a member of the National Rifle Association, consistently votes Republican, and counts Ronald Reagan and Mike Huckabee among his favorite politicians.

In many ways Laura is David's mirror opposite. While David lives in the Bible belt, Laura proudly resides in what she described as the "unchurched West where the outdoors is your chapel." David is happily married, and Laura is "proudly by myself." Laura fills her time with activities and hobbies in retirement; David hands out loans at the bank.

Laura labels herself a Christian as does David, but clearly she has something different in mind than he does. When asked to more specifically describe her personal religious or spiritual beliefs, Laura struggled. "I *am* a Christian . . . but I would also say that I am more spiritual than religious."

She imagines a world connected to a multitude of beneficial entities and higher powers, rather than a single, personified God, and she sees Jesus as a special being sent to Earth by high powers, not as the one and only son of God.

As someone who is strongly bound to conventional society, David is tentative and cautious in his paranormal belief. He believes in one subject only—Bigfoot—and is rankled by its definition as "paranormal." David wants to redefine Bigfoot as a purely zoological mystery as opposed to a supernatural one. He has no patience for UFOs, ghosts, astrology, or other paranormal matters. To believe in such things is a threat to his self image as a normal guy who just happens to hunt Bigfoot.

Laura is liberal and unconventional—and proudly so. Compared to David she is relatively free to explore "deviant" beliefs. She does not risk her career, her relationship, or contradict her personal faith by exploring alternative ideas. Her friends accept her varied interests, if they are to remain her friends. Where David is focused and driven to prove his quest is normal, Laura has long ago left concerns about normality behind. "People put so many blinders on themselves," she told us, "and I refuse to limit myself. I'm open to everything. Its all part of the fabric of life."

"I Refuse to Limit Myself"

Public discourse about the paranormal often tends to devolve into separating people who believe in the paranormal from people who do not. This distinction is not particularly useful. In previous chapters we found that it is difficult to predict who will be attracted to individual paranormal beliefs. After all, we have found that most Americans believe in something paranormal.

What truly distinguishes most Americans from one another is not *whether* they believe in a paranormal topic, but rather how many subjects they find credible. People who are very conventional otherwise are likely to believe in a single paranormal topic. These people are often indistinguishable from the average American in terms of their beliefs in other spheres and the way that they live their lives. Paranormal generalists who simultaneously believe in UFOs, ghosts, Bigfoot, astrology, psychic powers, and Atlantis are likely to be quite unconventional. They are not dangerous or mentally ill, they simply live in a different cultural universe than the rest of us.

7

Darkness and Light

As we have echoed, some might say bemoaned, throughout this book, the paranormal is a messy subject in many ways. The subjects themselves are elusive. Bigfoot is hard if not impossible to catch. Ghosts fade away, UFOs fly away before cameras are at the ready, and psychic powers rarely perform upon demand.

If that was not a big enough problem, agreed-upon definitions of our objects of study are equally elusive. When is something paranormal? One person's paranormal is another person's normal. Should Bigfoot be labeled paranormal? Some of the Bigfoot hunters we have talked to are baffled that we lump together with ESP, flying saucers, and ghosts what they consider to be an undiscovered animal.

Complicating matters further is the thorny issue of distinguishing religion and the paranormal. At first glance religious phenomena and paranormal phenomena appear to be one and the same. The belief that the Bible is God's word and belief in the physical resurrection of Jesus are just as resistant to scientific proof as astrology, auras, and flying saucers. Yet religious beliefs have the benefits of widespread acceptance, cultural continuity, and a strong organizational backing.

Previous research (and our study), has found that Americans tend to distinguish between these two realms of the supernatural. In American society religious beliefs are a sign of normality, paranormal beliefs a potential sign of deviance. Should you happen to mention to your new neighbors across the street that you are a Presbyterian, banker, and Cubs fan, none of these pieces of information elicit much concern from most people. Should you tell the neighbor that you are a banker, Cubs fan, and a practicing astrologer, they may consider you a bit kooky.

Unfortunately the subject of this chapter will complicate matters even further. There are a number of beliefs and experiences that straddle the border between religion and the paranormal. Consider once again the diverse collection of topics and subjects that appear in the New Age section of the local bookstore. Scattered among the UFO books, astrology training manuals, and collections of ghost tales you are likely to find books that discuss sightings of the Virgin Mary, stories of demons, possessions, and exorcism, collected tales of claimed miraculous healings and miraculous rescues by guardian angels.

Books on the same topics will also be found in most Christian bookstores and in the Christian section of general bookstores. An exorcism tale can carry different meanings depending upon the type of book in which it appears. A book targeted at Christian audiences is likely to frame exorcisms as proof of the reality of Satan and a warning to Christians to get right with God and avoid the "occult." A book meant for general audiences will treat exorcisms as a fascinating and frightening mystery but will avoid explicit religious overtones or suggestions that a conversion to Christianity is a means of avoiding possession. A Christian author may write of the power of Ouija boards, but rather than focus upon it as a potential means to contact a dead relative, the Ouija board is feared as an instrument through which demons may attack the unwary.[1]

Exorcisms, Virgin Mary sightings, guardian angel tales, and the like appear to serve as a potential bridging area between religion and the paranormal. Perhaps an interest in such topics will lead conservative Christians to develop an interest in paranormal subjects, such as UFOs and ESP, or maybe an interest in guardian angels could serve to draw an otherwise nonreligious person into a faith.

This chapter explores some of the contested ground between religion and the paranormal by examining who believes in manifestations of evil such as Satan, demons, possession, and Satanic conspiracies, and manifestations of "light" such as guardian angels, speaking in tongues and other powerful religious experiences.

Darkness: From Presidential Debates to Evil, Possession, and the End of the World

As part of the long run-up of public events preceding the 2008 presidential election in the United States, the two main contenders, Senators Barack Obama and John McCain, traveled to Saddleback Church, one of the largest megachurches in the country, to take questions from pastor and best-selling author Rick Warren. Rather than being a debate in the traditional sense, the evening consisted of separate interviews for both men. The candidates were not able to hear one another's responses.

Among the various topics covered, Warren asked each candidate about his understanding of the nature of evil in the world. Specifically, Warren asked "Does evil exist? And if it does, do we ignore it? Do we negotiate with it? Do we contain it? Do we defeat it?" The responses given by each candidate provided a glimpse into their moral framework of good and evil, and how these perceptions connected to policy issues.

Senator Obama responded:

Evil does exist. I mean, I think we see evil all the time. We see evil in Darfur. We see evil, sadly, on the streets of our cities. We see evil in parents who viciously abuse their children. I think it has to be confronted. It has to be confronted squarely, and one of the things that I strongly believe is that, now, we are not going to, as individuals, be able to erase evil from the world. . . . Now, the one thing that I think is very important is for to us have some humility in how we approach the issue of confronting evil, because a lot of evil's been perpetrated based on the claim that we were trying to confront evil.[2]

In effect then-Senator Obama claimed that evil did exist and was multifaceted, as it could take the form of genocide, poverty, crime, or child abuse. Although he believed that measures should be taken to confront these issues, he also qualified that evil could not be eradicated by humans, and that people should be careful about what is done in the name of confronting evil, as often the responses to such issues could also be morally reprehensible.

Senator McCain then took the stage for his interview and was eventually given the same question concerning evil, to which he responded:

Defeat it. A couple of points. One, if I'm president of the United States, my friends, if I have to follow him to the gates of hell, I will get bin Laden and bring him to justice. I will do that. And I know how to do that. I will get that done. No one, no one should be allowed to take thousands of American—innocent American lives. Of course, evil must be defeated. My friends, we are facing the transcended [*sic*] challenge of the twenty-first century—radical Islamic extremism. . . . And we have—and we face this threat throughout the world. It's not just in Iraq. It's not just in Afghanistan. Our intelligence people tell us Al Qaeda continues to try to establish cells here in the United States of America. My friends, we must face this challenge. We can face this challenge. And we must totally defeat it.

In arguing that evil must be defeated, McCain connected evil primarily to the issue of threats posed by radical Islamic sects and global terrorism. Related to this perception of evil and the broad issue of terrorism is an array of specific policy issues concerning war, border patrol, immigration, and attitudes toward methods of social control generally. The belief that evil must be defeated translated into approaching the issues that were linked to it with a veracity and tenacity necessary to achieve its defeat. Warren's question was an insightful way to draw out the differences between the two candidate's philosophies. Obama offered a more abstract concept of evil than did McCain (or did then-President Bush).

Ultimately Obama gathered 52.7 percent of the popular vote and won the presidency, but his narrow victory in the polls is reflective of many underlying differences between Americans, one of which is different underlying conceptions of evil. Americans are deeply divided on the nature of evil. Researchers have found that a person's views about the nature of evil and the role of evil in the world impact other behaviors and beliefs. For instance, beliefs about Satan were a strong predictor of participation in social movements, rallies, petitions, pickets, and membership associated with the Moral Majority. More recently, strong views of religious evil have been found to be associated with intolerance of homosexuality.[3] When it comes to Satan's power, Americans are split down the middle, with a little more than half expressing an absolute belief in the reality of a dark counterpart to God. A little less than half of Americans believe that Satan has access to an army of demons with which to further his goals (see fig. 7.1).

Like it or not, Satan is a part of American life, and his impact is felt in the pews and in popular culture. Belief in Satan is higher than in any of the paranormal topics we have discussed so far in this book. More people believe in a real Satan in the United States than in Bigfoot, psychics, and the power of astrology *combined.*

It is one thing to believe in the devil, another to grant him great power. Here Americans are a little more ambivalent. There are many ways that the devil might exert his will. The famous and terrifying film *The Exorcist,* and television shows such as the SCI-FI Network's *The Real Exorcist* give Satan the power to control unwary humans via demonic possession.

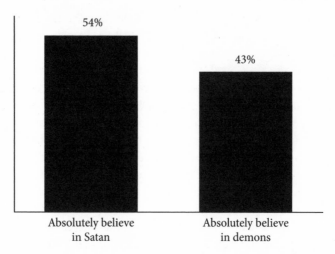

Fig. 7.1. Belief in Satan and demons in the United States (Baylor Religion Survey, Wave 2, 2007)

Some people believe that Satan is actively marshalling his demonic forces for an impending showdown with God's army. A fiery Armageddon will end Satan's reign but only after massive upheavals and tremendous death and destruction. Some Christians further believe that a "Rapture" will occur preceding Armageddon, wherein faithful Christians are immediately taken into heaven, leaving the remainder of humanity to suffer Satan's wrath until the final battle. While there is much speculation and disagreement about the specific sequence of events that will unfold, as well as when such occurrences will take place, nearly one-third of Americans believe these events *will occur* in some form or another. About one-fifth of Americans view happenings in the world through a supernatural lens, interpreting the presence of evil as evidence of Satan's power (see fig. 7.2).

Satanic Panics and Scares

Beliefs about Satan's power in the world have played an important role in American history. What constitutes the perceived earthly work of Satan evolves over time and varies from group to group, but when people come to believe that Satan is impacting the world directly (or via his minions), the effects of this belief can be quite powerful.

Perhaps the best known example of a scare related to Satan comes from the Salem witch trials, where from February 1692 to May 1693 more than 150 colonial settlers were arrested and charged with being witches.

The panic in Salem began when the young daughter of Reverend Samuel Parris, nine-year-old Betty Parris, and Parris's niece, eleven-year-old Abigail Williams, began acting strangely. They exhibited behavior somewhat akin to epileptic fits. The girls threw objects, screamed and cried, ran about the room, and crawled behind and under furniture. At times,

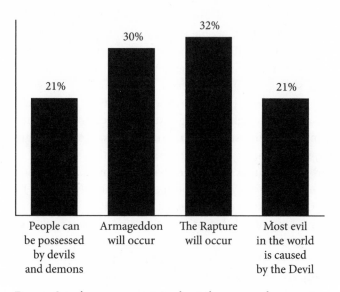

Fig. 7.2. Satan's power: certainty about the power of supernatural evil in the United States (Baylor Religion Survey, Wave 2, 2007)

Note: A series of questions on the Baylor Religion Survey, Wave 2 (2007) asked respondents about evil. For example, respondents were asked their level of agreement with the statement "It is possible for people to be possessed by devils/demons." Thirty-two percent of respondents agreed, and 21% strongly agreed. The remaining respondents were split between disagree (16%), strongly disagree (15%), and undecided (15%). When asked if they believe in Armageddon, 30.1% said absolutely. Another 27% think Armageddon is probably going to happen. Yet another 27% think Armageddon will probably not happen, and 15% are absolutely certain an Armageddon-like event will not occur. With regard to the Rapture, responses were as follows: Absolutely 32%, Probably 21%, Probably not 28%, Absolutely not 19%. Twenty-one percent of respondents agreed when asked if "most evil in the world is caused by the Devil"; 23% agreed, 9% were undecided, 26% disagreed, and 21% strongly disagreed.

they claimed to be pricked by invisible needles and pinched by unseen hands. When word traveled of the Parris girls' condition, other young women became similarly afflicted.

The Puritans of Salem found themselves in a new land, where even their previous religious identity, which centered around criticizing other groups, was placed into jeopardy. Without outside groups to castigate and define themselves against, the Puritans turned inward. When faced with a terrifying unknown, people often find or create a villain to explain their circumstances. This is especially true concerning an unknown involving people who are distinct in some way from the community in question. In other words, people who are viewed as fundamentally different or "other," compared to the majority of people comprising the community can become defined as the "them" that helps create and sustain the "us." A strong out-group offers a community a scapegoat for their trials and tribulations. Having a concrete villain upon which to place one's fears and direct righteous anger serves to comfort and bind together a community.[4] As the sociological truism goes, strong out-groups create strong in-groups. In Salem, rumors spread that witches were behind the disturbing and unexplained behavioral outbreak. Unfortunately, it is generally not satisfactory for a community to simply believe there is an enemy in their midst: the enemy must be identified and overcome. Sociologists have long noted that minority groups, or those who are already considered "strange" for some reason, are typically the first to be identified as the source of a new social problem.[5] In Salem, three women who were already community outcasts for various reasons were the first to be identified as witches.[6]

Each set of accusations multiplied into more as the community's fear spiraled out of control. The longer the panic continued, the greater the risk each person faced of being identified as a witch. Much of the problem had to do with reliance on so-called "spectral evidence." If a purported victim had a dream or vision in which the spirit of an accused witch appeared, the contents of the vision could be entered into court as evidence against the defendant. Since such dubious evidence was considered sufficient, it is not surprising that twenty-nine men and women were ultimately convicted of being witches. Nineteen of the convicted were hanged; one unfortunate soul was crushed to death under rocks. Ultimately the fear ran its course as accusations of witchery subsided and then stopped —particularly once the high-ranking and powerful members of the community began to face accusations themselves.

The Devil Comes to Olympia

The Salem witch trials have become emblematic of how panic can grip a community, a lesson in how unreasoned fear of evil can lead to terrible consequences. Yet, we often view the story of Salem with smug comfort and distance, mocking the backwards views of the Puritans and their fear of witches. We assume that, in our enlightened age, such things would not and could not happen again. And yet we have seen many similar incidents throughout U.S. history when people become convinced that Satan is active in the world.

Consider the Ingram case, where the young daughters of a prominent local citizen became convinced that they had been assaulted by a mysterious cadre of Satanists. Despite a complete lack of physical evidence, the girls' hazy recollections of Satanic ceremonies led to the arrest of their father, Paul Ingram, and two family friends. After a dramatic trial that included tales of mysterious underground Satanic cults, human sacrifice, forced abortions with swords, blood drinking, and demonic possession, Ingram was convicted—in Olympia, Washington, in 1988.

Prior to the events of 1988, the Ingram family had led normal lives by all appearances. Raised devoutly Roman Catholic, Paul Ingram met his future wife, Sandy, while attending Spokane Community College. Eventually they moved to Olympia to raise their four children: Paul Jr., Chad, Erika, and Julie. Over time Ingram became a pillar of the community and faithfully attended a local Pentecostal church called the Church of the Living Waters. A former president of the Thurston County Deputy Sheriff's Association and former chairman of the Thurston County Republican Central Committee, Paul was chief civil deputy of the Thurston County sheriff's office at the time of the accusations against him.

In the summer of 1988, Living Waters held a retreat for young, female members at Black Lake Bible Camp in Olympia. Erika, twenty-one at the time, and Julie, eighteen, attended. Karla Franko, a charismatic Christian from California who claimed to have "biblical gifts of healing and spiritual discernment" had been invited to speak. Over the course of the retreat, Franko claimed to have received several messages from the Holy Spirit indicating that some of those in attendance had suffered physical or sexual abuse. Franko's pronouncements created an emotionally charged atmosphere at the camp, with several girls sobbing and becoming hysterical.[7] On the last day of the retreat as attendants were boarding the bus to return home, Erika broke down and proclaimed that she had been sexually abused by her father. Eventually Julie corroborated Erika's claim of sexual abuse, adding that the abuse had been at the hands of several men.

Julie claimed that, since the age of four, she had been gang-raped by Paul and his friends who occasionally gathered at the Ingram home for poker games. The church reported the accusations against Paul to the sheriff's department. Soon after, he was brought into custody for questioning. Curiously, although Paul claimed that he could not remember a single incident where he molested his children, he admitted to the abuse. He reasoned that while he could not recall the crimes, they must have happened—because he had taught his children to be truthful.

As the prosecution interviewed various parties, the story grew increasingly tangled. Ingram admitted to the abusive poker parties reported by Julie and named several employees of the sheriff's department as participants in these games. Based on these "confessions," two of Ingram's closest friends, Jim Rabie and Ray Risch, were taken into custody. As interviews with family members continued, Erika expanded her allegations. She claimed that her mother had also participated in the abuse. The two Ingram sons, Chad and Paul Jr., added their own allegations. Eventually Paul and the Ingram children started talking of Satanic activity taking place along with the abuse.

In a December 1988 interview with sheriff's department detectives, Ingram remembered—though he could not give specific dates or times—standing near a fire with a person that he thought might be "the devil" next to him. He could hear wailing and moaning all around him as he stood on a platform that looked down on a fire. Ingram claimed he wore an apron with an upside-down cross on it and sacrificed a cat by slicing its stomach open and pulling out its heart.[8] Rabie and Risch, he said, were present at the meeting. Ingram claimed that Ray Risch's girlfriend at the time, Dana, was the "high priestess" of the ceremony, and as a reward for performing the sacrifice, he was allowed to have sex with Dana and another woman. Paul's wife, Sandra soon added her own stories of Satanism, including a bizarre instance in which Rabie allegedly held her by one hand and held an open book in the other, as blood purportedly flowed from the book, across his chest, and onto her.[9]

During the investigation of the Ingram case, detectives became convinced that the mysterious Satanists alluded to by the Ingrams must be practicing some form of mind control. This would explain why the Ingram family's stories often conflicted with one another and why Paul seemed to have great difficulty remembering the incidents of abuse, even though he admitted to being an abuser. It would also explain why Paul occasionally provided clearly false confessions. For example, at one point Ingram reported that he might be the Green River killer—a serial murderer accused of killing dozens of young women near the Seattle-Tacoma International Airport. Though characteristically hazy about dates or specific locations, he claimed that he and Rabie picked up a prostitute near the Sea-Tac airport and murdered her. The Green River Task Force investigated Ingram very briefly but quickly dropped him as a suspect.[10]

Working from their assumption of cultic mind control, the Thurston County prosecutor's office hired Dr. Richard Ofshe, a sociologist and expert on cult activity from the University of California at Berkeley. They hoped that Ofshe would testify for the prosecution about the ability of cults to affect a person's mind. However, Ofshe quickly became troubled by the investigation. His first concern was the credibility of Erika and Julie as witnesses. He was concerned with Erika Ingram's history of making and then dropping abuse charges, as well as with the content of her stories.[11] In particular, Erika's stories contained broad summaries of abhorrent events, but she failed to provide any other information about the group's ceremonies, Ofshe reported:

> Ms. Ingram has been consistently unable to provide me with any details about the content of the rituals or descriptions of even the most mundane events that occurred at the approximately 400 group meetings she claims to have been obliged to attend. Although Ms. Ingram is able to report watching numerous babies being killed, seeing the dead body of at least one adult woman, having undergone two backyard abortions and having to eat the flesh of her own fetus, she is unable to provide me with an account of the format of the group's meetings or any of the group's non-homicidal rituals. She reports that the group's meetings took about 3 hours. All that she can describe about their conduct is that "they chant."[12]

Further, Ofshe noticed that Paul only seemed to offer tales of Satanism *after* excessive prompting from detectives; therefore he decided to give Paul a test. In an interview with Ingram, Ofshe told Paul that one of his daughters and one of his sons claimed that Paul forced them to have sex together while he watched. In fact, no such charge had been made by the children. Ingram could not recall the event at first, but Ofshe pushed him, telling him that he "had to remember," just as detectives had done in previous interviews. When the two men met a day later, Ingram produced a confession:

> Mr. Ingram produced a written confession to acts of sexual abuse of his children in response to the influence of methods I employed. The tactics I used . . . resembled the interview procedures used in Mr. Ingram's interrogations.
>
> I subsequently confronted Mr. Ingram with the fact that he had produced a false confession. . . . Mr. Ingram became quite distraught but steadfastly maintained that the recollections he had in response to my suggestions were as real as his other recollections. Mr. Ingram succeeded in convincing me that this statement was true.[13]

Ofshe noted a similar process of persuasion at work in the recollections of Sandra Ingram. He was especially concerned with the influence of Jon Bratun, Paul and Sandra's minister at the Church of the Living Waters. Bratun counseled every member of the Ingram family, was allowed to visit Paul in jail, and had even performed a jailhouse exorcism on a distraught Paul. Ofshe was concerned that Bratun's influence had contaminated the case. Bratun admitted to acting as Sandra's spiritual advisor and telling her she was "80 percent evil." Perhaps even more troubling for the case, he provided Sandra with full details of Paul's confessions. Ofshe believed that Sandra provided stories of Satanism as a result of the intense spiritual and emotional pressure Bratun placed upon her. After spending a total of nine days interviewing prosecution witnesses, Thurston County detectives, friends of Erika and Julie Ingram, and John Bratun, Ofshe switched to the defense.

The interviews conducted with Paul's younger son Chad were also troubling. Consider the December 8, 1988, interview performed by two investigators, Dr. Richard Peterson and detective Brian Schoening. Peterson and Schoening started the interview by questioning Chad extensively about his childhood and probed him to remember any strange sexual encounters or abuse. Chad answered all of their questions in the negative, although he did reveal that he had become quite troubled during his teens, even attempting suicide once after a heated argument with his father. The incident piqued the interest of Dr. Peterson, who thought the suicide attempt was somehow related to suppressed memories of abuse. Peterson told Chad that he had been abused but simply couldn't remember it.[14]

As Chad continued to deny having memories of sexual or physical abuse, Peterson asked him if he could recall any strange or frightening dreams from his childhood. Chad recalled nightmares of a fat "witch" flying through his window and sitting on his stomach. Peterson and Schoening told Chad that this "dream" was a memory of a real event.[15]

In a turn strikingly similar to what occurred in Salem, Peterson and Schoening attempted to have Chad identify the witch in his dreams. At first, Chad could provide no information. He said the room was dark in his dream, so he could not see the witch's face. A frustrated Dr. Peterson asked Chad to "turn the lights on" in his dream, so that he could see the witch's face more clearly. Chad still could not identify the witch. The only details he could offer were that the witch was a female, had black hair, an oval-shaped face, and brown eyes. At that point Dr. Peterson pushed Chad further, with an interesting offer:

> *Peterson*: I'll tell you something, you'd have a, you have the right to sue these
>   f***** and get as much as you want from 'em.
> *Chad*: That'd be nice.
> *Peterson*: You'd *** rights [*sic*] it'd be nice. Pay for a college education.
> *Chad*: Yeah.
> *Peterson*: Pay for a nice car. Get you started in life.
> *Chad*: Well, I already got a nice car.
> *Peterson*: Yeah, do you have a BMW?[16]

Soon after this exchange, the cassette tape recording the conversation was turned off. When recording resumed, Chad named Jim Rabie as the witch —the same witch he had previously been certain was a female.

Even with the spectral evidence provided by Chad, the Thurston County sheriff's office was eventually forced to drop its case against Rabie and Risch. Thankfully unlike Salem, the courts in Washington could not be convinced to rely solely on the content of dreams to convict, and the prosecution found itself wholly without physical evidence. Erika and Julie Ingram claimed to have attended Satanic ceremonies at least three times a month for seventeen years, seeing hundreds of infants and animals sacrificed at these meetings, but investigators never found a single body, even after digging up the Ingram yard with backhoes. No skeletons, bodies, or any of the elaborate trappings of Satanic rituals were found. The investigators also failed to find a third-party witnesses to the large Satanic gatherings that purportedly took place over a twenty-year period. Further, physical examinations of Erika and Julie did not support their allegations of rape, mutilation, and forced abortions. In January 1989, Dr. Judith Ann Jacobsen of Providence Hospital in Seattle examined Erika and Julie, concluding that the girls did not appear to have suffered the abuse they reported.[17]

Despite the lack of evidence against him, Paul Ingram pled guilty to six counts of third-degree rape on May 1, 1988. As part of an agreement with the sheriff's office, Ingram accepted a plea bargain in exchange for an assurance that he would not be charged with any additional crimes that might arise from the investigation. Ultimately Ingram started serving his time in a Delaware prison in 1990 where he remained until he was released on parole in 2003. Sandra divorced Paul while he was in prison and, Paul claims, remained convinced of the claims of Satanism until her death in 2006.

Life as an Accused Satanist

On a recent Monday afternoon, Christopher met Paul Ingram and his new wife for lunch. Ingram was quite friendly, affable, and was willing to talk about his case. Over enormous plates of pasta at a Portland, Oregon, chain restaurant overlooking the Willamette River, we chatted about what life is like for the victim of a Satanic panic.

It took awhile for Paul to settle after his release, and he told us of some of his problems. At first he moved in with his sister in Spokane, where he was required to register as a sex offender. Although Paul's parole officer treated him well, he often felt unwelcome in the community. The local news stations aired details about his case and announced that the "notorious" Paul Ingram was headed to town. A neighbor who had heard of his case complained to the police that Paul was stalking her, driving by her home in the evenings in a black car. Paul explained to his parole officer that he had no driver's license and no car. The only vehicle that was at least theoretically available to him was his sister's tan sedan. Ultimately the matter was dropped, but Paul continued to feel the suspicion of his neighbors.

Paul found that his reputation even followed him into the pews. Shortly after visiting a small, nondenominational congregation in Spokane, he decided to join but thought it best to inform the pastor of the accusations against him first. To the pastor's credit he welcomed Paul into the congregation. Shortly after, a member of the church familiar with Paul's case recognized him and complained to the pastor about allowing a "known Satanist" to join the congregation. The pastor told a grateful Paul that he should remain with the church despite such objections, but Paul felt that his presence was dividing the church and chose to leave.

Not all was bad in Spokane. About the same time that Paul moved in with his sister, Catherine, a nurse from Boston, arrived in town. After years on the East Coast, Catherine had decided she needed a change, but she quickly grew depressed, bored, and lonely in Spokane. People made fun of her thick accent, and she had trouble making friends. Eventually, she joined a dating Web site and ran across Paul's profile. They emailed back and forth and finally set up a date.

The first date went well. Before their second date Paul asked Catherine if they could meet for lunch. As they sat down at a café the next day, Catherine could sense that Paul was very nervous and thought to herself "is he married?" "If only that had been the case!" she joked. Paul blurted out all of the details of his case and then excused himself to go the restroom. "I didn't expect her to be there when I got back. This was her chance to leave." Catherine stuck around. That evening she researched Paul's case online and became convinced that he was innocent of the horrifying charges against him. They had their third date.

Five years ago the couple married. They moved away from Washington State where Paul "never really felt comfortable" and settled in a small town near the Oregon coast. Paul is happy to have found a companion, but he often reflects upon the children from his first marriage. He has had no contact with Julie, Erika, Paul Jr., or Chad. Through extended family members he knows that he now has seven grandchildren, but has never seen any of them. On occasion he sends messages to his children through other family members, but he has never received a reply. Paul looks at the past with "no bitterness, just regret." He wishes that things were different and that he could see his kids, but is determined to make the best of his new life with Catherine.

They have joined a nondenominational church in his current town. Once again Paul's past threatened his membership, as several congregants complained to the pastor upon learning of the Ingram case. This pastor insisted that Paul and Catherine remain and instructed concerned congregants to research the Ingram case, which ultimately quieted the concerns about him. The couple remains active members.

As Paul's continued desire to find a church suggests, he has never lost his deep, personal faith despite all he has been through. It is this faith that gets Paul through "the rough patches," he told us. It was Paul's strong belief in the reality of personified evil that sealed his fate. Ingram completely trusted John Bratun, pastor of the Living Waters church, so when Bratun told him that Satan was clouding Paul's memories of his horrifying Satanic activities, Paul believed his pastor. The only way to release Satan's grip upon him, Bratun counseled, was to confess to the crimes against him, whether he could remember them or not. In the end, Paul admitted to being an evil Satanist to avoid becoming an evil pawn of Satan. The irony is not lost upon him.

Unfortunately, hysterical accusations of abuse by covens and Satanic cults have a long and storied history well beyond the Salem witch trials and Paul Ingram case.[18] Outlandish as Ingram's case may seem, it occurred during the height of a societal panic about the existence of powerful, underground Satanic groups and child abuse. The 1980s saw an incredibly fast rise in awareness about such groups and public fear that correlated with this menacing presence; however, as is often the case with such incidents of collective behavior, the response to the supposed threat far outweighed the actual threat in its impact on society. While the rumors of such groups were enough to produce specialists in law enforcement and psychotherapy designed to help patients "recover" memories of abuse, no physical evidence of such groups was ever produced.

The most notorious incident in regard to the moral panic was the McMartin Preschool trial, in which day care workers in California were accused of being members of an underground Satanic group possessing supernatural powers, which they used to engage in child abuse. Charges were brought against two workers, followed by a three-year investigation and a three-year trial, including the razing of the school in the search for evidence—none of which was found. Ultimately the trial, devoid of evidence, produced no convictions but not before costing in excess of $15,000,000 in public funds.

Such tales always appear ridiculous—after the fact. Yet their continual reoccurrence is evidence of the potential power of belief in evil, supernatural forces, regardless of whether such forces actually exist or are present in such cases.

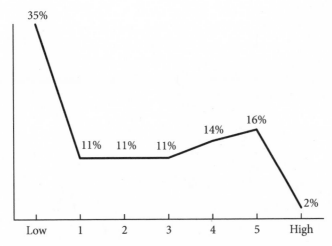

Fig. 7.3. Satan's tail: strength of belief in religious evil in the United States (Baylor Religion Survey, Wave 2, 2007; mean = 2)

Note: Each respondent to the Baylor Religion Survey, Wave 2 (2007) was given a score ranging from 0 to 6 based on his or her answers to earlier referenced questions about the existence of Satan, existence of demons, belief that Satan can possess humans, belief that Satan is the cause of evil, belief in Armageddon, and belief in the Rapture. A person scoring a 0 has not indicated strong belief in any of these things. A person with a 6 believes strongly in all six. Cronbach's alpha = .80. Mean = 2.1.

Who Believes in Supernatural Evil?

People differ to the extent that they see life as a true struggle with supernatural evil. Some believe in the reality of the devil but not that he has the power to possess people. Others view the Rapture and Armageddon as upcoming world events but do not think that Satan is the main cause of evil in the world. One way to see how much power an individual attributes to Satan and the forces of evil is to assign each respondent an "evil score" based on how many of these six items in which they express belief (see fig. 7.3).

A little more than a third of Americans (35%) do not ascribe much power to the forces of supernatural evil, having evil scores of zero. Such people dismiss the idea of Armageddon and the Rapture. They think the idea of possession is superstitious. They are skeptical about the existence of the devil and dismissive that he has a host of demons to command. They also believe that evil in the world is the work of humans, and when

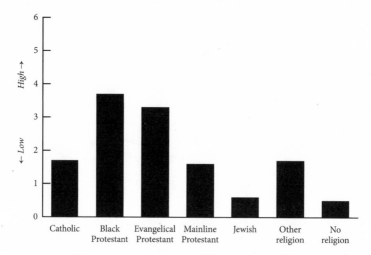

Fig. 7.4. Evil scores by religious tradition (Baylor Religion Survey, Wave 2, 2007)

bad things happen people are entirely to blame, not a supernatural force of evil.

Contrast this one-third of Americans with the small number (about 2%) at the other end of the spectrum. Such people attribute great power to the devil and clearly view the world in a different way than someone who is skeptical even about the devil's existence.

Not surprisingly, belief in devils, demons, and possession is strongly related to religious tradition. Evangelical Protestants and black Protestants have a much stronger belief in the reality of supernatural evil than do mainline Protestants, Catholics, Jews, those of other religions, and those who report no religion (see fig. 7.4).

The person most likely to believe in devils, demons, and possession will also be a person that takes the Bible literally. The average biblical literalist has an evil score more than four times that of a person who thinks of the Bible as a work of literature.[19] The more frequently a person attends religious services, the greater their belief in supernatural evil. Scores steadily and significantly increase with increasing church attendance (see fig. 7.5).

When it comes to social and personal characteristics, it can be a bit more difficult to predict who will see the world as a spiritual battleground.

Men are no more likely to hold such views than are women. Age is of no consequence—young and old alike are just as likely or unlikely to fear an impending Armageddon and believe in demons, devils, and other aspects of supernatural evil. Once we use statistical techniques to remove the effects of religiosity, race does not directly impact evil scores (more on this later). The married and the unmarried are not different in their levels of belief in evil.

What *does* matter when it comes to predicting beliefs about evil is a person's social status as measured by education and family income. The more education acquired, the less likely people are to believe in supernatural evil (see fig. 7.6). Belief that Satan is the primary cause of evil in the world declines steadily and dramatically with income (see fig. 7.7).

The person most likely to view the Earth as a spiritual battleground between good and evil is a conservatively/traditionally religious person who is not faring well in the socioeconomic status system by conventional standards. These patterns point to an interesting correspondence between conditions in the material world and one's perceptions about the nature of evil. Those occupying traditionally power-deprived social statuses are also

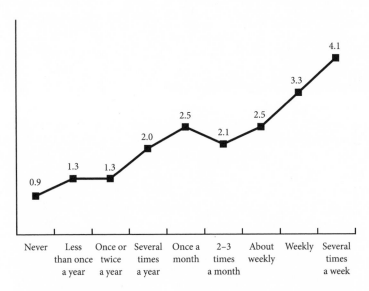

Figure 7.5. Church attendance and evil scores (Baylor Religion Survey, Wave 2, 2007)

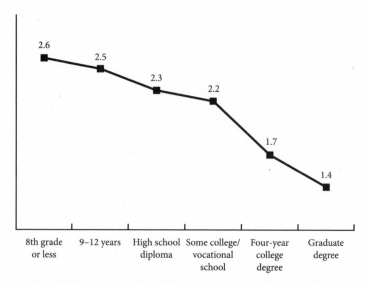

Fig. 7.6. Education and evil scores (Baylor Religion Survey, Wave 2, 2007)

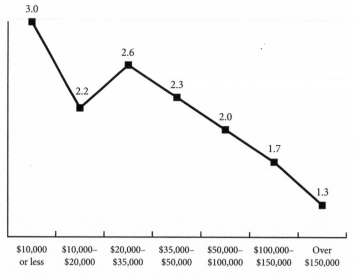

Fig. 7.7. Family income and evil scores (Baylor Religion Survey, Wave 2, 2007)

more likely to turn to religion as a coping mechanism to deal with the difficulties encountered in the world.[20] Christianity offers a ready-made explanation for one's suffering to those who desire such an answer—suffering, evil, and misery are the work of evil forces. In a certain way, this is a comforting answer. Their suffering is not meaningless or endless. The world is evil and controlled by Satan, it is not supposed to be fair or just. But Satan will be defeated at the battle of Armageddon, and those suffering now will be greatly rewarded later. Attribution literature in psychology suggests that when difficult situations occur, people are more likely to attribute the events to supernatural evil.[21]

But providing an explanation for suffering is only one of the rewards that religion can offer. We should not think that religions, even the most conservative and traditional, are focused solely upon the evil and demonic. One of the most powerful rewards religion can offer is direct access to the divine via religious experiences. Here again we enter the muddy waters separating religion from the paranormal.

Light: Speaking to God

Nestled in the foothills of the Blue Ridge Mountains in southern Appalachia, an unassuming Pentecostal church sits on the outskirts of a small city. The building is modern, but not fancy by any standard.

On a recent Sunday, Joseph and his wife attended services. We were greeted warmly by a well-dressed, middle-aged woman. The hallway from the foyer led directly into the sanctuary, a long room with a low ceiling, standing in direct contrast to the sweeping architecture and high ceilings of more traditional church buildings. Rows of padded folding chairs lined each side of the room. The aisles in the middle and down the side were wide enough to allow free movement, which proved necessary. Toward the front a large podium sat on a slightly elevated portion of the room. To its left a small booth with a drum kit, to the right a flat-screen television embedded in the wall. Directly behind it was large red banner displaying flames of fire and a flock of doves.

We took a seat toward the back as the pastor and several congregants gathered. Members shook our hands and offered warm greetings, doing their best to make us feel at home in a place where everyone else knows one another. Loud praise and worship music piped over the sound system.

The pastor and several members paced back and forth up front, praying aloud and moving their bodies to the frequent swells of the music. Others knelt in prayer or chatted with their families.

As start of services neared, we heard a commotion behind us at the entry to the sanctuary. An older man was clutching a young man in a tight embrace as others gathered around. The impromptu group began to loudly "speak in tongues."

The act of speaking in tongues or glossolalia is most frequently practiced in Pentecostal and charismatic churches. It consists of speaking phrases, noises, and sounds in an unknown language, usually during a period of religious ecstasy. Believers claim that when speaking in tongues they are using a special, holy language gifted to them by God. To skeptics, however, these utterances are simply incomprehensible gibberish produced as part of a religious trance induced by a highly emotional setting. For the most part this "language" is unintelligible to listeners, except for a select few who claim to have the gift of "interpreting."

On even rarer occasions a person will speak a recognizable language, such as French, that he claims not to know, a phenomenon called xenoglossolalia. We did not witness xenoglossolalia, but did watch someone earn the gift of speaking in tongues. During the service, James, a boy in his late teens with a slightly receding hairline, and dressed in jeans, work boots, and an untucked polo shirt, sat in front of us. He was closely flanked by Thomas, a slender, athletic boy with light blond hair who wore dress pants, a business shirt, and a tie. Near the end of the service, the pastor motioned for James to come to the stage. As James went forward, Thomas followed. The minister prayed over James, telling him that "the Holy Spirit" was all around him. James raised his hands—eyes closed—as those around him loudly spoke in tongues and prayed. The church band played on. For the next ten minutes the huddle prayed as the pastor told James that he was on the verge of baptism in the Holy Spirit, if we would only release his self-consciousness and "yield to it."

About twenty minutes after the pastor had called James forward, a young black man burst from the group and ran down the aisle. He was immediately followed by Thomas, who was drenched in sweat, tears streaming down his face. There was joyous pandemonium among the congregation as two men held a weak-kneed James up as he triumphantly spoke in tongues. After a couple of minutes, James ceased speaking in tongues and fell into a tight embrace with the pastor, who was visibly overjoyed by the events.

For They Heard Them Speak with Tongues (Acts 10:46)

Pentecostals share with Evangelicals, "fundamentalists," and other conservative Christians a tendency to view the Bible as the literal word of God, hold restrictive attitudes on moral issues, and focus upon born-again experiences.[22] But while Evangelicals and fundamentalists are strongly focused upon the bedrock of doctrine, Pentecostals emphasize the continual revelation of God's will through the dynamics of religious experience.[23] Pentecostals seek what they believe to be a baptism from the Holy Spirit, which can impart a number of spiritual "gifts" to the recipient. The ability to speak in tongues is but one of these gifts. Others include prophecy, the ability to sense the presence of demons or angels, and supernatural knowledge or wisdom.[24] In addition, one of the "gifts" is the ability to call upon God to heal the physical, emotional, and spiritual pains of the faithful, which we were able to witness that Sunday.

The congregation could barely contain its excitement when the preacher asked members to come forward to "testify." He asked a middle-aged woman to come forward and explained to the congregation that she had been enduring physical and spiritual troubles in her life. The pastor laid his hands on her as the praise-band leader put anointing oil on his hand and touched the woman's head. Soon more than twenty people gathered around her and prayed for her to be healed as she fell back into the arms of those gathered around her.

After almost two hours of singing, dancing, testifying, and religious experiences, the pastor had yet to deliver a sermon. The pastor stood before the group and said, "What more can I say? I could preach, but you all already did. The Lord has healed and we have rejoiced as a lost sheep returned to the fold. Young men have been baptized in Jesus Christ and the Holy Spirit. God is good! I hope we see y'all Tuesday night for Bible study. And don't you leave here without hugging everybody!" With that the extemporaneous, spirit-filled service came to a close.

Most recent estimates suggest that there are more than four million Pentecostals in the United States.[25] On any given Sunday, Pentecostals are communing with spirits and angels and speaking in unknown tongues. Yet these are marginal experiences even within the cultural context of Christianity (see fig. 7.8). When all the respondents to the BRS were asked if they have had a miraculous physical healing, have spoken in tongues during a religious service, or have directly heard the voice of God speaking to them, only a minority of Americans report such experiences.[26]

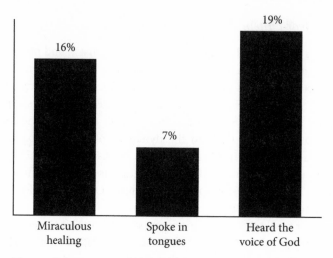

Fig. 7.8. Religious experiences in the United States (Baylor Religion Survey, Wave 2, 2007)

When we consider these three experiences together, about 30 percent of Americans claim having had at least one, if not more of them. And those Americans are distinct in many ways. First and foremost, those who claim such experiences are very religious. The more one attends church the more likely she is to report such experiences by a wide margin.[27] More than half (58%) of those who believe the Bible is God's literal word report such experiences compared to only a fifth (21%) of those who view the Bible in less literal terms. Evangelicals and black Protestants are much more likely to report speaking in tongues, miraculous healings, and hearing the voice of God than are members of other religious traditions.

It should come as no surprise that such experiences generally occur in a religious setting. Religious experiences are a product of the contextual environment in which they occur. These settings stress specific experiences, are high in emotional intensity, and draws upon specific religious doctrines and narratives to frame the experiences.

There are also some social factors that are associated with religious experiences. We do not find age or education to predict religious experiences. We do find that females are more likely to claim such experiences than males (34% versus 23%), and unmarried people are slightly more likely (33%) to have religious experiences than married people (27%).

We found that income was a strong predictor of beliefs about evil, and it is an equally powerful predictor of religious experiences (see fig. 7.9). Almost half of those who make $10,000 a year or less report speaking in tongues, miraculous healings, and/or hearing the voice of God. From there the likelihood of reporting such experiences decreases dramatically. Only about a third of those making $20,000 to $35,000 a year report one or more of these experiences. Individuals at the highest level of income (more than $150,000 a year), are half as likely to speak in tongues, have a healing, or hear the voice of God as those at the lowest levels of income.

Why might religious experiences be of greater appeal to those at the lowest levels of income? Our visit to another small Pentecostal church provided insight into this matter.

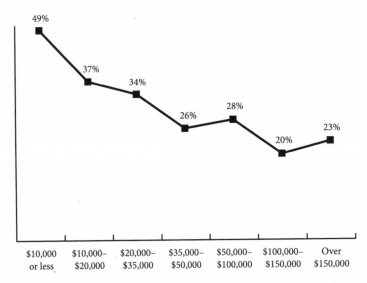

Fig. 7.9. Having a religious experience, by yearly family income (Baylor Religion Survey, Wave 2, 2007)

Note: Percentage indicates what percentage of respondents at given income level have spoken in tongues and/or received a miraculous healing and/or heard the voice of God speaking to them. Forty-nine percent of those making less than $10,000 a year reported at least one such experience.

A Gift of Faith from the Lord

About an hour north of Austin, Texas, sits a classic, small, rural church covered in flaking white paint. The Pentecostal House is the kind of simultaneously quaint and nondescript house of worship that is easy to pass by on the interstate with barely a glance.[28] On a recent Wednesday evening, we pulled off the highway access road and into its grass-covered parking lot to attend a service.

We were met by the pastor, Buddy, and his assistant, Tom. Buddy, forty-five years old with sandy brown hair, penetrating eyes, and a crooked smile, has been with the church for twenty years. His wife greeted us warmly and introduced us to their son and young daughter. Tom, a tall man in his sixties with gray hair, served terms as pastor at a variety of conservative churches around Texas before finally settling onto a farm near the Pentecostal House. Numbering only fifteen consistent members, the congregants were very excited by our visit, in spite of the fact that we had told them we were there primarily for observation purposes —we were not looking to join. Nevertheless, they hoped that a passionate Wednesday night worship session might change our minds and net three unexpected new members. By all accounts they were welcoming and friendly.

Ricky, a tall, imposing, fifty-year-old maintenance worker, firmly shook our hands. He did not look the part of a small country church member. He was dressed in faded jeans and a well-worn black T-shirt. His arms were banded with tattoos, and his boots were those of a working man, smattered with the remnants of construction and hard labor. "This is a church where you meet the Lord," he told us. "We don't judge people by how they look," he said, chuckling as he showed off his tattoos. "Just come three times and you're a member."

Ricky sat near the back with his wife, and another older couple next to them. In front of us three older women shared a pew with an older Hispanic male. The women were stay-at-home moms and secretaries for small businesses. The men worked construction, in factories, or in other forms of manual labor. To them, as one member told us, "worshipping the Lord is fun after a hard day's work." The minister too was empathetic to the plight of a working-class lifestyle, starting his message to the congregation by saying, "I'm not gonna ask ya to stand," his voice rising in volume, "I know y'all worked hard today. So stay in your seats, but rise up in your hearts to praise Him!"

It was clear from talking to members that they strongly believe in the power of direct contact with the supernatural, and this contact is extremely important to them. A stack of pamphlets in a rack near the doorway testified to "The Truth about the Holy Spirit Baptism." With sufficient faith and obedience, the tract promises, anyone can develop a special relationship with the Lord whereupon they may speak with tongues, lay their hands on one another in healing, and prophesy the future.

Pastor Buddy convinced a soft-spoken man named Gary to tell us of his healing. It seems that Gary had suffered a massive stroke two years ago that had left him unable to walk, speak, or squeeze with his hands. Doctors couldn't help him. In an effort have the supernatural intervene in Gary's life, the group had prayed over him during an impassioned service, laying their hands upon him as they called for God's mercy. Gary felt "a charge" and is convinced that God interceded on his behalf. From that point on he steadily improved. He now walks, although he still favors one side of his body. He seems embarrassed by the slight droop on one side of his mouth, but he speaks without difficulty. And he vigorously and happily shook each of our hands several times throughout the night, demonstrating that his ability to grip has fully recovered. "A gift of faith from the Lord," he told us.

During the service the pastor repeatedly called upon members to continually seek a new connection to the divine and not rest on past experiences. Tom would shout at the top of his voice "If you are hungry for God's glory then you can see God's glory! We want a bigger touch! A new touch! A fresh touch of his love!" All this was a reminder that they must not content themselves with the past, but continually seek to renew their connection to the divine with new experiences.

The call to experience God's love was couched in a warning. Pastor Tom warned of a coming judgment: the once-mighty dollar is losing its clout, evil is rampant. The world is like a tree that has been eaten from the inside by insects, he exhorted. It may look strong from the outside, but a coming storm will knock it down, revealing its inner corruption. Sinners will be placed in a "fiery furnace." Neither is it enough to be born again. People must still work hard to convert others and do God's work or they will not be among the favored in Heaven. "Anyone in America can be rich if they just work at it," Buddy said, "If you aren't rich already you just haven't tried hard enough. But what's important is to spend your time getting rich in the right way. I'd rather have my treasures stored up in Heaven. I'm too happy worshipping the Lord to worry 'bout getting rich here!" The rewards offered by God to Buddy, Gary, and the other working-class congregants were otherworldly, both in contemporary experiences and eternal bliss.

Scholars of religion have suggested that the economically disadvantaged will be the most open to intense religious experiences.[29] Religious groups in which most of the members are lower on the socioeconomic ladder tend to have a strong focus upon the rewards offered in the next life. Promises of chariots in heaven and the riches of salvation offer some recompense for the sufferings of this life.

Within these churches, speaking in tongues, receiving healings, and other religious experiences confer status. As we noticed in our observations of Pentecostal churches, those who spoke in tongues received enormous attention and respect from other church members. Those at the lower end of the economic ladder have much to gain from such experiences, with less conventional social status to lose from claiming an encounter with the otherworldly. A surgeon who believes she has had religious visions and experienced miraculous healings may well have difficulty convincing her social network that her experiences are the product of divine intervention and not an issue of mental malfunction. A long history of studies indicates that people of lower social status are more likely to be drawn to sects where intense emotive experiences are integrated into the religious culture of the group.[30] In general, such experiences are not typically found in more "traditional" or liturgical congregations on a Sunday.

Angels: Gateway to the Paranormal?

One of the big surprises we encountered while investigating American paranormal beliefs and experiences was the commonality of the belief that one has been saved by a guardian angel. Angels pervade popular culture in books, television shows, and movies. Publications such as *Angels on Earth* are dedicated to communicating stories about angels in the world. More than half of Americans have seen the popular television show, *Touched by an Angel.*[31] Believers exchange informal testimonials in newsletters and interpersonal conversations about the potential power of angels to influence the world, and more than half of Americans (53%) believe that they have personally been saved from harm by a guardian angel.

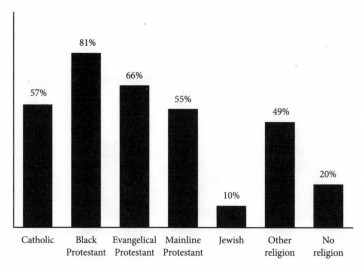

Fig. 7.10. Guardian angel experience by religious tradition (Baylor Religion Survey, Wave 2, 2007)

The presence of guardian angels offers a supernatural explanation for events that seem inexplicable. How and why did I survive that accident? Why did I miss the train on the day it crashed? How did I survive my tour of military duty? Stories about angelic intervention are as varied as those who tell them, but all such stories contain a common element: the belief that the supernatural broke through to influence the material world for the benefit of the believer. Anthropologists have found the belief in intentional agents of the divine is one of the most common supernatural beliefs among humans in general.[32]

While speaking in tongues, miraculous healings, and hearing the voice of God are mostly confined to the realm of conservative Christianity, the guardian angel experience appears to have much wider appeal (see fig. 7.10). The majority of Christians in all traditions (Catholics, mainline Protestants, evangelical Protestants, and black Protestants) claim to have been protected from harm by a guardian angel. Nearly half of those in non Judeo-Christian traditions also claim guardian angel encounters. Even one-fifth of those who claim no religion believe that they have been rescued by angelic forces.

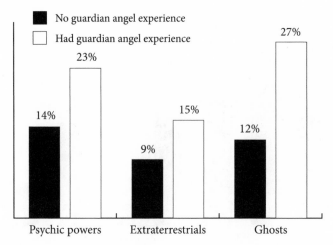

Fig. 7.11. Paranormal beliefs and guardian angel experiences (Baylor Religion Survey, Wave 2, 2007)

While books about angels are quite popular on the Christian shelves, angels also find their way into the New Age sections of bookstores. Guardian angel belief is one that could appeal to both "conventional" and "unconventional" supernatural worldviews, perhaps even serving as a gateway between religion and the paranormal. Indeed, quite unlike other religious experiences, people who claim to have been protected by guardian angels are *more likely* to believe in paranormal subjects such as ghosts, extraterrestrials, and psychic phenomena than those who have not had such an experience (see fig. 7.11). For example only 12 percent of those people who have never had a guardian angel experience believe in ghosts. Those who *have* had a guardian angel experience are more than twice as likely to believe in ghosts and spirits.

Good and Evil

The Christian world is filled with experiences, beliefs, and events that are certainly beyond the "normal." By their very definition religious experiences are the perception of direct contact between an individual and that which is otherworldly. The aspect that fundamentally distinguishes "religious" experiences from "paranormal" experiences is where the individual attributes the source of their otherworldly experience.[33] One might there-fore expect that someone who is actively experiencing the supernatural in their church services and believes in the reality of personified evil has simply become accustomed to magical thinking, willing to believe in any-thing, from demons to flying saucers.

But the guardian angel experience appears unique among religious experiences. The relationships between paranormal experiences and other religious experiences is haphazard and often insignificant (see fig. 7.12). Ghosts are somewhat more appealing to those who have spoken in tongues, but someone who has spoken in tongues is no more likely to believe in extraterrestrials than someone who does not. People who speak in tongues are no more or less likely to believe in the reality of psychic phenomena than anyone else.

With the exception of guardian angels, most religious experiences ap-pear to exist within a fairly narrow segment of the population—conser-vative Christians, particularly those lower on the socioeconomic ladder. This same population tends to believe in the reality of Satan, demons, possession, and the power of evil forces (see fig. 7.13). Nearly all (85%) of those who claim to have spoken in tongues believe in the absolute real-ity of demons. Less than half of those people who have never spoken in tongues (42%) believe in Satan's helpers. Why do these beliefs and experi-ences cluster together and what purpose do they serve?

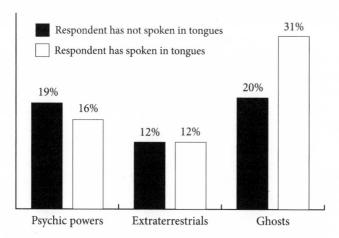

Fig. 7.12. Paranormal beliefs and speaking in tongues (Baylor Religion Survey, Wave 2, 2007)

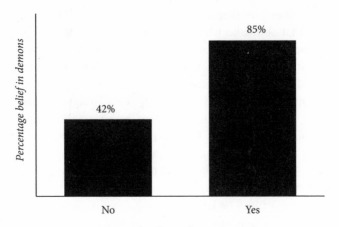

Fig. 7.13. Belief in demons and speaking in tongues (Baylor Religion Survey, Wave 2, 2007)

A person who believes that God sometimes imparts special languages to a chosen few or is willing to heal the faithful also believes in a world of active supernatural forces. It serves as a spiritual compensator. Being a spiritual warrior on the side of righteousness is a very important role, especially in the lives of people for whom important roles are often lacking. It makes sense that people who imagine a very active God will also imagine God's counterpart in order to account for misfortune. Taken together, beliefs about Satan and religious experiences are complementary for those suffering in this world. The presence of a real and powerful evil force provides an explanation for worldly suffering. The countervailing presence of good felt via palpable religious experiences proves to those receiving the experience that there is a God that will reward his followers for maintaining faith in the face of such evil.

8

Out on a Limb

January 1989

More than twenty years ago Christopher found himself in the passenger seat of a decrepit, rusted van as it hurtled through the woods near the town of Carson in Washington State. The driver did his best to avoid trees, boulders, ditches, and other obstacles as he navigated toward a small hunting cabin deep in the woods. Wiping mud from my eyes, I looked down at my feet, only to realize that part of the rusted floorboard had given way. I spent the remainder of the terrifying ride balancing my feet on the rough edges. Each time the van sped through a puddle, dirty water shot through the hole. Eventually the van came to a lurching stop at the bottom of a hill and the driver, Datus Perry, stepped out.

Datus was a spry, sometimes cranky, seventy-six-year-old Bigfoot witness. On this day, he wore a green winter jacket and corduroy pants that were patched in places with duct tape. Thick boots protected his feet from the mud, and a safari hat rested atop a thick mound of snowy-white hair. A long white beard completed the picture of a backwoods eccentric. A large patch on his jacket reading "Sasquatch Country" provided a clue to his particular interest.

Datus parted the brush to reveal an overgrown path heading up a hill, and we hustled away. I struggled to keep pace with a man three times my age. At frequent intervals Datus stopped to scan the nearby ridges. Suddenly he grunted and moved off the path. Standing near a large evergreen tree, he peered into the distance. Determined not to miss a potential Bigfoot sighting, I ran to his side. When I realized that Datus was urinating on the tree, I retreated to the trail, embarrassed. He snorted, giggled, zipped his fly, and resumed the hike.

A few weeks earlier, while cleaning the old cabin, Datus had spotted a nine-foot-tall, black shape in a stand of trees about 150 feet away. Assuming the shape to be a curious Bigfoot, he waved and said "Come on down, Sasquatch!" As the creature remained motionless Datus questioned its motives. Perhaps it was a female, he thought, and he did not know how "sexy she might want to get." He decided to ignore the beast and went back to work as the creature continued to stand motionless in the distance. The stalemate continued until evening, when he lost sight of it in the enveloping darkness.

Datus was somewhat unique among Bigfoot witnesses in that he claimed at least a dozen Bigfoot sightings and believed that he knew how the creature thinks. When I arrived at Perry's home earlier that morning, he proudly retrieved from his garage a large cardboard cutout he had made of Bigfoot. Standing at least seven feet tall and in the shape of a large man, the cutout was topped off by a sharply triangular head. "That's how you know when someone is hoaxing a Bigfoot sighting," Datus told me, "because it has a sharp sagittal crest. If someone says Bigfoot doesn't have a pointy head they are a hoaxer." This was only one of several beliefs Datus held that proved controversial in Bigfoot circles. Bigfoot has been reported in a number of different hair colors, various shades of brown or black. Even the occasional reddish and gray-colored Bigfeet have been seen. "Bigfoot only comes in black," Datus reported. All other colors people have seen are the result of the creature wearing coats made of animal skins. It was also common knowledge among Bigfoot enthusiasts that the creature has a powerful smell. "Nonsense," said Datus. "If Bigfoot smells it's because of rotten meat on the animal hides that it wears. Or maybe Bigfoot is farting."

Earlier in the day I had sat in Datus's living room as he packed his van for our trip to the cabin. In one corner of the room sat an easel with a large tablet upon it. I paged through it while waiting for Datus and found the easel filled with sketches of Bigfoot, each one captioned with the creature's thoughts. On one page was a crude drawing of the head and shoulders of an apelike creature with an astonishingly pointy head and black fur, a grimace on its face. An assortment of captions surrounding the face:

You won't find any bigger than I am.
I am 11 ft. tall.
I was here FIRST. I am real.
I don't want to be bothered. Don't pick on me little man.
Let me eat your pig or your dog.
I am black and very dark.

I will see you first and I'll watch you from a bush.
Throw me a fish!

On the next page was a full-body sketch of a Sasquatch with "I am always looking for something to eat," written sideways down the page. A profile of Bigfoot's face on the next page was titled "I am not the missing link." On the bottom of the page was Datus's attempt to spell out the way Bigfoot yells: "YEE-TEE-E-E-E-EE!!!"

When we finally reached the ramshackle cabin after our perilous van ride, we found three moss-covered walls and a collapsed door about the size of a storage unit. Datus told me about his many sightings as we stood among the trees. He claimed that the creature regularly came on to his property to steal rabbits from his pens and that he often heard it whistling and screaming in the woods surrounding his farm. His closest visual encounter with Bigfoot occurred when he was traveling in Canada and came within a few feet of a creature standing on a riverbank, but most of his other encounters took place while walking through the woods near his home, several near this cabin.

Datus had become so accustomed to Bigfoot's behaviors and habits during his many experiences that he had developed techniques for

Datus Perry with his model of Bigfoot

spotting the creature. And here was the purpose of our visit. We stood near the dilapidated cabin as Datus instructed me to calm my breathing and be very quiet. We needed to sit still for some time. If a Bigfoot is in the area, he instructed, it will become curious as to what encroaching humans are doing. It will stealthily follow the trespasser, staying far enough away as to avoid being seen. If a person walks around looking for Bigfoot, he will never see one, Datus told me. Should he see the person turn around, Bigfoot will stand completely still, its black fur and pointy head making it indistinguishable from the dark trees around it. Our best hope was to wait, immobile, in the hopes that a Sasquatch would become so curious as to our intentions that it would finally wander into our line of site as it investigated.

No such luck on this day. We sat and waited. And waited. Finally Datus sighed and gave up. "They must not be around today."

We made our way back down to his van. A light rain had started as we were waiting for Bigfoot's appearance, making the downward climb treacherous and slippery. One flat tire (Datus had run over something while barreling through the woods) and a few geysers of mud through the floorboards later we arrived back at his home. "Come back again," Datus told me, "maybe next time."

Over the next few years I did return to see Datus, but he was never able to draw Bigfoot into view. He died in the late 1990s, his passion for Bigfoot never earning him more than a reputation as a crackpot in his community and the occasional footnote in Bigfoot history.

Spending time in the realms of the paranormal in the course of writing this book led us to reflect on how much has changed since the 1980s. Back then the Internet was in its infancy, not filled with Web sites, blogs, and discussion forums devoted to paranormal subjects. The *X-Files* had yet to appear on television. There was no *MonsterQuest* or *GhostHunters*, let alone the seemingly endless clones and spin-offs that have appeared in their wake. Not that the paranormal is new, far from it. *In Search Of* was a fairly popular pre-1990 paranormal show. In 1992 CBS relaunched *Miracles and Other Wonders*, hosted by Darren McGavin. Magazines such as *Fate* and *Argosy* (now defunct) brought the ghosts and psychic powers to the newsstands.

What appears to have changed is the degree of societal interest in the paranormal and the extent to which this interest has organized. Two decades ago an attempt to investigate the paranormal nearly always led to someone like Datus Perry. Almost every community had "that guy who sees UFOs," or the "family who thinks their house is haunted." Few people knew of the organized paranormal groups in existence at the time, such as the Mutual UFO Network and National Investigations Committee on Aerial Phenomena (NICAP), so local inquiries usually led to colorful, eccentric dead ends.

It is clear that increased interest in the paranormal has gone hand in hand with greater media attention and the rapid diffusion of the Internet. If you live in a city or town of any size, you are likely to find an organized local or regional group of ghost hunters, a group for developing one's psychic potential, a UFO investigation club, and depending on the region, a Bigfoot hunting organization. If your area does not have its own paranormal organization or club, it is probably home to a regional chapter of a national one. Twenty years ago a visit to a reputed haunted house in a community was a lonely affair. Today one may find competition for the ghosts' attentions with a local ghost-hunting group, a documentary crew, or a radio show.

While we doubt many will argue with us when we claim that interest in the paranormal has increased over the last few decades, it is very difficult to prove so with any certainty. Beliefs about the paranormal have only rarely been subjected to detailed scrutiny. When survey researchers have asked Americans if they believe in paranormal topics or have had paranormal experiences, the way in which the questions have been asked, the population to whom the questions have been asked, and even the subjects asked about have varied so dramatically that it is impossible to know for certain how much interest in the paranormal has increased. What we *can* say for certainty is that we live in a paranormal America. Put another way, the paranormal is normal.

It is important that we be very clear what we mean by this statement, as it may be open to misinterpretation. Most books about the paranormal are written from a base underlying assumption regarding the reality of the phenomena under discussion. A number of skeptics and scientists have written books bemoaning increased interest in the paranormal as a sign that our culture is losing its critical reasoning skills. Michael Shermer's *Why People Believe Weird Things* and the late Carl Sagan's *The Demon Haunted World* assume that paranormal phenomena are not objectively real and therefore try to explain what leads people to lose their common sense and believe in fallacious subjects.[1] Books written by paranormal believers attempt to present evidence, often in the form of personal accounts or eyewitness testimony, in an attempt to prove the reality of the phenomenon in question. Conservative Christian authors vary—some arguing that paranormal phenomena are not real while others claim that the paranormal is a tool of Satan.

In the course of researching this book and presenting its findings we have been accused of being (1) too skeptical by some paranormal believers who wish we would attest to the reality of UFOs or Bigfoot, and (2) not skeptical enough by some colleagues who wish we would "call out" lapses in logic among the people we have studied.

We could have presented arguments against the objective reality of UFO abductions. The first widely publicized abduction case of Betty and Barney Hill (see chap. 3) has been the subject of intense debate. For example, Betty claimed to have copied a "star map" shown to her by her abductors. Skeptics and believers have argued ever since whether the map truly displays a star system (and if so, which one) or is simply a random selection of dots produced by a deluded person.

From our perspective, there was little point in entering such debates. One aspect of the Hill case that few disagree with is that the couple truly believed themselves to have been abducted. From a sociological perspective, that is the important factor. The Hill's apparent sincerity amid their astonishing claims proved to be a formative moment in what ultimately became a popular phenomenon in the late seventies. Sociologists have long observed that people act upon their strongly held beliefs, whether those beliefs represent "reality" or not.

When we report that the paranormal is normal, therefore, it should not be taken as an implicit or explicit statement for or against the reality of UFOs, psychic phenomena, ghosts, Bigfoot, or any other paranormal topics. We simply mean that the paranormal is no longer a fringe subject. Need proof? Reflect back on the data we have presented in this book: only 32 percent of Americans report no paranormal beliefs, and half of the population reports belief in two or more paranormal phenomenon.[2] Statistically, those who report a paranormal belief are not the oddballs; it is those who have *no beliefs* that are in the significant minority. Exactly which paranormal beliefs a person finds convincing varies, but whether it is UFOs and ghosts or astrology and telekinesis, most of us believe more than one. If we further consider strong beliefs in active supernatural entities and intense religious experiences the numbers are even larger. Thus we can say with great confidence that the paranormal is here to stay and is no longer a marginal phenomenon. Whether future authors wish to bemoan or cheer the ascension of the paranormal, their arguments will be strengthened by a clear understanding of who believes in and experiences the paranormal, and in what ways. This has been the goal of our project.

Key Findings

Given the diversity and amount of data we have presented in this book, a summary of its key findings is in order.

Individual Paranormal Beliefs and Experiences

Scholars have presented contrary hypothesis regarding who should believe in paranormal subjects or report paranormal experiences. Some theorize that marginalized people (low income or education, minorities) will be more likely to believe in the paranormal, either because marginalized people have little to lose from participating in deviant beliefs or activities or because some paranormal subjects provide the believers with a sense of control over their circumstances. Other scholars suggest that paranormal interest will be more prevalent amongst the upper classes for they have the resources to indulge experimentation with fringe beliefs.

The correct answer appears to be much more complicated. What is very clear is that it is incorrect to stereotype believers in the paranormal, for the people involved vary quite a bit by subject. People who believe in UFOs are not always the same types of people who believe in astrology. The following are the clear patterns we find with regards to paranormal beliefs and experiences:

- With the exception of belief in UFOs, women are more likely to believe in paranormal subjects than are men.
- There is limited evidence that marginalized people will gravitate toward certain paranormal beliefs, specifically beliefs in psychic powers, ghosts, and astrology.
- Females also appear more likely to have or seek out paranormal experiences, as they are significantly more likely to consult horoscopes and psychics, use Ouija boards, and to believe they have lived in or visited a haunted house.
- There is limited evidence that elites are more likely to have some paranormal experiences, specifically out-of-body experiences and UFO sightings.

Religious Beliefs and Paranormal Beliefs

The relationship between religious beliefs and paranormal beliefs has also been subject to competing hypotheses. Some scholars have argued that religious beliefs should open a person up to the paranormal, since someone who is willing to believe in the supernatural in one realm should be more willing to do so in another. Others have argued that religious beliefs provide a specific worldview and belief system, which is in conflict with the paranormal; therefore religious people should show lower levels of belief in paranormal topics and have fewer paranormal experiences.

We find that much of the confusion has to do with the fact that the relationship with religion and the paranormal varies by levels and types of religiosity. People who are open to religious ideas but hold more liberal views are more likely to believe in the paranormal than nonreligious people. So in a certain sense religious beliefs do condition a person to accept paranormal beliefs. But people who have very strict religious views are less likely to believe in the paranormal than others.

- Evangelical Protestants and Jews show the lowest levels of belief in paranormal subjects.
- Belief in paranormal topics is at its highest levels among people with more liberal views of the Bible.
- Belief in paranormal topics is at its lowest levels among people who believe the Bible is the literal word of God.
- The likelihood of holding a paranormal belief or having a paranormal experience is greatest among infrequent church attenders (once a month) and lowest among the most frequent church attenders (several times a week).

Paranormal Researchers

In chapter 5 we explored the world of paranormal subcultures with a particular emphasis on Bigfoot researchers. By spending time reading the literature of Bigfoot hunters, visiting their Web sites, attending their conferences, and joining in on Bigfoot hunts, an additional complexity regarding the paranormal became apparent to us: the people varied depending on what type of Bigfoot-related activity in which they engaged. For example, African Americans are more likely to believe in Bigfoot than those of other races, and females in general exhibit slightly higher levels of belief than males. Yet when it comes to reading books about Bigfoot, watching Bigfoot documentaries, or visiting related Web sites, younger males corner the market, while the Bigfoot hunters we spent time with tended to be middle-aged white men in white-collar occupations.

We do not know if this level of variance would be found in other paranormal subcultures, but we can boil down these observations into a single statement:

- The type of person interested in a paranormal subject may vary depending upon her level of involvement in the subject. Those who simply believe in a paranormal topic are not necessarily the same types of people who research the subject, have related experiences, or engage in related practices.

Paranormal People

In our studies of the paranormal we were struck by the different types of people we met. We met some who were highly conventional people who believed in psychic powers, ghosts, or some other paranormal subject. What struck us is the fact that those who had more to lose by engaging in the paranormal did not necessarily avoid it altogether. Rather, they tended to limit their beliefs. A middle-class, married banker with conventional religious beliefs may believe strongly in UFOs because of a personal interest or experience, but that same banker is unlikely to also believe in Bigfoot, ghosts, astrology, and psychic powers.

We met people, such as Laura, who were very unconventional and often proud of the fact that they didn't "quite fit in." Without as much to lose from embracing paranormal beliefs, such people seemed more willing to accept numerous paranormal topics and even claim multiple different kinds of paranormal experiences.

- In a statistical sense, it is not deviant to believe in a paranormal subject. More than two-thirds of Americans (68%) believe in at least one.
- Individuals vary in their stakes in conformity as measured by conventional attachments, investment in conventional society (education and income), and conventional beliefs.
- Stakes in conformity strongly predict how many paranormal beliefs a person accepts. Highly conventional people report signifi-

cantly fewer paranormal beliefs and experiences than highly unconventional people.

Supernatural Evil and Religious Experiences

In chapter 7 we examined the muddy waters between religion and the
paranormal, exploring beliefs about the devil, demons, possession, Armageddon and the Rapture, and such powerful religious experiences as
speaking in tongues, miraculous healings, and hearing the voice of God.
It was immediately clear, with one exception, that such beliefs and experiences do not make one more likely to believe in paranormal subjects. We
can much more clearly explicate who will believe in supernatural evil and
claim religious experiences:

- People who are conservatively religious and marginalized in terms
  of education and income will be the most likely to believe in the
  reality of supernatural evil forces such as Satan and demons.
- People who are conservatively religious and marginalized in
  terms of education and income are also the most likely to report
  religious experiences such as speaking in tongues and miraculous
  healings.
- Belief in supernatural evil is strongly related to religious experiences. In other words, someone who believes in a real Satan also
  tends to be the same type of person who will speak in tongues or
  hear the voice of God.
- While other religious experiences have inconsistent effects on
  paranormal beliefs, believing that one has been saved from harm
  by a guardian angel appears to be a crossover experience. People
  who claim this experience are more likely to believe in paranormal subjects.

Out on a Limb

A key figure in the New Age and paranormal is the actress and author
Shirley MacLaine. In 1983 she released *Out on a Limb,* an autobiographi-
cal work in which she reveals how troubles in her life sparked a journey
of self-exploration that led her to delve into subjects such as channeling,
reincarnation, and UFOs. MacLaine was widely ridiculed and became

the target of jokes on late-night talk shows, but for those in the New Age community, she was a brave trailblazer. Whether one considers MacLaine to be kook or a visionary, one thing is clear: releasing *Out on a Limb* was a very bold and risky move on her part.

We would like to end this journey into the paranormal with our own (relatively) risky move, predicting what the paranormal will look like in the United States in the future.

What will be the state of affairs twenty, thirty or even forty years from now? Will people still believe? Will there be greater emphasis on paranormal beliefs? Will the level of interest in the paranormal slip? Will the ever-shifting demographic and religious composition of the U.S. population lead to a different type of paranormal? Let's get out our crystal ball and take a peek to see what the future portends.

In chapter 6 we showed that the number of paranormal beliefs a person subscribes to varies quite significantly by education, race/ethnicity, age, gender, income, and religiosity (see table A6 in the appendix). Over the next twenty to forty years the sociodemographic and religious composition of the United States will change. The forces of changing fertility patterns, increased life expectancy, and immigration mean that the United States of 2040 or 2050 will not resemble the United States of 2010. If we hope to predict the extent of paranormal belief in the future, we will have to make some assumptions about what the demographics of the United States will look like many years from now.

The current population of the United States is approximately 296 million. By 2050, that number is projected to increase by 48 percent, or a net gain of 142 million people.[3] However, the vast majority (82%) of that growth is projected to come from immigration, and by 2050, one in five persons will be foreign born. Currently, white, non-Hispanics comprise 67 percent of the population, but by 2050 this group is expected to represent only 47 percent of the population.

These trends are important for future levels of paranormal beliefs. White respondents report significantly fewer paranormal beliefs than do nonwhite respondents. Therefore, any decrease in the relative size of the white population would presumably result in an increase in paranormal beliefs.

Yet there are other future trends that may offset such projected changes in racial/ethnic composition. We have found that age decreases the reported number of paranormal beliefs. Older respondents to our surveys are much less likely to believe in Bigfoot, ghosts, psychic abilities, etc.

Currently, the elderly (age sixty-five and older) comprise 12 percent of the population in the United States, but by 2050 this age group is projected to represent 19 percent of the total population. Given our current understanding of the relationship between age and paranormal beliefs, an increase in the percentage of elderly will have a net, negative effect on the overall level of paranormal beliefs. Of course this assumes that these are effects of age generally and not generational cultural shifts.

The second demographic trend that may reduce the future level of paranormal belief is that of expected gains in educational attainment and subsequent gains in income. Census projections show that the percentage of the adult population (twenty-five and older) with a college degree is expected to increase from 22 percent in 2003 to 25 percent by 2030. Since those who have more education, on average, have higher incomes, we expect that real income should climb during that period as well. Since both of these measures are negatively related to the number of reported paranormal beliefs (see table A6 in appendix), then a net gain for the nation as a whole in both education and income over the next twenty to forty years should predict a net decline in paranormal beliefs.[4]

As we have found, conservative religion has a dampening effect upon paranormal belief. Therefore, changes in the religious makeup of the United States will impact the paranormal. There is no strong consensus regarding how the religious landscape will change in America over the next twenty to forty years. We know from past experience that mainline protestant congregations have been declining in membership, and that evangelical Christian denominations have been growing.[5] Along with this growth in evangelicals, there has been an uptick in the percentage of people who respond "no religion" on national surveys.[6] Further, the publicity of New Age and alternative spiritual experiences/practices leads people to believe that "spiritual but not religious" has been an increasing trend.

Over the next thirty years Roman Catholics, Protestants, non-Judeo-Christian religions, and secularists are all predicted to grow in absolute numbers. Recent projections about the American religious landscape indicate that immigration and differential fertility patterns will restructure the religious composition of the nation. As noted earlier, 82 percent of all population growth over the next forty years is expected to be through immigration, specifically Hispanic immigration. As a result, Catholics are expected to grow from 28 percent to 32 percent of the total population during this time frame. Protestants, taken as a whole, are expected to decline in representation by 12 percent during the first half of the twenty-first century, but conservative evangelical Protestants are expected to decline by only 3 percent. Those who affiliate with other religions are expected to double in their representation in the U.S. population. Those with no religion are expected to grow as a proportion of the U.S. population by .5 percent.[7]

The predicted tailoring off of religious conservatives is particularly interesting, as two of the most important predictors of paranormal beliefs are church attendance and biblical literalism. Religious conservatism is positively correlated with both of these measures.[8] Therefore, if religious conservatives decline somewhat over the next forty or so years, it is reasonable to assume that biblical literalism and church attendance might also decline, to a judicious degree.

If we move forward based on such assumptions, what does it mean? Sixty-eight percent of Americans currently report at least one paranormal belief. The average American holds slightly more than two (2.1) paranormal beliefs. By weighting the relative importance of the demographic and religiosity variables that predict paranormal beliefs, and considering the predicted changes in the demographic and religious landscape over the next thirty to forty years, we prognosticate that by 2050, 72.7 percent of Americans will report at least one paranormal belief, and that the average number of paranormal beliefs reported will by respondents to such surveys will be 2.45.[9] This equates to a 14 percent increase in the mean number of reported paranormal beliefs in the United States.

We realize that we have gone out on the proverbial limb here by making assumptions about future changes in the United States. Those assumptions are based upon current research on population trends, and the relationships are strong. The actual change in paranormal beliefs we experience may be slightly smaller or somewhat larger. What our models decidedly do not predict, however, is the elimination of paranormal belief in our society or even a dramatic reduction.

Whether we like it or not, we have become and will remain a paranormal America.

Appendix

Data, Methods and Findings

For readers concerned about methodological issues this appendix provides details on the sources of our data—extensive fieldwork and two waves of the Baylor Religion Survey, and the statistical analyses that lie behind our presentation.

The Baylor Religion Surveys

Funded by the John Templeton Foundation, the Baylor Religion Survey (BRS) is an in-depth survey of religious beliefs and attitudes administered to the U.S. general population. Most other national surveys, such as the General Social Survey (GSS) and National Election Study, include limited questions on religion.[1] That is not to say that the developers of these surveys do not feel that religion is important; rather it is a question of focus. The BRS was designed to try to fill this gap with the inclusion of dozens of new religion questions. Most important for the purposes of this book, the BRS includes multiple questions on paranormal beliefs, experiences, and practices.

This book utilizes data from the first two waves of the BRS. Wave 1, collected in the fall of 2005 consists of a random sample of 1,721 Americans. Wave 2, collected in the fall of 2007, provides responses from a random sample of 1,648 Americans. In the interests of space we have not reproduced the full survey booklets for each wave in this volume. Interested readers can view the questionnaires at the Web site for Baylor's Institute for Studies of Religion (ISR): http://www.baylor.edu/ISR. Researchers can also download the surveys at http://thearda.com.

Data Collection

The Gallup Organization administered the Baylor Religion Survey. Even though the BRS includes many religion questions, it was *not* administered only to highly religious people, or to a certain type of religious person. The Gallup Organization called a random sample of people around the country in order to solicit their participation in the survey. As such, every person in the United States with a phone had an equal chance of being selected for the survey. While Americans are overwhelmingly Christian, people of non-Christian religions and atheists completed the survey as well.[2]

For both waves, Gallup used a mixed-mode sampling design (telephone and self-administered mailed surveys). The recruitment and administration of the BRS can be broken down into three distinct phases: (1) initial recruitment through random-digit dialing; (2) phone interviews on a randomly selected subsample of participants to determine bias in initial refusals; and (3) the mailed survey. Given the number of different stages in the process, we will focus upon Wave 1 in our description below and present a table to summarize both waves.

The Gallup Organization conducted phone recruitment requesting participation in a survey project which is designed to "investigate the values and beliefs of Americans." The Gallup Organization did not indicate that the BRS was specifically about religion or that Baylor University was involved in the study for fear that this might bias the response rate. The random-digit telephone sample was drawn from telephone exchanges serving the continental United States. In order to avoid various other sources of bias, a random-digit procedure designed to provide representation of both listed and unlisted (including not-yet-listed) telephone numbers was used. The design of the sample ensures representation of all telephone numbers by randomly generating the last two digits of numbers selected on the basis of their area code, telephone exchange, and bank order.

The mailed survey consisted of a sixteen-page booklet including a cover page titled, "The Values and Beliefs of the American Public—A National Study."[3] Questionnaires included a cover letter explaining the study's objectives and a number to call if participants had any questions or comments. In appreciation of their participation, potential mail survey respondents were offered a $5.00 incentive to complete the self-administered questionnaire and return it to the Gallup Organization. A follow-up reminder postcard was sent to all those who did not respond to the initial survey mailing.

For Wave 1 the Gallup Organization contacted 7,041 households by phone and 3,002 people agreed to participate in the study. The response rate for the initial recruiting phase is calculated according to the American Association for Public Opinion Research (AAPOR) RR1 definition: $RR1 = 3,002 / 7,041 = 42.6\%$. Of the 2,603 surveys mailed, 1,721 were completed and returned. Consequently, the return rate for the mailed surveys is 66.1% (1,721 / 2,603). When these three phases of data collection (initial recruitment, phone interviews, and mailed surveys) are pooled to calculate the response rate for the mixed-mode method per AAPOR RR1, it becomes 24.4% (1,721 / 7,041 = 24.4%).[4] Using the same formula, the response rate for the mixed-mode method per AAPOR RR1 for Wave 2 is 24.94% (1,648 / 6,604).

$$RR1 = \frac{I}{(I + P) + (R + NC + O) + (UH + UO)}$$

I = Complete interview; P = Partial interviews; R = refusals and break-offs; NC = Non-contact; O = Other; UH = Unknown if household occupied; UO = Unknown, other. This response rate for multimethod surveys accounts for nonresponse at all levels of data collection.

The Gallup Organization asserts that these response rates fit within the normal parameters for reliable national survey data. In addition, all demographic variables compare favorably to other national surveys. To search for such bias we compared our respondents to those of the 2004 General Social Survey on key religious indicators such as attendance and denomination. The respondents to the two surveys were similar. For example, there was no evidence of a systematic bias toward more conservative denominations in the BRS. For the thirty-seven groups for which comparison are possible between the BRS and GSS, the two surveys differ by less than 1 percent.[5] The largest differences were for Roman Catholics (the GSS had 4% more), Baptists (5% more in the GSS), and those with no religion (14.8% in the GSS, 11% in the BRS). Other religion indicators were equally comparable. Respondents to both surveys attend church at about the same rate, with BRS data having a slightly higher number that never attend.

With the exception of being slightly more educated on average than GSS respondents (16% of BRS respondents have had some graduate study compared to 10% in the GSS), our sample also looked very similar to the GSS with regards to employment status, marital status, and education. In sum, differences between the BRS and GSS were small and certainly not sufficiently worrisome as to suggest we have an overly religious sample that does not represent the general population.[6] We are confident that the BRS data can be used to present a portrait of current religious beliefs in the United States.

The Gallup Organization created weights for each wave using a ratio estimation program. By using a statistical algorithm, the overall (marginal) distributions as well as the interrelationships among several variables are simultaneously adjusted by assigning weights to individual respondents in order to bring all of the distributions into alignment with population parameters, or "true distributions" of these variables and their relationships with one another. The Gallup Organization used the most recent national data available from the Bureau of the Census Current Population Survey (CPS) for gender, race, region, age, and education. In the first step of the weighting a full weighting matrix of region by gender by age by education is derived from the CPS information. The second step involved a full weighting matrix of region by gender by race. All of our analyses are weighted using these constructed weight variables.

Field Research

In order to aid in our understanding of the subject of this book, we felt it necessary to supplement our statistical findings with field research. This book draws upon field research conducted by the lead researcher over the last twenty years and several new fieldwork endeavors engaged in specifically for this project.

Our methodologies varied by situation, but we most often engaged in participant observation by joining a group in its activities, whether that be a Bigfoot hunt or services at a Pentecostal church. We approached all potential subjects as social scientists interested in study paranormal and supernatural beliefs and experiences. At no time did we present ourselves as anything other than sociologists or attempt to claim a paranormal experience in question to gain increased access to a group.

Our descriptions of events are primarily based on our field notes. In some of these instances only one researcher was present. When more were present each took extensive field notes, which we then compared. At times our fieldwork led to other methods, such as the survey of TBRC conference attendees described in chapters 5 and 6.

In order to avoid bogging down this book in dates and locations, we have avoided discussing the exact details of different field excursions in the main body of the text. For the interested reader, the following is a list of key groups and locations and the dates on which we visited (see table A.1).

TABLE A.1

Summary of Fieldwork and Related Projects

Purpose	Location	Date(s)
Chapter 1		
Author (Baker) takes a course in ghost hunting	Greenville, TX	July 31, 2007
Overnight Ghost watch/hunt at the Big Cypress Coffee House	Jefferson, TX	December 5–6, 2007
Chapter 2		
Observation/participation in the Dallas Psychic Fair	Dallas, TX	December 7, 2008
Chapter 3		
Observation of the UFO Contact Center International, a UFO abduction support group	Federal Way, WA	1989–1991 1997–1998 December 12, 2009
Survey of members of the UFO Contact Center International	Mailed to affiliates of the UFOCCI around the U.S.	1990
Chapter 4		
Interview with Laura Cyr, UFO Contactee	Federal Way, WA	December 12, 2009
Chapter 5		
Observations of meetings and conferences of the Texas Bigfoot Research Conservancy (TBRC)	Tyler, TX	2005–2006
Bigfoot hunt with members of the TBRC	Big Creek Scenic Area, Sam Houston National Forest	December 8, 2006
Observation, presentation and survey administered at the 9th Annual Meeting of the TBRC	Tyler, TX	September 25–26, 2009
Chapter 7		
Observation of services at a small Pentecostal Church	Johnson City, TN	July 19. 2009
Observation of services at a small Pentecostal Church	Bruceville-Eddy, TX	August 26, 2009
Interviews with key figures in Paul Ingram ritual abuse case	Olympia, WA	1991
Meeting/interview with Paul Ingram	Portland, WA	July 20, 2009
Chapter 8		
Observations of and interviews with Datus Perry	Carson, WA	1989–1990

The Analyses

In chapters 3 through 8 we reference analyses that are not presented in the respective chapters. In this section we include more detail on those analyses. The analyses in those chapters used a standard set of predictor variables to estimate respondents reported paranormal beliefs, practices, and experiences. The standard model included both demographic and religiosity measures. Those measures, and their operationalization, are presented in table A.2.

Figures 3.6 and 3.7 present contingency analyses of paranormal beliefs by gender (3.6) and race/ethnicity (3.7). Table A.3 provides the chi-square and p values for each analysis. Each of the differences is statistically significant at the $p < .05$ level, with the exception of belief in the power of astrology by race/ethnicity categories.

TABLE A.2

Demographics

Gender, Age (measured in years), *Race* (White, African American, Other), *Marital Status* (5 categories): Currently married, single never married, divorced/separated, cohabitating, widowed.

Region

East
New England:	ME, NH, VT, MA, RI, CT
Middle Atlantic:	NY, NJ, PA, MD, DE, WV, DC

Midwest
East Central:	OH, MI, IN, IL
West Central:	WI, MN, IA, MO, ND, SD, NE, KS

South
Southeast:	VA, NC, SC, GA, FL, KY, TN, AL, MS
Southwest:	AK, LA, OK, TX

West
Rocky Mountain:	MT, AZ, CO, ID, WY, UT, NV, NM
Pacific:	CA, OR, WA

Education

What is the highest level of education you have completed?
1. 8th grade or less,
2. 9th–12th grade (no high school diploma)
3. High school only
4. Some college, trade/technical/vocational training
5. College degree (no postgraduate work)
6. Postgraduate degree

Income

By your best estimate, what was your total household income last year before taxes?
1. $10,000 or less,
2. $10,001 to $20,000,
3. $20,001 to $35,000
4. $35,000 to $50,000,
5. $50,000 to $100,000,
6. $100,001 to $150,000,
7. $150,000 or more

Religiosity Measures

CHURCH ATTENDANCE

How often do you attend religious services?
1. Never
2. Less than once a year
3. Once or twice a year
4. Several times a year
5. Once a month
6. 2–3 times a month
7. About weekly
8. Several times a week

RELIGIOUS TRADITION[a]

Includes the following 7 categories: Evangelical Protestants, Catholics, Black Protestants, Mainline Protestants, Jewish, Other religion, No religion.

BIBLICAL LITERALISM

Which ONE statement comes closest to your personal beliefs about the Bible?
1. The Bible is an ancient book of history and legends.
2. The Bible contains some human error.
3. The Bible is perfectly true, but it should not be taken literally, word for word. We must interpret its meaning.
4. The Bible means exactly what it says. It should be taken literally, word for word on all subjects.

BELIEFS ABOUT GOD

Which ONE statement comes closest to your personal beliefs about God?
1. I have no doubts that God exists.
2. I believe in God, but with some doubts.
3. I sometimes believe in God.
4. I believe in a higher power or cosmic force.
5. I don't believe in anything beyond the physical world.

[a] This measure uses the Steensland et al. (2000) model.

TABLE A.3
Chi-Square Values for Figures 3.6 and 3.7

	Figure 3.6: Gender		Figure 3.7: Race	
Atlantis	43.3	p < .001	31.2	p < .001
Telekinesis	23.8	p < .001	29.1	p < .001
Psychic powers	72.4	p < .001	20.4	p < .01
Astrology	58.8	p < .001	6.69	p = .57
Mediums	83.3	p < .001	41.3	p < .001
Ghosts	74.3	p < .001	20.3	p < .01
UFOs	29.3	p < .001	25.3	p < .01
Monsters	37.1	p < .001	45.1	p < .001

TABLE A.4

Fig. 3.10 Logistic Regression: Demographic and Religiosity Predictors of Paranormal Experiences

	Consulted horoscope	Consulted psychic	Haunted house	Out-of-body experience	Used Ouija board	Witnessed UFO
Demographics						
Female	1.073 ***	1.57 ***	0.422 **	0.041	1.135 ***	-0.097
White	-0.201	-0.257	0.062	-0.844 ***	-0.573	-0.392
Age	-0.023 ***	-0.008	-0.035 ***	-0.003	-0.032 ***	-0.0007
Education	-0.025	0.066	-0.052	0.085	-0.055	-0.007
Income	-0.028	-0.04	-0.27 ***	-0.239 ***	-0.205 **	-0.226 ***
Married	0.538 ***	0.206	-0.024	-0.189	0.026	0.252
Region of country						
East	0.31	0.356	-0.146	0.499 *	1.003 **	-0.25
South	0.001	-0.292	0.097	0.465 *	0.839 *	0.111
Midwest	0.309	-9	-0.11	0.266	0.492	-0.108
Religiosity						
Church attendance	-0.233 ***	-0.155 ***	-0.124 ***	-0.095 **	-0.158 ***	-0.111 ***
Religious tradition						
Catholics	0.155	0.163	0.24	0.221	0.153	-0.07
Evangelicals	-0.148	-0.104	-0.102	-0.189	-0.009	0.091
Black Protestant	-0.079	-2.169 *	-0.77	-0.298	-15.3	0.167
Jewish	0.439	-0.6	-0.3	-1.502	-0.743	0.225
Other religion	0.615 *	0.767 *	0.156	1.274 ***	0.661	0.567
No religion	-0.691 ***	-0.277	-0.675 **	0.235	-1.15 **	-0.453
Biblical literalism	-0.251 ***	-0.156	-0.242 **	-0.157	-0.385 **	-0.312 ***
Intercept	-1.4 *	2.72 ***	0.094	0.912	1.089	
R-square	0.213	0.18	0.169	0.112	0.212	0.094
N	1462	1462	1462	1462	1462	1462
Model chi-square	235.08 ***	146.91 ***	169.66 ***	95.577 ***	134.89 ***	83.789 ***

$* p < .05; ** p < .01; *** p < .001$

In table A.4 we present the regression analysis for figure 3.10, the key demographic predictors of paranormal experiences. Using the 2005 Baylor Religion Survey, we predict paranormal experiences using demographic, church attendance, religious tradition, and biblical literalism (see table A.2) to predict six paranormal experiences. These experiences are taken from the following questions on the 2005 Baylor Religion Survey:

Have you ever had an experience when you felt at one with the universe? (yes or no). Have you even had an experience where you felt that you left your body for a period of time? (yes or no). As an adult, have you ever consulted an Ouija board to contact a deceased person or spirit? (yes or no). As an adult, have you ever witnessed an object in the sky that you could not identify? (yes or no). As an adult, have you ever visited or lived in a house or place believed to be haunted? (yes or no). As an adult, have you ever called or consulted a medium, fortune-teller, or psychic? (yes or no). As an adult, have you ever consulted a horoscope to get an idea about the course of your life? (yes or no). Each of these variables were operationalized as a binary variable (1 = yes; 0 = no), and regression equations were estimated using logistic regression.

The parameter estimates for each are presented in table A.4.

In chapter 5 we present a contingency analysis of paranormal research activities by gender (fig. 5.3). Table A.5 presents the chi-square and p values for each bar chart in this graph. The data show that all relationships are statistically significant at p < .05.

Figure 5.8 shows the important predictors of who researches the paranormal. The data from that figure are presented in table A.6. In this analysis we use the base model of demographics and religiosity (not including beliefs in God) to predict the following:

Have you ever read a book, consulted a Web site, or researched:
Mediums, fortune-tellers, or psychics (yes or no)
UFO sightings, abductions, or conspiracies (yes or no)
Ghosts, apparitions, haunted houses, or electronic voice phenomena (yes or no)
Mysterious animals, such as Bigfoot or the Loch Ness Monster (yes or no)
Astrology (yes or no)
The prophecies of Nostradamus (yes or no)
The new age movement in general (yes or no)

Each variable was operationalized as a binary (yes = 1, no = 0) variable. Logistic regression was used to predict the probability of researching each of these topics. The parameter estimates are presented in table A.6.

TABLE A.5
Chi-Square Values for Figure 5.7: Gender and and Paranormal Research

	Chi-square	P value
The New Age	8.1	p < .01
Psychics, fortune tellers, mediums	45.6	p < .001
Astrology	38.1	p < .001
Prophecies of Nostradamus	15.5	p < .001
UFO sightings, abductions, conspiracies	38.1	p < .001
Bigfoot, Loch Ness Monster, and other creatures	7.1	p < .01

TABLE A.6

Fig. 5.8 Logistic Regression: Demographic and Religiosity Predictors of Paranormal Research

	UFOs	Psychic	Ghosts	Monsters	Astrology	Nostradamus	New Age
Demographics							
Female	−0.609 ***	1.23 ***	0.249	−0.286 *	1.056 ***	−0.339 **	0.64
White	−0.131	−0.561 *	−0.166	−0.183	−0.67 **	−0.405 *	−0.411 ***
Age	−0.007	−0.0126 *	−0.025 ***	−0.015 ***	−0.011 *	0.0013	0.0005
Education	0.063	0.109	0.039	0.051	0.015	−0.058	0.16
Income	−0.185 ***	−0.2249 ***	−0.181 ***	−0.12 *	−0.2 ***	−0.029	−0.239 **
Married	0.017	0.1928	0.276	0.204	0.443 *	−0.036	0.358 ***
Region of country							
East	0.003	0.215	−0.056	−0.033	0.073	−0.281	−0.824
South	−0.219	0.118	0.117	−0.273	−0.242	0.357 *	−0.138
Midwest	0.033	0.1	−0.159	−0.491 *	−0.102	0.244	−0.238
Religiosity							
Church attendance	−0.113 ***	−0.145 ***	−0.086 **	−0.071 *	−0.183 ***	−0.01 ***	−0.018
Religious tradition							
Catholics	−0.059	0.472	0.092	−0.036	−0.035	0.353 *	0.283
Evangelicals	0.047	−0.132	−0.02	0.031	−0.366	−0.211 *	0.216
Black Protestant	−0.391	−0.865	−1.26 **	−0.257	−0.459	−0.934 *	0.572
Jewish	−0.96	−0.478	−0.544	−0.912	−1.46 *	−0.914	0.292
Other religion	0.735 **	0.668	0.316	−0.07	0.257	0.359	1.209 ***
No religion	−0.149	−0.196	−0.674 **	−0.445	−0.869 ***	−0.645 **	0.315
Biblical literalism	−0.251 **	−0.343 ***	−0.304 ***	−0.228 **	−0.275 ***	−0.215 **	−0.65 ***
Intercept	1.28 *	0.049	1.962 ***	1.146 *	1.824 ***	0.925	−0.229
R-square	0.123	0.18	0.135	0.079	0.201	0.085	0.173
N	1462	1462	1462	1462	1462	1462	1462
Model chi-square	124.29 ***	146.27 ***	139.91 ***	76.42 ***	215.69 ***	88.614 ***	141.33 ***

* $p < .05$; ** $p < .01$; *** $p < .001$

Table A.7 shows an analysis that is used to support the conclusions presented in chapter 6. We present a count model that estimates the number of reported paranormal beliefs, and how this report varies by demographic and religiosity measures. Consistent with the conclusions presented in chapter 6, we find in the count analysis that those with more education and income report fewer paranormal beliefs, as do older respondents, males, and whites. Those who attend church more often also report fewer paranormal beliefs, as do those who take the Bible literally. Among Christians, Roman Catholics and Mainline Protestants report greater paranormal beliefs, while those with no religion report the fewest. Those with other religions report the greatest number of paranormal beliefs, all things equal. The data in table A.8 show the regression results that are used to generate conclusions for chapter 7.

Projections: Chapter 8

Here we project that the percent of the population reporting at least one paranormal belief will grow from 68 percent to 72.7 percent over the next thirty to forty years. We base this projection on the assumption that the relative effects of demographic and religiosity variables that predict the number of reported paranormal beliefs will not change over time. Working from this assumption, we create relative weights for each significant variable in table A.7 by multiplying the regression coefficient by the standard deviation of the respective variable, and dividing that product by the standard deviation of the dependent variables (number of reported paranormal beliefs). This quotient was then converted into the relative weight by estimating the total reduction in error under the null hypothesis is

TABLE A.7	
Chapter 6 Poisson Regression:	
Count of New Age Beliefs	
	Estimate
Demographics	
Female	0.194 ***
White	−0.247 ***
Age	−0.007 ***
Education	−0.028 *
Income	−0.051 ***
Married	−0.058
Region of country	
East	0.084
South	−0.004
Midwest	0.021
(West is omitted)	
Religiosity	
Church attendance	−0.049 ***
Religious tradition	
Catholics	0.247 ***
Mainline Protestant	0.181 ***
Black Protestant	−0.083
Other religion	0.393 ***
No religion	−0.177 ***
Biblical literalism	−0.083 ***
Log likelihood	717.4
N	1370
Reduction in error	0.23

* p<.05; ** p<.01; *** p<.001

TABLE A.8	
Chapter 7 Regression of Satan's Power on	
Demographic and Religiosity Predictors	
	Satan's power
Demographics	
Female	0.045
White	−0.238
Age	0.001
Education	−0.072 *
Income	−0.083 **
Married	0.078
Region of country	
East	−0.28 *
South	0.273 *
Midwest	−0.089
Religiosity	
Church attendance	0.219 ***
Religious tradition	
Catholics	−0.759 ***
Mainline Protestant	−0.829 ***
Black Protestant	0.038
Jewish	−1.515 ***
Other religion	−0.869 ***
No feligion	−1.206 ***
Biblical literalism	1.244 ***
Intercept	2.36 ***
R-square	0.2304 ***
N	1288

* p<.05; ** p<.01; *** p<.001

TABLE A.9
Relative Importance of Predictors of Paranormal Beliefs

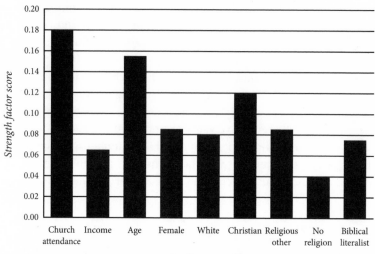

accounted for by each significant demographic and religiosity variable. Table A.9 provides the relative weights for each.

These weights are used in standardized fixed effects regression models where we first estimate a relative factor score based on the results from the BRS. Then we adjust the effects of the relative weights based on predicted changes in race/ethnic composition of the United States, changes in religious landscape, educational attainment and income, as well as church attendance and biblical literalism (the latter two we set at a very conservative 3% relative drop in the next thirty to forty years). We then re-estimate the model once these adjustments have been made. The last effort produced an overall 7 percent increase in the absolute value of the predicted relative factor score. If the adjustments in the demographic and religious composition of the United States occur as other scholars are predicting, then we expect that paranormal beliefs, on the aggregate level, will increase by 7 percent over the next thirty to forty years. We apply this factor to both the percent who currently believe in at least one paranormal phenomenon (68%) and the mean reported number of beliefs (2.1) and arrive out our speculation that the percent reporting paranormal beliefs by year 2050 will be 72.7 percent.

Notes

1. A number of factors contributed to Jefferson's decline including the development of the railroads and the removal of an enormous blockade of trees from the Red River by the U.S. Army Corps of Engineers. This last dropped the water level of the Big Cypress Bayou sufficiently as to make its use by large ships dangerous.

2. Wlodarski and Wlodarski (2001, 121).

3. See http://historicjeffersonhotel.com/ghost.htm.

4. Duane is using a turn of phrase here: we did not pay to spend the evening.

5. A Ouija board is a game board printed with letters and numbers. Users place their fingers upon a "planchette" (a piece of plastic with an acrylic window in the middle) and ask questions of the board. The planchette then moves around the board spelling out answers. Skeptics argue that the effects of the board are simply due to unconscious movement on the part of the users. Believers claim that the board opens a line of communication to the spirit world. Parker Brothers holds the patent on the design and markets an official version.

6. See Vigil (2006).

7. Ibid.

8. See Barrett (2001). Barrett references both Gallup data and the NORC General Social Survey.

9. See Goode (2000) for a discussion of popular perceptions of paranormal believers.

10. During an October 30, 2007, Democratic Presidential Debate in Philadelphia, the moderator Tim Russert asked Dennis Kucinich if he had seen a UFO. The question was prompted by the recent release of a book by Shirley MacLaine, which reported that Kucinich witnessed a large, triangular UFO hovering over her Washington State home in the 1980s. Kucinich admitted to the experience, noting that former president Jimmy Carter had also claimed a UFO sighting.

11. Most UFO researchers trace the beginnings of the modern age of UFO sightings to the June 1947 sighting by Private Kenneth Arnold. While flying over

the Cascade Mountains in Washington State, Arnold reported sightings of nine delta-shaped objects flying in formation. The story received extensive press coverage at the time.

12. The anthropologist David J. Daegling (2004) concludes that the existing evidence for Bigfoot is insufficient for proving the creature's existence.

13. Detailed sampling and methodological information about the Baylor Religion Survey is available from Bader, Mencken, and Froese (2007) and in the appendix.

14. See, for example, Mears and Ellison (2000); Wuthnow (1978); Glendinning (2006). Wuthnow (1978) is a sample of Berkley, CA; Mears and Ellison (2000) is a sample of Texas; Glendinning (2006) is a sample of Scotland.

15. See Laubach (2004) and Bainbridge (2004). Bainbridge is a nonrandom sample; Laubach (2004) is limited to paranormal experiences.

16. See, for example, Rice (2003); Orenstein (2002); McKinnon (2003). Each used data that are now at least ten years old.

17. Several religious groups with UFO-based theologies have appeared since in the 1950s, see chap. 4.

18. The phrase "superempirical," used by Smith (2003) in his theoretical treatise about the nature of morality and belief, is apt here.

19. See, for example: Stark and Bainbridge (1985); Lewis and Melton (1992).

20. Brown (1992), Lewis (1992).

21. Iannaccone (1995a).

22. Melton (1995).

23. Desmond and Adamski (1953).

24. See Sparks (2001); Orenstein (2002); or Bainbridge (2004) for an overview of these positions.

25. Graham (1992, 148). Note: est is a form of hypnotic therapy.

26. See Wuthnow (1978), Rice (2003).

27. See, for example, Donahue (1993); Orenstein (2002); Rice (2003); Sparks (2001).

28. Bainbridge (2004) and Orenstein (2002) have already begun to explore this possibility.

29. See Redfern (2004).

30. We are not the first to use the metaphor of a cafeteria to refer to people who sample a variety of different religious and supernatural beliefs and practices. See, for example, Roof, Carroll, and Roozen (1995). We must also note here that some people are interested in only one paranormal subject while others are interested in many, a topic we address in chap. 6.

31. Nathan (1991).

32. For example, the McMartin daycare abuse case, which received national attention (running from 1984 to 1990 including preliminary investigations) involved allegations that hundreds of children had been physically and sexually

abused at the hands of staff involved in Satanic ceremonies at the center. The case ultimately cost millions of taxpayers' dollars.

33. The appearance of the Church of Satan in the 1960s provided the media with endless tales and images for use in cautionary stories about the rise of Satanism. Popular films such as *Rosemary's Baby* projected the image of a secretive Satanic cult operated by powerful members of the upper class. Tales of Satanism also appeared in Christian literature throughout the 1960s and 1970s, such as Mike Warnke's (1972) *The Satan Seller*, in which he claims to have joined an underground Satanic cult in the 1960s, rising to the rank of high priest. Also famous in panic lore is *Michelle Remembers* (1980), co-written by a medical doctor. See Russell (1991) and Stevens (1991). The classic work on Satanic panic in sociology is Erikson's work on the Salem witch trials (1966).

34. See, for example, Victor (1994), Richardson, Best, and Bromley (1991).

35. The most famous examples of the real costs of a Satanic panic are the one hundred fifty accused witches imprisoned during the Salem witch trials, nineteen of whom were hanged.

NOTES TO CHAPTER 2

1. Many scholars have wrestled with the difficult task of developing a definition of what beliefs and ideas constitute New Age. See, for example, Lewis (1992); Melton (1992); Melton, Clark, and Kelly (1991) and tracing the historical roots of New Age concepts, Alexander (1992); Melton, Clark, and Kelly (1991).

2. To answer the reader's question before it is posed, neither of us saw anything. We seem to have bad luck that way—Bigfoot, ghosts, UFOs, and the like are never around when we show up to see them.

3. Evans (2002, 1). The cognitive anthropologist Pascal Boyer (2001) suggests that concepts such as ghosts are especially good at sticking around in people's memories, and therefore in culture as well.

4. Finucane (1984, 40–41).

5. This is not meant to suggest that there are no differences between the ghosts of today and the ghosts of yore. Some ghost motifs have fallen away over time, and the manner in which people interpret the meaning of ghosts has changed. We do not hear much today about a ghost appearing because it is angry to be sharing cemetery space with a sinner, a fairly common tale when a Christian burial was a privilege and the segregation of cemeteries common. See Finucane (1984, 43–44).

6. Sociologists have noted that consumption patterns often reveal their structural placement in the larger social fabric. See Bourdieu (1984).

7. Of course, certain genres complicate matters further. There have been many academic and/or skeptical explorations of New Age beliefs such as Hines (1988), Lewis and Melton (1992), Denzler (2001), and others that we would not consider examples of New Age beliefs. There is also a minor genre within Christian

publishing that examines New Age beliefs from a Christian perspective (often arguing that New Age phenomena are demonic in nature). See, for example, the books of Texe Marrs (1988, 1989, 1991, 2000), Cumby (1985), or Noonan (2005).

8. Indeed, at times New Age/paranormal topics have managed to attract the interest of prominent institutions and academics. For example, during the 1960s and 1970s, J. B. Rhine of Duke University conducted controlled experiments designed to test for evidence of ESP and psychokinesis. The late John Mack, a Harvard professor of psychiatry, interviewed purported UFO abductees and reported that such experiences could not be explained away as hallucinations or psychotic episodes. See Mack (1994). See Northcote (2007) for boundary maintenance between science and the paranormal. For a general overview of the cultural boundaries of science and their maintenance see Gieryn (1999).

9. Our definition is very similar to that used by Gray (1991) and Hines (1988). Goode (2000, 24) also notes a common thread shared by paranormal beliefs in that "traditional science regards their existence or validity as so improbable as to be all but impossible."

10. Goode (2000) would disagree with us here. He distinguishes between the paranormal, which by his definition would include astrology and psychic powers, and belief in Bigfoot, which he classifies as pseudo-science. We see no need to make this distinction for our purposes.

11. This is not to say that New Age beliefs or practices cannot become the focus of religious movements. Indeed, the belief in extraterrestrials has spawned several new religious movements, such as the Aetherius Society, Unarius, and the Raëlian movement. However, none of these movements have gained enough members to be a significant force in the American religious landscape.

12. For example, Evans (1984) includes a full chapter on religious visions, such as encounters with the Virgin Mary. However, he considers such visions to be similar in nature to experiences with extraterrestrials, ghosts, faeries, demons, the Men in Black, and so on. Connell (1996) recounts many of the same reported visions as Evans, but she treats such experiences as authentic encounters with the divine and proof of the tenets of Christianity. Consequently her book is filed in the religion section of most bookstores.

13. People who believe they have psychic powers use a variety of labels to describe themselves, including psychic, clairvoyant, sensitive, and intuitive.

14. Correspondence via email with the authors, January 2009.

15. The cyclical Mayan calendar ends in the year 2012, prompting concern among millennialists and New Agers that the world will end or dramatically change in 2012. Cheryl imagines 2012 as bringing great enlightenment to the world; others fear an apocalypse. As the Web site www.survive2012.com says "To some people this [2012] means a positive, spiritual change. [Others] consider that a catastrophic event may have been predicted."

16. Astral travel purportedly occurs when an individual's consciousness leaves

the body and travels to another location. Someone in the midst of astral travel might claim to view her body from above.

17. The powers attributed to different gems and stones vary depending upon the source consulted. For example, although a flyer from "Power of the Rainbow, a "rock shop" in Arlington, Texas, " told us that amethyst aids with psychic powers and dream recall, a guide to the mystical powers of gems and stones that we consulted suggested amethyst to control one's temperament (Edgar Cayce Foundation 1987, 11).

18. As of this writing, Daniel Weatherbee has a Web site at: http://www .authenticauraphoto.com/.

19. Weatherbee also acts as a clinical hypnotherapist, offering to hypnotize clients to help them quit smoking or lose weight.

20. Descriptions are from a flier, "Authentic Aura Photography," provided by Daniel Weatherbee.

21. See, for example, Melton, Clark, and Kelly (1991). Of course, there are benefits to having a committed membership over allowing experimentation. As Stark and Finke (2000) and Stark and Bainbridge (1985) note, religious organizations that require commitment from members tend to grow faster than those that do not. Making requirements of members chases away "free riders," those who want the rewards of church membership without providing anything in return (Iannaccone 1992). What remains is a committed core willing to give their time, money and effort toward growing the organization.

22. This is not to say that people interested in the New Age never develop a commitment to a particular belief or practitioner. Many develop longtime relationships with a certain psychic or spiritual therapist. But it appears assumed within the subculture that such relationships are not exclusive. Someone is free to search for other sources of enlightenment, even if he has regular meetings with a particular psychic.

23. Stark and Bainbridge (1985) note that much of the interest in New Age/paranormal phenomena occurs through the mass media and within a loosely organized lecture circuit, which they label as "Audience Cults" (26–27). Some beliefs gather enough momentum that they develop into "Client Cults," in which a practitioner provides a specific service (such as foretelling the future) in exchange for money (28–29).

24. Judging by what the readers charged for their services at their own establishments, the fair seemed to be a good deal for visitors. Two of the readers the authors consulted charged $75 and $80 for readings outside of the fair.

25. Flyer provided by the astrologer Leighton Haverty at a reading in December 7, 2008, in Dallas, Texas.

26. Paulos named the effect after the famous psychic Jeane Dixon. See Paulos (1991). Dixon wrote a bestselling book (*Jeane Dixon: My Life and Prophecies* [Wm. Morrow, 1969]), and she became famous for purportedly predicting the assassi-

nation of John F. Kennedy and consulting for Richard Nixon and the Reagans. Skeptics have long decried the fact that her many incorrect predictions (such as her prediction that World War III would start in 1958) were quickly forgotten in favor of publicizing her hits. Dixon died in 1997.

27. Cold reading is a technique used by mentalists, magicians, and some psychics, astrologers, and the like. It involves watching for very subtle cues in body language, facial expression, voice inflection, and even dress and appearance, which might provide insight into the personality. A reader adept at cold reading her client would greatly cut down on incorrect statements (assuming she is not actually using psychic means to acquire information).

28. Northcote (2007, 63).

29. Duane labels himself a high priest of Wicca and uses the spiritual name of "Gwydian," which means "Storm Brewer."

30. In our experience, photos of "orbs" are the evidence most commonly produced by ghost hunters. Searching the Internet for orb photos produces thousands of hits. Skeptics often contend that photos of orbs are the result of a camera flash or natural light reflecting off of dust particles.

NOTES TO CHAPTER 3

1. Irving (1981, 90).

2. For example, in November 1896 a dark structure encased in bright light slowly passed over Sacramento, Folsom, and San Francisco, California. See Story (1980, 8–9).

3. Denzler (2001, 7).

4. Ibid., 4.

5. Arnold and Palmer (1957, 10–11).

6. See Denzler (2001), 4. It should also be noted that the concept of extraterrestrial contact had a long tradition pre-Arnold. For example, some occult traditions involve the concept of communication with "spiritual masters" on other planets (see Lewis 2000, 28). Arnold's sighting, however, spurred massive public interest in the phenomenon. See Partridge (2003) for an excellent overview of extraterrestrials in occultic groups.

7. The origin of this term is also unclear (see Denzler 2001, 4). Of course, the term "UFO" simply refers to an object seen in the sky, which has not yet been conclusively identified. The object need not be extraterrestrial. In popular literature, however, a UFO is generally assumed to be from another world.

8. As Story (1980b, 14) notes, Charles Fort, Richard Shaver, Morris K. Jessup, and others put forth the thesis that extraterrestrials had visited Earth in ancient times. According to Story, it was Louis Pauwels and Jacques Bergier who first "enumerated and synthesized" supposed examples of ancient extraterrestrial contact in their 1960 book *The Morning of the Magicians* (New York, 1968).

9. We will not delve into the theories of author Zecharia Sitchin. Similar to Daniken, Sitchin hunts for examples of extraterrestrial intervention in Earth's history. However, he has developed a more cohesive cosmology than has Daniken. He believes that Sumerian culture is the product of interference by aliens from the planet Nibiru and who may one day return to reclaim the planet.

10. Palmer (2004).

11. This event drew media attention, but some thought it was a gimmick to attract young converts (Palmer 2004).

12. Daniken (1974b, 60).

13. For example Daniken (1974b, 41) includes an image of a twenty-inch high, Incan copper figure in a sun-shaped headdress. Strange features of the figure lead Daniken to an interesting conclusion. The figure has normal human proportions but "only four fingers and four toes on hands and feet. The serious scientific explanation? An adding machine!"

14. See Stiebing (1984) and Story (1980b) for critical discussions of ancient astronaut claims.

15. See Harrold and Eve (1995).

16. Lemuria and Mu are two additional lost "lands." They have not gained much currency in wider popular culture but are often subjects within the New Age/paranormal circles. The concept of Lemuria was originally proposed to explain the spread of species, particularly lemurs, fossils of which are found in India and Madagascar. However, this theory was rendered unnecessary with increased understanding of plate tectonics. The writings of the theosophist Helena Blavatsky resuscitated Lemuria as an occult concept. She claimed that a lost continent of Lemuria was home to a race of seven-foot-tall beings in ancient times (see Melton 1990, 258–61). Mu was popularized through the books of James Churchward, which drew upon legend, myth, and mysterious tables he claimed to have read at a temple in India. Similar to the legend of Atlantis, Mu was supposedly an ancient advanced civilization destroyed by a natural disaster. See Churchward (1938), which has been reprinted many times.

17. See Donnelly (1882).

18. We are indebted to J. Gordon Melton's (1990, 44–48) *New Age Encyclopedia* for its excellent summary of the Atlantis myth.

19. See, for example, Greeley (1975); Ben-Yehuda (1985); Saliba (1995); Hay and Morisy (1978); Orenstein (2002); MacDonald (1995).

20. For example, J. W. Fox (1992) does not find a relationship between income, age, race/ethnicity, or marital status and the number of reported paranormal experiences. He does find that education increases the likelihood of reporting a déjà vu experience and that females, on average, report more paranormal experiences more than males. See also Mencken, Bader, and Stark (2008).

21. See, for example, Wuthnow (1978); Hay and Morisy (1978).

22. Wuthnow (1978) examined correlates of the paranormal in San Francisco

and found that having an ESP-like experience varied slightly by age and education but not by race/ethnicity or gender.

23. A number of studies utilize samples of college students. See for example Weeks, Weeks, and Daniel (2008); Bainbridge and Stark (1981).

24. Stark and Bainbridge (1987) formalized the concept of religious compensators. A compensator is simply a belief or promise in a forthcoming reward. People can be motivated to work for compensators. For example, a parent may promise a child a reward for good grades ("A good report card earns you a trip to the pizza parlor, young lady!"). The hope is that the child will be sufficiently excited by the prospect of this reward that she will feel compensated for the hard work she must do *now*. Some compensators are more abstract, such as compensators humans have created to explain the meaning of human existence: "Act properly now and be rewarded with Heaven later."

25. Legerski, Cornwall, and O'Neil (2006); Phares (2001).

26. We also recognize the possibility that those who have high levels of an internal locus of control are the ones that are socially successful in the first place. As with most theoretical issues in the social sciences, we have an issue of reflexivity, wherein psychological dispositions influence the external actions and the results of these actions correspondingly influence psychological dispositions and patterns.

27. Ross and Mirowsky (2002).

28. Stinchcombe (1990).

29. See Pargament (1997); Schieman and Plickert (2008); Schieman and Bierman (2007); Schieman, Nguyen, and Elliot (2003); Schieman et al. (2006). Here, we are not talking about a pure sense of fatalism, where everything is determined by fate. See Caudill (1962); Whelan (1996).

30. Stark (2008).

31. Stark and Bainbridge (1981).

32. Chaves (2004).

33. J. W. Fox (1992).

34. Saliba (1995).

35. See Kemp (1994).

36. Women in general are more religious and spiritual than men on most measures. See Miller and Hoffman (1995); Stark (2002). Perhaps spirituality is perceived as a form of femininity, making women more likely to embrace paranormal beliefs. See also Sjodin (2002); Stark (2002) for review. Novel religious movements tend to be quite disproportionately female (Stark and Bainbridge 1985). Women may also be less stigmatized than men when they report such beliefs (Stark 2002, Mears and Ellison 2000; J. W. Fox 1992).

37. See the appendix.

38. The Hill sighting was, in fact, investigated by Project Blue Book, a now-

defunct U.S. government project to investigate UFOs based at Wright Patterson Air Force Base in Ohio. The project concluded that the Hills likely misidentified the planet Jupiter. See Clark (1996, 238).

39. See Clark (1996, 242).

40. See Fuller (1966, 87).

41. Ibid., 260.

42. The "star map" became one of the most controversial aspects of the case. In 1968 the school teacher Marjorie Fish attempted to match the stars in Betty's drawing to known systems. By creating a three-dimensional representation of the map, Fish became convinced that the aliens' home planet was in the neighborhood of Zeta Reticuli 1 and 2. See Rimmer (1984, 88–92) and Klass (1989, 21–23).

43. Fuller (1966, 188).

44. Arguably the first UFO encounter involving abduction was also reported by Antonio Villa Boas, a farmer. In 1957 he claimed that aliens pulled him aboard their ship wherein he had intercourse with a humanlike woman (see Spencer 1991). However, Boas's tale did not become widely known until after the Hills achieved fame.

45. Hopkins (1981, 401).

46. We should note a few caveats here. One early abductee Betty Andreasson did claim multiple contacts with the same gray beings. However, her experience was more similar to contactee tales (with friendly interactions) than the horrifying tales of abduction that had become so popular in the 1980s. Her mixture of contactee and abduction elements were more popular in the 1990s. See Fowler (1979) for a discussion of the Andreasson events (which were continued in a series of further books). Further, Betty Hill did believe that she had seen alien craft after her encounter, though she never claimed another abduction-type experience (see Hill 1995, chap. 14).

47. Hopkins (1981, 214).

48. Hopkins (1987, 282).

49. See Lavigne (1995), Bryant and Seebach (1991) and Mitchell (1994) for some examples of UFO abduction therapy manuals.

50. See Klass (1989).

51. See Pritchard et al. (1992) for the proceedings of this conference. Note that although the conference took place at MIT, most of the presenters were not, in fact, academics. Many were UFO authors or researchers such as Budd Hopkins and Jenny Randles, and/or people who claimed UFO abductions.

52. Edwards (1988, ii).

53. Brochure produced by the UFO Contact Center International, Federal Way, Washington.

54. The author observed the UFOCCI at intermittent monthly meetings between 1989 and 1997.

55. Conroy (1989, 279).

56. The case of Betty Andreasson (see n. 46) is one of the earliest examples of a reported positive abduction-type encounter. See Fowler (1979).

57. Boylan and Boylan (1994, 4).

58. For full details of this project see Bader (2003).

59. In our reading of the UFO literature, abductions remain a primarily "white affair." The authors are aware of very few African American abductees.

60. Our numbers for average Americans are from the 1990 General Social Survey. For full tables, see Bader (2003).

61. See Larsen (1962).

62. Historically speaking, the New Age movement represents a relatively recent idea in the American religious marketplace. While some argue that it has an origin in the nineteenth-century spiritualist movement (Hess 1993), Melton (1992) traces the modern New Age movement to the counterculture of the 1960s and the elimination in 1965 of the Asian Exclusion Act. What ideas and beliefs actually constitute the New Age is the source of academic debate (Lewis and Melton 1992).

63. See Ben-Yehuda (1985); Greeley (1975); MacDonald (1995).

64. See Smelser (1962); Stark and Bainbridge (1985); Wuthnow (1978).

65. Kelly (1992) notes that new religious movements tend to be created by those that express creativity in all other fields—middle- and upper-class intellectuals. See also Mencken, Bader, and Stark (2008).

66. O'Dea (1957).

67. Alexander (1992).

68. Melton (1992).

69. Adler (1979).

70. See Hirschi (1969). Hirschi's Social Control Theory speaks to this issue (see also chap. 6 for more on his work).

71. Zeleney (2008).

72. Cornwell (2003).

73. In a 2000 interview with AlienZoo.com.

74. We must recognize that schizophrenics (or those with other severe mental issues) may be unlikely to complete a sixteen-page questionnaire and mail it in. So it is at least theoretically possible that a host of mentally unstable paranormal experiences are unaccounted for.

75. Lofland and Stark (1965) outline a step-by-step process by which a person would be likely to affiliate with a deviant religious group. They note that the potential convert must be at a "turning point" in life; a time in which their life is undergoing dramatic changes that may lead to the search for answers. For example, the death of a loved one might lead one to search for new answers to the meaning of life. By observing some of the original converts to the Unification Church (popularly known as the Moonies), Lofland and Stark outlined seven progressive

steps necessary for conversion. Brainwashing is not one of them. More recently see Cowan (2008) and Anthony and Robbins (2004).

NOTES TO CHAPTER 4

1. Italic emphasis added.

2. According to the Baylor Religion Survey, Wave 1 (2005), 22 percent of Americans report that they never attend religious services; 29 percent report that they attend less than once a year, once or twice a year, or several times a year. The remaining half of Americans attend once a month, two to three times a month, about once a week, weekly, or several times a week. Percentages do not add up to 100 percent due to rounding error.

3. When coding the reported religious traditions of Americans, 21 percent report being a Catholic, 5 percent belong to a traditionally African American Protestant denomination, 34 percent belong to Evangelical denominations such as the Southern Baptists and Assemblies of God and another 22 percent to Main-line denominations such as the Presbyterian Church USA and Episcopal Church. The remaining 18% of Americans are split between various branches of Judaism (3 percent), those in other religions such as Hinduism, Buddhism and smaller groups such as Wicca (5 percent). The remaining 11 percent report having no religion. See Steensland et al. (2000) for a discussion of religious traditions in the United States.

4. When asked if they believe in God, 69 percent believe in God without doubts. Another 12 percent believe in God, although they may occasionally have doubts. Fourteen percent believe in a "cosmic force." The remaining 4 percent do not believe in anything beyond the physical world.

5. Leslie and Adamski (1954, 172).

6. Ibid., 188.

7. Ibid., 194–95.

8. Ibid., 197.

9. Clark (1992, 3).

10. Adamski recounts details of this meeting in his final book *Flying Saucers Farewell* (1961). Adamski also claimed to have met Pope John XXIII in May 1963, but the Vatican denied such a meeting occurred. See Clark (1992, 4).

11. Adamski (1961, 110).

12. Clark (1992, 4).

13. In addition to the examples provided in this chapter, there were dozens of contactees. Some of the more famous examples include Howard Menger, Orfeo Angelucci, Frank Stanges, Robert Short, Cedric Allingham, and Buck Nelson.

14. See Tumminia (2005, 3) for a detailed definition of UFO contactee religion.

15. King formed the Aetherius Society (www.aetherius.org) in 1956 after claim-

ing that a "Master of Yoga" had helped him develop the ability to communicate with a Venusian named Aetherius. See Saliba (2003, 129) and Scribner and Wheeler (2003, 157).

16. See King (1961, 11) for this tale.

17. Brown (1992) notes that New Age belief systems draw upon many religious traditions, including Eastern and Judeo-Christian beliefs.

18. Stark and Iannaccone (1997).

19. Bushman and Bushman (1999).

20. The LDS Church grew by 19 percent in the United States alone between 1990 and 2000, placing it in the top twenty-five fastest growing denominations in the United States for that time period. See the Associated of Religion Data Archives: http://www.thearda.com/mapsReports/reports/US_compare_change.asp.

21. Palmer (2004).

22. See Goode (2000) and Bainbridge (2004).

23. In Wuthnow's (1978, 71) analysis of the relationship between religious experiences and ESP beliefs, he concludes that "one kind of supernatural belief reinforces another." See Mencken, Bader, and Kim (2009).

24. Chapter 7 discusses *religious* experiences, such as speaking in tongues and miraculous healings.

25. Steensland et al. (2000) further subdivide Protestants into Mainline Protestants, Evangelical Protestants, and Black Protestants.

26. Green et al. (1996).

27. Iannaccone is one of several scholars that have developed the so-called rational choice perspective on religion. See Iannaccone (1992, 1995a, 1995b), Stark and Bainbridge (1987), Stark and Finke (2000).

28. Iannaccone (1995a), 285.

29. Ibid., 288.

30. We will provide a different perspective on the holding of diverse religious portfolios in chap. 6—another reason why people may experiment with the paranormal is having a low stake in conformity, of which religion plays a part.

31. Iannaccone (1992); Iannaccone (1995a).

32. Iannaccone (1995a), 287.

33. Of course, there are some paranormal writers who believe that UFOs are mentioned throughout the Bible. See chap. 8.

34. Bainbridge (2004).

35. A host of books from a Christian perspective address the perceived threat of the New Age. Among these are *Ransomed From Darkness: The New Age, Christian Faith, and the Battle for Souls* (Noonan 2005); *Des Masquerade: An Expose on Satan in the New Age Movement* (Hardy 1999); *Inside the New Age Nightmare* (Baer 1989); *The Hidden Dangers of the Rainbow: The New Age Movement and Our Coming Age of Barbarism* (Cumbey 1985); and multiple titles from the author Texe Marrs.

36. Rabey (1988).

37. Rhodes (1998, 198–99). Emphases and quotes in original.

38. See, for example, Larson (1997).

39. Lesage (1998).

40. Hutchings, Spargimino, and Glaze (2000), 156.

41. Historically, African American denominations, such as the African Methodist Episcopal Zion Church, tend to be theologically conservative but socially progressive. Approximately one-fifth (18 percent) of Americans do not belong to a Christian denomination but (see the chart) are Jewish, another religion such as Hinduism, Buddhism, Islam, or any number of small, religious movements, and those who claim no religion.

42. Stark and Bainbridge (1980) hypothesized that Christian and paranormal beliefs are negatively related and found that paranormal beliefs tend to be strongest in areas where traditional Christianity tends to be weak and vice versa. Wuthnow (1978) and Hess (1993) make similar arguments.

NOTES TO CHAPTER 5

1. See Charles Y. Glock and Rodney Stark (1965), 23–35.

2. Organizations such as the Committee for Skeptical Inquiry (www.csicop .org) are devoted to trying to inject skeptical discourse about the paranormal into the public sphere. There are also a number of celebrities, such as James Randi (The Amazing Randi) and Benjamin Radford, who regularly appear as the skeptical voice on programs related to paranormal subjects. The late Philip J. Klass was a thorn in the side of UFO believers for years.

3. Daegling (2004, 233–34).

4. See Coleman (2003) for an overview of Native American traditions related to Bigfoot. See also Rigsby (1977).

5. Eberhart (2002, 473).

6. Bord and Bord (1982, 17) includes an excellent historical overview of Bigfoot sightings reported in the 1800s.

7. Roosevelt's book is the only original source for this tale, and he did not provide a full name for Bauman or his partner. The story has been repeated countless times in books about Bigfoot.

8. Our version of this tale is from a reissue of Roosevelt's book, Roosevelt (1927).

9. Beck's encounter was first reported by the Portland *Oregonian* on July 13, 1924, under the title "Fight with Big Apes Reported by Miners." The article was reproduced in J. Green (1980, 45). In 1967 Beck self-published his own version of the events. The above quote is from Beck (1967, 2)

10. Ibid., 4.

11. For example, those who desire to visit Ape Canyon can visit the Ape Canyon

Trail in the Gifford Pinchot National Forest (http://www.fs.fed.us/gpnf/recreation/trails/locations/msh-0234-ape-canyon.shtml).

12. The Bigfoot researcher John Green was contacted by Albert Ostman in 1957, after Ostman saw stories written by Green in the newspaper.

13. This tale is repeated in several Bigfoot-related books, including Coleman (2003) and J. Green (1980).

14. The contractor on the Klamath job was Ray Wallace. As Coleman (2003, 66–74) notes, Wallace ultimately became notorious for his Bigfoot hoaxes.

15. Indeed, much of Bigfoot's earlier history coalesced after the Crew incident, as people who claimed pre-1958 experiences came forward and Bigfoot enthusiasts scanned newspaper archives. See Daegling (2004, 24–33).

16. For reasons of space we cannot adequately cover Bigfoot's history. For example, entire books have been devoted to the dissection of a purported film of Bigfoot taken by Roger Patterson and Bob Gimlin in 1967. See also Patterson and Murphy (2005) and Long (2004). Interested readers are referred to J. Green (1978), Coleman (2003), and Daegling (2004).

17. The Seattle Supersonics moved to Oklahoma City before the 2008/2009 season, where they are now known as the Oklahoma City Thunder.

18. Eberhart (2003, 52).

19. Bigfoot's reported appearance has changed over time. Some of the earliest reported encounters (such as the Ape Canyon incident) feature creatures that could best be described as Neanderthal in appearance. Today Bigfoot is typically reported with more gorilla-like features.

20. For example, the purported film of Bigfoot taken by Patterson and Gimlin shows a hairy creature with obvious breasts (see n. 16). The late William Roe provide a sworn account of his sighting of a female Bigfoot in British Columbia (see J. Green 1978, 52–56).

21. www.bfro.net

22. See Farnsworth (1996), Murphy (2006), Opsasnick (2004), Holyfield (1999), Michael (undated), J. Smith (2003) and M. Green (2002), respectively.

23. The late Grover Krantz of Washington State University and Jeffrey Meldrum of Idaho State University, both anthropologists, are among the few academics who have openly supported the possibility of Bigfoot's existence.

24. See Quast (2000).

25. Baylor Religion Survey, Wave 1 (2005)

26. See Mears and Ellison (2000), and Denzler (2004).

27. Of course, the fact that the hunts for Bigfoot and UFOs have not, to date, provided conclusive physical evidence is one of the primary arguments against their reality used by skeptics.

28. Quote from Craig Woolheater's online bio at the Bigfoot-related Web site *Cryptomundo.* http://www.cryptomundo.com/craigwoolheater/.

29. This is, indeed, the same town that claims the Big Cypress Coffee House and numerous other haunted locations. Apparently Jefferson is a promising location in which to begin a paranormal investigation.

30. Retrieved from Melissa Hovey's blog "The Search for Bigfoot" (http://txsasquatch.blogspot.com/2009/05/when-it-rains-it-pours.html). John Green is considered a pioneer of Bigfoot research. His book *Sasquatch: The Apes among Us* was the first Bigfoot book owned by many enthusiasts we talked to.

31. Many Bigfoot books provide an account of the Patterson-Gimlin encounter. See for example, Patterson and Murphy (2005, 184–87).

32. Various Bigfoot experts (skeptical, believers, and undecided) have attempted to estimate the height of the creature in the Patterson-Gimlin film via various means. Their estimates range from the late Grover Krantz's calculation of 6 feet tall to Jeff Glickman's estimate of 7.3 feet in height. See Patterson and Murphy (2005, particularly 234) for a discussion of varying height estimates. See also Long (2004, 383–84).

33. Patterson died in 1972.

34. See, for example, Long (2004) and Patterson and Murphy (2005) for books about the Patterson-Gimlin film. Almost every Bigfoot book that discusses the phenomenon in general discusses that film, at least in passing.

35. When asked "How credible do you find the following pieces of evidence for Bigfoot's existence: The Patterson-Gimlin Film," 57 percent of respondents selected "very credible," 24 percent "somewhat credible," 8 percent "doubtful," 2 percent "probably untrue," 2 percent "a hoax," and 9 percent said "I don't know what this is."

36. The TBRC helped us to prepare this list, which included the items mentioned above and others, such as the Patterson-Gimlin film dermal ridges.

37. MMORPGs are Massively Multiplayer Online Role-Playing Games, or games in which the player connects to a server hosting the game and creates a character. He then plays the game alongside other players—in most cases fighting monsters in a fantasy world to acquire treasure and become more powerful. World of Warcraft is the most popular such game (so far) with several million players. In turn-based combat, combat takes place in turns or rounds with the focus upon strategy. In real-time combat all participants attack simultaneously, thus there is a greater focus upon speed and movement.

38. A residual haunting is akin to a videotape—it is believed that a traumatic event might somehow be imprinted upon an environment and "replayed" at particular times. The ghost(s) involved in a residual haunting are not assumed to have independent thought. An intelligent haunting involves ghosts that are aware of their surroundings. Here, a ghost could theoretically choose when, where, and to whom it appears. Human entities are assumed to be the ghosts of deceased humans. Inhuman entities are assumed to be demons or elementals. EVP stands for

electronic voice phenomena. Many ghost hunters carry handheld tape recorders around haunted sites hoping that the voice ghost will appear on their recordings.

39. Legget (2009).

40. By our accounting Keith personally consumed five large sausages, two packages of beef jerky, and a rack of ribs in twenty-four hours. He earned the appellation "Dr. Meat."

41. David had warned us several times about the bitter cold we would experience, but we never spent the evening outdoors in a Texas winter.

42. For the full report of this excursion, see http://www.texasbigfoot.org/reports/report/detail/455 .

NOTES TO CHAPTER 6

1. This 68 percent is a conservative estimate. We coded all of those who did not respond to the paranormal belief questions as nonbelievers. Therefore, our numbers represent the percentage of Americans willing to go on record in a survey as believing in paranormal phenomena. It is possible that some of those respondents who did not answer these questions also have paranormal beliefs. Since they did not state so when given the opportunity to respond to this survey, we are going to classify them as nonbelievers.

2. Email correspondence with Laura Cyr.

3. Ibid.

4. See Buhs (2009, 199–203) for a discussion of this issue.

5. Meldrum (2006), 45.

6. UFO researcher Stan Gordon provides his summary of the events on his Web site: http://web.archive.org/web/20051028050624/http://www.westol.com/~paufo/features/scary+ufo+story.htm

7. For an example of a blog devoted to a paranormal theory of Bigfoot, see http://www.blogcatalog.com/blog/frame-352.

8. Johnson and Shapiro (1987, 10).

9. Ibid., 28.

10. Many of the arguments made by believers in a biological version of Bigfoot highlight that they believe there are only a handful of these creatures in existence. To this they add that the animals would presumably be found in very dense and forest area uninhabited by humans, and that the Bigfeet are very intelligent, purposefully avoiding humans. Additionally they point to the immense number of sightings as evidence that humans have in fact encountered these creatures at various points.

11. Several other Bigfoot researchers have hypothesized that this creature is not simply an undiscovered ape. For example, Jack Lapseritis claims to have developed a psychic link with both friendly Bigfoot creatures and extraterrestrials (see Lapseritis 2005). Clark and Coleman (2006) outline several cases in which

Bigfoot emerged from a flying saucer or appeared to exhibit the ability to disappear into thin air.

12. For example, the authors attended a November 2006 monthly meeting of TBRC meetings in Tyler, Texas. A good portion of the meeting was devoted to relating the case of a man who believed that a camera he had placed near a deer feeder had captured pictures of a Bigfoot's eyes glowing in the darkness. TBRC investigators were able to demonstrate that the "eyes" were merely reflections off of the deer feeders.

13. One comes away with very different ideas about Bigfoot depending upon the books that one reads. Books by authors that prefer a naturalistic explanation for Bigfoot often do not include cases that suggest a connection between Bigfoot and UFOs and other phenomena or which strip those cases of untoward elements. For example, in chapter 5 we discussed Fred Beck's claim that several Bigfeet attacked his mining cabin in 1924. In his book Beck claims that he is a clairvoyant and once talked to the "Great Spirit" in a cave. He also reports that Bigfoot will never be caught because the creature can become immaterial. The Beck case is considered a classic and appears in nearly every Bigfoot book.

14. Zahn and Sagi (1987) and Jenkins (1994).

15. See Canter, Missen, and Hodge (1996) and J. A. Fox and Levin (1999).

16. Taylor and Sorenson (2002).

17. Hirschi (1969).

18. Hirschi's control theory owes a particular debt to the works of Reiss (1951), Nye (1958), Reckless (1962), and Toby (1957).

19. The concept of a "stake in conformity" first appeared in Toby's study of academic achievement. Toby argued that youth who are doing poorly in school would be more likely to break the law. Students with low academic achievement, he argued, risk less by engaging in deviance than students who perform well in school. Therefore, such students will be more likely to give in to the temptation to engage in deviance. A key predictor of deviance then, is the extent to which a person is invested in conformity. The greater someone's "stake in conformity," the more they risk by engaging in deviance, and the less attractive deviance becomes. Toby (1957).

20. Wu and Hart (2002); Sherman, Smith, Schmidt, and Rogan (1992).

21. Respondents to the Baylor Religion Survey, Wave 1 (2005) were asked how they felt about the morality of a number of different behaviors. When asked about "Living with a partner before marriage," 26.8 percent said that it is "always wrong," 11.9 percent said it is "almost always wrong," 18.1 percent believe that living together is "only wrong sometimes." The remaining 43.2 percent report that living together is "not wrong at all." The question, however, assumes marriage at some point, "living together *before marriage*." It is likely that Americans are more conservative when it comes to beliefs about cohabitation as a permanent lifestyle choice.

22. Abramowitz and Saunders (2006).

23. See, for example, Greeley (1995); Stark (2001); Bader and Froese (2005); Froese and Bader (2007, 2008); Froese, Bader, and Smith (2008).

24. See discussion in Vold, Bernard, and Snipes (1998).

NOTES TO CHAPTER 7

1. For example, in *Spellbound: The Paranormal Seduction of Today's Kids*, Montenegro (2006) notes that the purported effects of Ouija boards may be the result of the unconscious mind or involuntary body movements by the participants. She then puts forth another possibility "[another] view should be the biblical one—that in some cases, the responses are from fallen angels. This would explain some of the strange and dangerous experiences people have had when using the board" (187).

2. See http://transcripts.cnn.com/TRANSCRIPTS/0808/17/se.01.html for a full transcript of the forum at Saddleback Church.

3. See Wilcox, Linzey, and Jelen (1991) and Wilson and Huff (2001). Swatos (1988) found the belief that Satan is responsible for pornography is related to the picketing of stores carrying erotic materials.

4. Kai Erikson provides an excellent overview of the Salem witch trials, as well as a classic study in theories of deviance. In seventeenth-century Massachusetts almost everyone followed strict codes of conduct, and there was little fear of violence or crime within the community. However, this bucolic life fostered the birth of a wholly fictitious moral enemy—the dreaded witch. Yet, instead of tearing the community apart, Erikson argues that these acts of betrayal and murder strengthened the unity and resolve of the "good" colonists. Erikson (1966).

5. See Goode and Ben-Yehuda (1994).

6. Sarah Good, Sarah Osborne, and a slave named Tituba were the first to be accused of being witches. Good was impoverished and often begged neighbors for food. Osborne rarely attended the local church and had married her servant. Tituba was dark skinned, of South American descent, and had lived in the Caribbean, adding rumors of voodoo to her already outcast racial and social statuses.

7. Wright (1994, 24–25).

8. Ibid., 59.

9. Thurston County Sheriff's Office (1989a).

10. Ibid., 1988, 14.

11. In his report Ofshe (1989) notes that prior to the charges against her father, Erika made a charge of improper sexual advances against a church youth counselor while at a church retreat. Curiously, Erika reported the advances to Jim Rabie, who at that time was head of the Thurston County sex crimes department. She eventually dropped the charges against the counselor.

12. Ofshe (1989, 2–3).

13. Ibid., 7.

14. Thurston County Sheriff's Office (1988b, 14).

15. Ibid., 48.

16. Expletives replaced with asterisks.

17. Jacobsen (1989, 1).

18. See Russell (1991), Stevens (1991), and Victor (1993) for historical overviews of Satanism and witchcraft panics.

19. The mean "evil score" for people who believe the Bible is an ancient book of stories and fables is .36, compared to 4.1 for those who believe the Bible to be the literal word of God.

20. See Krause and Chatters (2005); Pargament (1997); Pargament and Hahn (1986); Spilka et al. (2003).

21. Lupfer, Tolliver, and Jackson (1996).

22. Woodberry and Smith (1998).

23. Pentecostals are often confused with Charismatics. Both Pentecostals and Charismatics have a strong focus upon personal religious experiences, but the two movements have different histories. The Pentecostal movement began in the early 1900s with the ministry of the Rev. Charles Parham of Topeka, Kansas. It ultimately spawned several distinct denominations such as the Assemblies of God, Church of God Mountain Assembly, and the Holiness Church of God, among others. See Cox (1995) for an overview of the Pentecostal movement. Any congregation—regardless of affiliation—might contain a charismatic movement. For example, in 1959 a small group of Episcopalians in a California church began speaking in tongues, ultimately resulting in the First National Episcopal Charismatic Conference in 1973 (Rosten 1975, 591; see also Melton and Baumann 2002).

24. See Melton (2003) and Poloma (1989).

25. Both the 1990 National Survey of Religious Identity (Kosmin and Lachman 1993) and the 2001 American Religious Identity Survey (Kosmin, Mayer, and Keysar 2001) included a question that asked respondents if they identify with the label "Pentecostal/charismatic." This resulted in an estimated 3.2 million in 1990, and 4.4 million by 2001 (about 1.8% of the adult population and 2.1% of the Christian population in 1990, and 2.1% of the adult population or 2.8% of the Christian population in 2001). The 2007 BRS reports that 5.3 percent of respondents answered that the term "Pentecostal" described them "very well," indicating the rising popularity of this form of Christianity.

26. The experiences examined here are all "intense" religious experience that involve the direct intervention of the supernatural in the physical world or an experience that transcends religious feeling alone. Other experiences such as "being filled with the spirit" or "feeling called by God to do something" deserve inquiry in their own right but will not be considered here. See Baker (2009) for a discussion of the distinction between deviant and normative religious experiences and multivariate analyses of these issues.

27. For example, only 11 percent of those who never attend church reported

one or more of these experiences, compared to nearly 65 percent of those who attend more than once a week.

28. We use pseudonyms for the name of the church and its members.

29. Stark and Bainbridge (1987).

30. For an introduction to this line of inquiry see Chaves (2004); Iannaccone (1988); Niebuhr ([1929] 1957); Troeltsch ([1912] 1932); Weber ([1922] 1991).

31. In the first wave of the Baylor Religion Survey (2005) we asked respondents if they had seen the television show *Touched by an Angel*. Fifty-seven percent had seen the show.

32. See Boyer (2004); Kaneko (1990); Scott (1977); Trachtenberg ([1939] 2004); Williams (1980).

33. For definitions and discussions of what constitutes religious experiences cf. Hood et al. (1996); Glock and Stark (1965); James ([1902] 1961); Poloma (1995); Proudfoot (1985); Yamane (1998, 2000).

NOTES TO CHAPTER 8

1. See Sagan (1997) and Shermer (2002).

2. Thirty-two percent of the 2005 BRS sample reported neither agreed nor strongly agreed with the possibility of any of the nine following paranormal phenomena: (a) that Atlantis or other ancient advanced civilizations once existed, (b) telekinesis, (c) psychic abilities, (d) predictive power of astrology, (e) communication with the dead, (f) UFOs, (g) monsters such as Bigfoot, (h) we are approaching a radical new age, and (i) haunting.

3. Passel and Cohn (2008).

4. Cheeseman Day and Bauman (2000).

5. Stark (2008).

6. See Sherkat (2001).

7. Kaufmann (forthcoming).

8. Froese and Bader (2007).

9. The methodology for these estimates is reported in the appendix. Also, we want to caution that this prediction assumes that the relative importance of the demographic and religiosity variables will not change over the next thirty to forty years, an assumption that will obviously open our estimates to criticism from future sociologists.

NOTES TO THE APPENDIX

1. The National Opinion Research Center (NORC) has conducted the General Social Survey (GSS) since 1972. The GSS was administered to random samples of the U.S. population on a yearly basis from 1972 to 1994 with the exceptions of 1979, 1981, and 1992. Starting in 1994 the survey has become biannual with ad-

ministrations in 1994, 1996, 1998, 2000, 2002, 2004, and most recently 2006. The GSS provides in-depth coverage on particular topics through the use of rotating content modules. It has included content modules on religion on several occasions. For example, in 1988 the GSS included a special module on religion with items related religious socialization (e.g., religion in the family) and religious beliefs and behaviors.

2. For details of the methodology behind the Baylor Religion Survey, see Bader, Mencken, and Froese. (2007). .

3. A copy of the mailed survey instrument can be found at www.baylor.edu/isr.

4. See the American Association for Public Opinion Research (2006).

5. We were unable to definitively located respondents in the GSS 2004 that were Baha'i, Chinese folk religion, Christian and Missionary Alliance, Christian Science, or Salvation Army.

6. For a full report on how BRS respondents compare to the GSS, see Bader, Mencken, and Froese (2007).

References

Abramowitz, Alan J., and Kyle L. Saunders. 2006. "Exploring the Bases of Partisanship in the American Electorate: Social Identity vs. Ideology." *Political Research Quarterly* 59:175–87.

Adamski, George. 1955. *Inside the Space Ships*. New York: Abelard-Schuman.

———. 1961. *Flying Saucers Farewell*. New York: Abelard-Schuman.

Adler, Margot. 1979. *Drawing Down the Moon: Witches, Druids, Goddess-Worshippers, and Other Pagans in America Today*. New York: Penguin.

Alexander, K. 1992. "Roots of the New Age." In *Perspectives on the New Age*, ed. James R. Lewis and J. Gordon Melton, 30–58. Albany: State University of New York Press.

Anthony, Dick, and Thomas Robbins. 2004. "Conversion and 'Brainwashing' in New Religious Movements." In *The Oxford Handbook of New Religious Movements*, ed. J. R. Lewis, 243–97. New York: Oxford University Press.

Angelucci, Orfeo. 1955. *The Secret of the Saucers*. Amherst, WI: Amherst Press.

Arnold, Kenneth, and Ray Palmer. 1957. *The Coming of the Saucers*. Boise, ID and Amherst, WI: self-published.

Auerbach, Loyd. 2003. *How to Investigate the Paranormal*. Berkeley, CA: Ronin.

Bader, Christopher. 2003. "Supernatural Support Groups: Who are the UFO Abductees and Ritual Abuse Survivors?" *Journal for the Scientific Study of Religion* 42(4): 669–78.

Bader, Christopher, and Paul Froese. 2005. "Images of God: The Effect of Personal Theologies on Moral Attitudes, Political Affiliation, and Religious Behavior." *Interdisciplinary Journal of Research on Religion* 1, article 11:v.

Bader, Christopher D., F. Carson Mencken, and Paul Froese. 2007. "American Piety 2005: Content and Methods of the Baylor Religion Survey." *Journal for the Scientific Study of Religion* 46 (4): 447–63.

Baer, Randall N. 1989. *Inside the New Age Nightmare*. Lafayette, LA: Huntington House.

Bainbridge, William Sims. 2004. "After the New Age." *Journal for the Scientific Study of Religion* 43:381–94.

Bainbridge, William Sims, and Rodney Stark. 1980. "Scientology: To Be Perfectly Clear." *Sociological Analysis*. 41:128–36.

Bainbridge, William Sims, and Rodney Stark. 1981. "The Consciousness Reformation Reconsidered." *Journal for the Scientific Study of Religion* 20:1–16.

Baker, Joseph. 2008a. "An Investigation of the Sociological Patterns of Prayer Frequency and Content." *Sociology of Religion* 69 (2): 169–85.

———. 2008b. "Who Believes in Religious Evil? An Investigation of Sociological Patterns of Belief in Satan, Hell, and Demons." *Review of Religious Research* 50 (2): 206–20.

———. 2009. "The Variety of Religious Experiences." *Review of Religious Research.*

Balzano, Christopher. 2009. *Picture Yourself Ghost Hunting.* Boston: Course Technology.

Barrett, Greg. 2001. "Can the Living Talk to the Dead?" *USA Today,* June 20.

Baxter, Marla. 1958. *My Saturnian Lover.* New York: Vantage.

Baer, Randall N. 1989. *Inside the New Age Nightmare.* Lafayette, LA: Huntington House.

Barker, Gray. 1956. *They Knew Too Much About Flying Saucers.* New York: University Books.

Barkun, Michael. 2003. *A Culture of Conspiracy: Apocalyptic Visions in Contemporary America.* Berkeley: University of California Press.

Baylor University. 2005. *The Baylor Religion Survey, Wave 1.* Waco, TX: Baylor Institute for Studies of Religion.

———. 2007. *The Baylor Religion Survey, Wave 2.* Waco, TX: Baylor Institute for Studies of Religion.

Beck, Fred. 1967. *I Fought the Apemen of Mt. St. Helens.* Kelso, WA: R. A. Beck.

Ben-Yehuda, Nachman. 1985. *Deviance and Moral Boundaries.* Chicago: University of Chicago Press.

Bender, Albert K. 1962. *Flying Saucers and the Three Men.* Clarksburg, WV: Saucerian Books.

Berger, Peter L. 1967. *The Sacred Canopy: Elements of a Sociological Theory of Religion.* New York: Anchor Books.

Berger, Peter L., and Thomas Luckmann. 1967. *The Social Construction of Reality: A Treatise in the Sociology of Knowledge.* Garden City, NY: Doubleday.

Berlitz, Charles, and William L. Moore. 1980. *The Roswell Incident.* New York: Grosset and Dunlap.

Birnes, William. 2002. "The Day After Corso." In *MUFON 2002 International UFO Symposium Proceedings,* ed. Barbra Maher and Irena Scott, 33–49. Morrison, CO: Mutual UFO Network.

Bivins, Jason. 2008. *Religion of Fear: The Politics of Horror in Conservative Evangelicalism.* New York: Oxford University Press.

Bord, Janet, and Colin Bord. 1982. *The Bigfoot Casebook.* Harrisburg, PA: Stackpole Books.

Bourdieu, Pierre. 1984. *Distinction: A Social Critique of the Judgment of Taste.* Trans. R. Nice. Cambridge, MA: Harvard University Press.

Boyer, Pascal. 2004. *Religion Explained: The Evolutionary Origins of Religious Thought.* New York: Basic Books.

Boylan, Richard J., and Lee K. Boylan. 1994. *Close Extraterrestrial Encounters: Positive Experiences with Mysterious Visitors.* Tigard, OR: Wild Flower.

Bromley, David. 1991. "Satanism: The New Cult Scare." In *The Satanism Scare,* ed. James T. Richardson, Joel Best, and David G. Bromley, 49–72. New York: Aldine de Gruyter.

Brown, Susan L. 1992. "Baby Boomers, American Character, and the New Age: A Synthesis." In *Perspectives on the New Age,* ed. James R. Lewis and J. Gordon Melton, 87–96. Albany: State University of New York Press.

Bryant, Alice, and Linda Seebach. 1991. *Healing Shattered Trauma: Understanding Contactee Trauma.* Tigard, OR: Wild Flower.

Buhs, Joshua Blu. 2009. *Bigfoot: The Life and Times of a Legend.* Chicago: University of Chicago Press.

Bushman, Claudia L., and Richard L. Bushman. 1999. *Building the Kingdom: A History of Mormon's in America.* New York; Oxford University Press.

Canter, David, Christopher Missen, and Samantha Hodge. 1996. "A Case for Special Agents?" *Policing Today* 2:23–27.

Carey, Thomas J., and Donald R. Schmitt. 2007. *Witness to Roswell: Unmasking the Sixty-Year Cover-Up.* Franklin Lakes, NJ: New Page Books.

Caudill, Harry. 1962. *Night Comes to the Cumberlands: A Biography of a Depressed Area.* Boston: Little, Brown.

Chaves, Mark. 2004. *Congregations in America.* Cambridge, MA: Harvard University Press.

Cheeseman Day, Jennifer, and Bauman, Kurt J. "Have We Reached the Top? Educational Attainment Projections of the U.S. Population." Population Division, U.S. Bureau of the Census. May 2000. Population Division Working Paper 43.

Churchward, James. 1938. *The Lost Continent of Mu.* New York: Washburn.

Clark, Jerome. 1992. *The Emergence of a Phenomenon: UFOs from the Beginning through 1959. The UFO Encyclopedia,* vol. 2. Detroit, MI: Omnigraphics.

———. 1996. *High Strangeness: UFOs from 1960 through 1979. The UFO Encyclopedia,* vol. 3. Detroit, MI: Omnigraphics.

Clark, Jerome, and Loren Coleman. 2006. *The Unidentified and Creatures from the Outer Edge.* San Antonio, TX: Anomalist Books.

Coleman, Loren. 2003. *Bigfoot! The True Story of Apes in America.* New York: Paraview Pocket Books.

Connell, Janice T. 1996. *Meetings with Mary: Visions of the Blessed Mother.* New York: Ballantine.

Conroy, Ed. 1989. *Report on Communion.* New York: Avon.

Cornwell, Rupert. 2003. "In God He Trusts—How George Bush Infused the White House with a Religious Spirit." *Independent,* UK, September 21.

Corso, Philip J., and William J. Birnes. 1997. *The Day after Roswell*. New York: Pocket Books.

Cowan, Douglas E., and David G. Browley. 2008. *Cults and New Religions: A Brief History*. Malden, MA: Blackwell.

Cox, Harvey. 1995. *Fire from Heaven: The Rise of Pentecostal Spirituality and the Reshaping of Religion in the Twenty-First Century*. Cambridge, MA: De Capo.

Cumby, Constance. 1985. *Hidden Dangers of the Rainbow: The New Age Movement and Our Coming Age of Barbarism*. Lafayette, LA: Huntington House.

Daegling, David J. 2004. *Bigfoot Exposed: An Anthropologist Examines America's Enduring Legend*. New York: AltaMira.

Daniken, Erich von. 1974a. *The Gold of the Gods*. New York: Bantam.

———. 1974b. *In Search of Ancient Gods: My Pictorial Evidence for the Impossible*. New York: G. P. Putnam's Sons.

Dean, Jodi. 1998. *Aliens in America: Conspiracy Cultures from Outerspace to Cyberspace*. Ithaca, NY: Cornell University Press.

Denzler, Brenda. 2001. *The Lure of the Edge: Scientific Passions, Religious Beliefs, and the Pursuit of UFOs*. Berkeley: University of California Press.

Donahue, Michael J. 1993. "Prevalence and Correlates of New Age Beliefs in Six Protestant Denominations." *Journal for the Scientific Study of Religion* 32:177–84.

Donnelly, Ignatius. [1882] 1981. *Atlantis: The Antediluvian World*. New York: Harper's.

Durkheim, Emile. [1912] 1995. *The Elementary Forms of Religious Life*. Trans. Karen E. Fields. New York: Free Press.

Eberhart, George M. 2002. *Mysterious Creatures: A Guide to Cryptozoology*, vol. 2, M–Z. Santa Barbara, CA: ABC-CLIO.

Edgar Cayce Foundation. 1987. *Gems and Stones: Based on the Edgar Cayce Readings*. Virginia Beach, VA: A.R.E.

Edwards, Aileen. 1988. *On the (UFO) Road Again: Case Histories of Close Encounters of the Third Kind*. Seattle, WA: UFO Contact Center International.

Erikson, Kai T. 1966. *Wayward Puritans: A Study in the Sociology of Deviance*. New York: Macmillan.

Evans, Hilary. 1984. *Visions, Apparitions, Alien Visitors: A Comparative Study of the Entity Enigma*. Northamptonshire, UK: Aquarian.

———. 2002. *Seeing Ghosts: Experiences of the Paranormal*. London: John Murray.

Farnsworth, Susan A. 1996. *The Mogollon Monster: Arizona's Bigfoot*. Mesa, AZ: Southwest.

Finucane, R. C. 1984. *Appearances of the Dead: A Cultural History of Ghosts*. Buffalo, NY: Prometheus Books.

Fowler, Raymond E. 1979. *The Andreasson Affair*. New York: Bantam.

Fox, James Alan, and Jack Levin. 1999. "Serial Murder: Popular Myths and Empirical Realities." In *Homicide: A Sourcebook of Social Research*, ed. M. Dwayne Smith and Margaret A. Zahn, 167–75. Thousand Oaks, CA: Sage.

Fox, John W. 1992. "The Structure, Stability, and Social Antecedents of Reported Paranormal Experiences." *Sociological Analysis* 53 (4): 417–31.

Frazier, E. Franklin. 1963. *The Negro Church in America*. New York: Schocken Books.

Friedman, Stanton T., and Don Berliner. 1992. *Crash at Corona: The U.S. Military Retrieval and Cover-up of a UFO*. St. Paul, MN: Paragon House.

Froese, Paul, and Christopher D. Bader. 2007. "God in America: Why Theology Is Not Simply the Concern of Philosophers." *Journal for the Scientific Study of Religion* 46 (4).

———. 2008. "Unraveling Religious Worldviews: The Relationship Between Images of God and Political Ideology in a Cross-cultural Analysis." *Sociological Quarterly* 49 (4): 689–718.

Froese, Paul, Christopher D. Bader, and Buster Smith. 2008. "Political Tolerance and God's Wrath in the United States." *Sociology of Religion* 69 (1): 29–44.

Fukuyama, Francis. 1995. *Trust: The Social Virtues and the Creation of Prosperity*. New York: Free Press.

Fuller, John G. 1966. *Interrupted Journey: Two Lost Hours "Aboard a Flying Saucer."* New York: Dial.

Geertz, Clifford. 1973. *The Interpretation of Cultures*. New York: Basic Books.

Gieryn, Thomas F. 1999. *Cultural Boundaries of Science: Credibility on the Line*. Chicago: University of Chicago Press.

Glendinning, Tony. 2006. "Religious Involvement, Conventional Christian, and Unconventional Nonmaterialist Beliefs." *Journal for the Scientific Study of Religion* 45: 585–95.

Glock, Charles Y., and Rodney Stark. 1965. *Religion and Society in Tension*. Chicago: Rand McNally.

Goldberg, Robert A. 2001. *Enemies Within: The Culture of Conspiracy in Modern America*. New Haven, CT: Yale University Press.

Goode, Erich. 2000. *Paranormal Beliefs: A Sociological Introduction*. Prospect Heights, IL: Waveland.

Goode, Erich, and Nachman Ben-Yehuda. 1994. "Moral Panics: Culture, Politics, and Social Construction." *Annual Review of Sociology* 20:149–71.

Graham, Billy. 1977. *Angels*. New York: Simon and Schuster.

———. 1992. *Storm Warning*. Dallas, TX: Word.

Gray, William D. 1991. *Thinking Critically about New Age Ideas*. Belmont, CA: Wadsworth.

Greely, Andrew. 1975. *The Sociology of the Paranormal*. Studies in Religion and Ethnicity, vol. 3. Beverly Hills, CA: Sage.

———. 1995. *Religion as Poetry*. New Brunswick, NJ: Transaction.

Green, John. 1978. *Sasquatch: The Apes among Us*. Blaine, WA: Hancock House.

———. 1980. *On the Track of Sasquatch*, Book 1. British Columbia, Canada: Cheam.

Green, John C., James L. Guth, Corwin E. Smidt, and Lyman A. Kellstedt. 1996. *Religion and the Culture Wars*. Lanham, MD: Rowman and Littlefield.

Green, Mary A. 2002. *Fifty Years with Bigfoot: Tennessee Chronicles of Co-Existence*. Cookeville, TN: Green and Coy Enterprises.

Hardy, Diana. 1999. *Des Masquerade: An Expose on Satan in the New Age Movement*. Kirkwood, MO: Impact Christian Books.

Harrold, Francis B. and Raymond A. Eve, eds. 1995. *Cult Archeology and Creationism: Understanding Psuedoscientific Beliefs about the Past*. Iowa City: University of Iowa Press.

Hay, David, and Ann Morisy. "Reports of Ecstatic, Paranormal, or Religious Experience in Great Britain and the United States." *Journal for the Scientific Study of Religion* 17 (1978): 255–68

Heelas, Paul. 1996. *The New Age Movement: The Celebration of Self and the Sacralization of Modernity*. Oxford: Blackwell.

Hess, David J. 1993. *Science in the New Age: The Paranormal, Its Defenders and Debunkers, and American Culture*. Madison: University of Wisconsin Press.

Hill, Betty. 1995. *A Common Sense Approach to UFOs*. Greenland, NH: self-published.

Hines, Terence. 1988. *Pseudoscience and the Paranormal: A Critical Examination of the Evidence*. Buffalo, NY: Prometheus Books.

Hirschi, Travis. 1969. *Causes of Delinquency*. Berkeley: University of California Press.

Hofstadter, Richard. 1966. *The Paranoid Style in American Politics and Other Essays*. New York: Knopf.

Holyfield, Dana. 1999. *Swamp Bigfoot: Tales of the Louisiana Honey Island Swamp Monster*. Pearl River, LA: Honey Island Swamp Books.

Hood Jr., Ralph W., Peter C. Hill, and W. Paul Williamson. 2005. *The Psychology of Religious Fundamentalism*. New York: Guilford.

Hood Jr., Ralph W., Bernard Spilka, Bruce Hunsberger, and Richard Gorsuch. 1996. *The Psychology of Religion: An Empirical Approach*, 2nd ed. New York: Guilford.

Hopkins, Budd. 1981. *Missing Time: Documented Stories of People Kidnapped by UFOs and Then Returned with Their Memories Erased*. New York: Richard Marek.

———. 1987. *Intruders: The Incredible Visitations at Copley Woods*. New York: Ballantine.

Hout, Michael, and Claude S. Fischer. 2002. "Why More Americans Have No Religious Preference: Politics and Generations." *American Sociological Review* 67 (2): 165–90.

Hutchings, Noah, Larry Spargimino, and Bob Glaze. 2000. *Marginal Mysteries: A Biblical Perspective*. Oklahoma City: Hearthstone.

Iannaccone, Laurence R. 1988. "A Formal Model of Church and Sect." *American Journal of Sociology* 94:S241–S268.

———. 1992. "Sacrifice and Stigma: Reducing Free Riding in Cults, Communes and Other Collectives." *Journal of Political Economy* (April): 271–91.

———. 1995a. "Risk, Rationality and Religious Portfolios." *Economic Inquiry* 23: 285–95.

———. 1995b. "Voodoo Economics? Reviewing the Rational Choice Approach to Religion." *Journal for the Scientific Study of Religion* 34 (1): 76–89.

Irving, Washington. [1893] 1981. *The Life and Voyages of Christopher Columbus.* Boston: Twayne.

Jacobsen, Judith A. 1989. *Medical Report of Erika Ingram.* Seattle, WA: Harbourview Hospital.

James, William. [1902] 1961. *Varieties of Religious Experience: A Study in Human Nature.* New York: Collier Macmillan.

Jenkins, Philip. 1994. *Using Murder: The Social Construction of Serial Homicide.* Hawthorne, NY: Aldine de Gruyter.

Johnson, Stan, and Joshua Shapiro. 1987. *The True Story of Bigfoot.* Pinole, CA: J&S Aquarian Networking.

Jung, Carl G. 1979. *Flying Saucers: A Modern Myth of Things Seen in the Sky.* Princeton, NJ: Princeton University Press.

Kaneko, Satoru. 1990. "Dimensions of Religiosity among Believers in Japanese Folk Religion." *Journal for the Scientific Study of Religion* 29 (1): 1–18.

Kaufmann, Eric. Forthcoming. "Secularism, Fundamentalism or Catholicism? The Religious Composition of the United States to 2043." *Journal for the Scientific Study of Religion.*

Kelly, Aidan A. 1992. "An Update on Neopagan Witchcraft in America." In *Perspectives on the New Age,* ed. James R. Lewis and J. Gordon Melton, 136–51. Albany: State University of New York Press.

Kemp, Alice Abel. 1994. *Women's Work: Degraded and Devalued.* Englewood Cliffs, NJ: Prentice Hall.

King, George. 1961. *The Twelve Blessings: The Cosmic Concept as Given by the Master Jesus.* London: Aetherius.

Klass, Philip J. 1989. *UFO Abductions: A Dangerous Game.* Buffalo, NY: Prometheus Books.

Knight, Peter. 2002. "Introduction: A Nation of Conspiracy Theorists." In *Conspiracy Nation: The Politics of Paranoia in Postwar America,* ed. Peter Knight, 1–20. New York: New York University Press.

Kosmin, Barry A., Egon Mayer and Ariela Keysar. 2001. *American Religious Identification Survey.* New York: Graduate Center of New York University.

Kosmin, Barry A., and Seymour P. Lachman. 1993. *One Nation Under God: Religion in Contemporary Society.* New York: Harmony.

Krause, Neal, and Linda M. Chatters. 2005. "Exploring Race Differences in a Multidimensional Battery of Prayer Measures among Older Adults." *Sociology of Religion* 66:23–43.

Lapseritis, Jack. 2005. *The Psychic Sasquatch and Their UFO Connection*. Mills Spring, NC: Wild Flower.

Larsen, Otto N. 1962. "Innovators and Early Adopters of Television." *Sociological Inquiry* 32 (S): 16–23.

Larson, Bob. 1997. *UFOs and the Alien Agenda*. Nashville, TN: Thomas Nelson.

Laubach, Marty. 2004. "The Social Effects of Psychism: Spiritual Experience and the Construction of Privatized Religion." *Sociology of Religion* 65:239–63.

LaVigne, Michelle. 1995. *The Alien Abduction Survival Guide*. Newberg, OR: Wild Flower.

Legerski, Elizabeth, Marie Cornwall, and Brock O'Neil. 2006. "Changing Locus of Control: Steelworkers Adjusting to Forced Unemployment." *Social Forces* 84:1521–38.

Legget, Mike. 2009. "Texas Bigfoot Conference More Boring Than You Would Think." *Austin-American Statesman*, October 4.

Lesage, Julia. "Christian Media." In *Media, Culture, and the Religious Right*, ed. L. Kintz and J. Lesage, 21–50. 1998. Minneapolis: University of Minnesota Press.

Leslie, Desmond, and George Adamski. 1954. *Flying Saucers Have Landed*. New York: The British Book Centre.

Lewis, James R. 1992. "Approaches to the Study of the New Age Movement." In *Perspectives on the New Age*, ed. James R. Lewis and J. Gordon Melton, 1–14. Albany: State University of New York Press.

———, ed. 2000. *UFOs and Popular Culture: An Encyclopedia of Contemporary Myth*. Santa Barbara, CA: ABC-CLIO.

Lewis, James R., and Gordon Melton, eds. 1992. *Perspectives on the New Age*. New York: State University of New York Press.

Lincoln, C. Eric. 1974. *The Black Church Since Frazier*. New York: Schocken Books.

Lincoln, C. Eric, and Lawrence H. Mamiya. 1990. *The Black Church in the Africa-American Experience*. Durham, NC: Duke University Press.

Lofland, John, and Rodney Stark. 1965. "Becoming a World-Saver: A Theory of Conversion to a Deviant Perspective." *American Sociological Review* 30:862–74.

Long, Greg. 2004. *The Making of Bigfoot: The Inside Story*. Amherst, NY: Prometheus Books.

Lupfer, Michael, Donna Tolliver, and Mark Jackson. 1996. "Explaining Life-Altering Occurrences: A Test of the 'God-of-the-Gaps' Hypothesis." *Journal for the Scientific Study of Religion* 35 (4): 379–91.

MacDonald, William L. 1995. "The Effects of Religiosity and Structural Strain on Reported Paranormal Experiences." *Journal for the Scientific Study of Religion* 34:366–76.

Mack, John E. 1994. *Abduction: Human Encounters with Aliens*. New York: Charles Scribner's Sons.

MacLaine, Shirley. 1986. *Out on a Limb*. New York. Bantam Books.

Marrs, Texe. 1988. *Mystery Mark of the New Age: Satan's Design for World Domination*. Wheaton, IL: Crossway Books.

———. 1989. *Ravaged by the New Age: Satan's Plan to Destroy Our Kids*. Austin, TX: Living Truth.

———. 1991. *New Age Cults and Religions*. Austin, TX: Living Truth.

———. 2000. *Dark Secrets of the New Age: Satan's Plan for a One World Religion*. Austin, TX: Rivercrest.

Mason, Fran. 2002. "A Poor Person's Cognitive Mapping." In *Conspiracy Nation: The Politics of Paranoia in Postwar America*, ed. Peter Knight, 40–56. New York: New York University Press.

Maudlin, Michael G. 1989. "Holy Smoke! The Darkness is Back." *Christianity Today* 15 (December): 58–59.

McAndrew, James. 1997. *The Roswell Report: Case Closed*. Washington, DC: U.S. Government Printing Office.

McKinnon, Andrew. 2003. "The Religious, the Paranormal, and Church Attendance: A Response to Orenstein." *Journal for the Scientific Study of Religion* 42:299–303.

Mears, Daniel P., and Christopher G. Ellison. 2000. "Who Buys New Age Materials? Exploring Sociodemographic, Religious, Network, and Contextual Correlates of New Age Consumption." *Sociology of Religion* 61 (3): 289–314.

Meldrum, Jeff. 2006. *Sasquatch: Legend Meets Science*. New York: Tom Doherty Associates.

Melley, Timothy. 2000. *Empire of Conspiracy: The Culture of Paranoia in Postwar America*. Ithaca, NY: Cornell University Press.

———. 2002. "Agency Panic and the Culture of Conspiracy." In *Conspiracy Nation: The Politics of Paranoia in Postwar America*, ed. Peter Knight, 57–84. New York: New York University Press.

Melton, J. Gordon. 1990. *New Age Encyclopedia*. Detroit: Gale Research.

———. 1992. "New Thought and the New Age." In Perspectives on the New Age, ed. J. Lewis and G. Melton, 15–29. Albany: State University of New York Press.

———. 1995. "The Contactees: A Survey." In *The Gods have Landed: New Religions from Other Worlds*, ed. James R. Lewis, 1–13. Albany: State University of New York Press.

———. 2003. "Pentecostal Family." *The Encyclopedia of American Religions*. 7th ed. Detroit: Gale Research.

Melton, J. Gordon, and Martin Baumann. 2002. *Religions of the World: A Comprehensive Encyclopedia of Beliefs and Practices*. Santa Barbara, CA: ABC-Clio.

Melton, J. Gordon, Jerome Clark, and Aidan Kelly. 1991. *New Age Almanac*. Canton, MI: Visible Ink.

Mencken, F. Carson, Christopher Bader, and Ye Jung Kim. 2009. "Round Trip to Hell in a Flying Saucer: The Relationship between Conventional Christian and Paranormal Beliefs in the United States." *Sociology of Religion* 70:65–85.

Mencken, F. Carson, Christopher Bader, and Rodney Stark. 2008. "Conventional Christian Beliefs and Experimentation with the Paranormal." *Review of Religious Research* 50:194–205.

Menger, Howard. 1959. *From Outer Space to You*. Clarksburg, WV: Saucerian Books.

Michael, Jay. Undated. *Bigfoot in Mississippi*. Laurel, MS: self-published.

Miller, Alan S., and John P. Hoffman. 1995. "Risk and Religion: An Explanation in Gender Differences in Religiosity." *Journal for the Scientific Study of Religion* 34 (1): 63–75.

Mills, C. Wright. [1959] 2000. *The Sociological Imagination*. Oxford: Oxford University Press.

Mitchell, Karyn K. 1994. *Abductions: Stop Them, Heal Them, Now!* St. Charles, IL: Mind Rivers.

Montenegro, Marcia. 2006. *Spellbound: The Paranormal Seduction of Today's Kids*. Colorado Springs, CO: Cook Communications Ministries.

Moseley, James. W., and Karl T. Pflock. 2002. *Shockingly Close to the Truth!* Buffalo, NY: Prometheus Books.

Murphy, Christopher L. 2006. *Bigfoot Encounters in Ohio: Quest for the Grassman*. Blaine, WA: Hancock House.

Mustapa, Margit. 1960. *Spaceship to the Unknown*. New York: Vantage.

———. 1963. *Book of Brothers*. New York: Vantage.

Nathan, Debbie. 1991. "Satanism and Child Molestation: Constructing the Ritual Abuse Scare." In *The Satanism Scare*, ed. James T. Richardson, Joel Best, and David G. Bromley, 75–94. New York: Aldine de Gruyter.

Newport, Frank. 1997. *What If Government Really Listened to the People?* Retrieved from http://www.gallup.com/poll/4594/What-Government-Really-Listened-People.aspx, March 3, 2008.

Niebuhr, H. Richard. [1929] 1957. *The Social Sources of Denominationalism*. New York, NY: Meridian Books.

Noonan, Moira. 2005. *Ransomed from Darkness: The New Age, Christian Faith, and the Battle for Souls*. El Sobrante, CA: North Bay Books.

Northcote, Jeremy. 2007. *The Paranormal and the Politics of Truth: A Sociological Account*. Charlottesville, VA: Imprint-Academic.

Nye, F. Ivan. 1958. *Family Relationships and Delinquent Behavior*. New York: John Wiley and Sons.

O'Dea, Thomas F. 1957. *The Mormons*. Chicago: University of Chicago Press.

Ofshe, Richard. 1989. Report from Dr. Richard Ofshe to Gary Tabor, Prosecutor. Olympia, WA.

Opsasnick, Mark. 2004. *The Maryland Bigfoot Digest: A Survey of Creature Sightings in the Free State*. Self-published: Xlibris.

Orenstein, Alan. 2002. "Religion and Paranormal Belief." *Journal for the Scientific Study of Religion* 41:301–12.

Pagels, Elaine. 1995. *The Origin of Satan*. New York: Random House.

Palmer, Susan J. 2004. *Aliens Adored: Raël's UFO Religion*. New Brunswick, NJ: Rutgers University Press.

Pargament, Kenneth I. 1997. *The Psychology of Religion and Coping: Theory Research, Practice*. New York: Guilford.

Pargament, Kenneth I., and June Hahn. 1986. "God and the Just World: Causal and Coping Attributions to God in Health Situations." *Journal for the Scientific Study of Religion* 25:193–207.

Parish, Jane, and Martin Parker, eds. 2001. *The Age of Anxiety: Conspiracy Theory and the Human Sciences*. Oxford: Oxford University Press.

Partridge, Christopher, ed. 2003. *UFO Religions*. New York: Routledge.

———. 2003. "Understanding UFO Religions and Abduction Spiritualities." In *UFO Religions*, ed. Christopher Partridge, 3–42. London: Routledge.

Passel, Jeffrey S., and Cohn, D'Vera. 2008. *U.S. Population Projections: 2005–2050*. Pew Research Center, Washington, DC. www.pewresearch.org

Patterson, Roger, and Christopher Murphy. 2005. *The Bigfoot Film Controversy*. Blaine, WA: Hancock House.

Paulos, John Allen. 1991. *Beyond Numeracy*. New York: Vintage.

Phares, Jerry. 2001. "Locus of Control." In *The Corsini Encyclopedia of Psychology and Behavioral Science*, vol. 2, ed. W. E. Craighead and C. B. Nemeroff, 889–91. New York: John Wiley and Sons.

Pipes, Daniel. 1997. *Conspiracy: How the Paranoid Style Flourishes and Where It Comes From*. New York: Simon and Schuster.

Poloma, Margaret. M. 1989. *The Assemblies of God at the Crossroads: Charisma and Institutional Dilemmas*. Knoxville: University of Tennessee Press.

———. 1995. "The Sociological Context of Religious Experience." In *Handbook of Religious Experience*, ed. R. W. Hood Jr., 161–82. Birmingham, AL: Religious Education Press.

Pritchard, Andrea, David E. Pritchard, John E. Mack, Pam Kasey, and Claudia Yapp, eds. 1992. *Alien Discussions: Proceedings of the Abduction Study Conference Held at MIT, Cambridge, MA*. Cambridge, MA: North Cambridge Press.

Proudfoot, Wayne. 1985. *Religious Experience*. Berkeley: University of California Press.

Putnam, Robert D. 2000. *Bowling Alone: The Collapse and Revival of American Community*. New York: Simon and Schuster.

Quast, Mike. 2000. *Big Footage: A History of Claims for the Sasquatch on Film*. Moorhead, MN: self-published.

Quine, Williard V., and J. S. Ullian. 1978. *The Web of Belief*. New York: Random House.

Rabey, Steve. 1988. "Spiritual Warfare, Supernatural Sales." *Christianity Today* 9 (December): 69.

Raboteau, Albert J. 1997. "The Black Experience in American Evangelicalism: The Meaning of Slavery." In *African-American Religion*, ed. Timothy E. Fulop and Albert J. Raboteau, 89–106. New York: Routledge.

Reckless, Walter C. 1962. "A Non-Causal Explanation: Containment Theory." *Excerpta Criminologica* 2:131–32.

Redfern, Nick. 2004. *Three Men Seeking Monsters: Six Weeks in Pursuit of Werewolves, Lake Monsters, Giant Cats, Ghostly Devil Dogs, and Ape-Men*. New York: Pocket Books.

Reiss, Albert J. 1951. "Delinquency as the Failure of Personal and Social Controls." *American Sociological Review* 16:196–207.

Rhodes, Ron. 1998. *Alien Obsession*. Eugene, OR: Harvest House.

Rice, Tom W. 2003. "Believe It or Not: Religious and Other Paranormal Beliefs in the United States." *Journal for the Scientific Study of Religion* 42:95–106.

Richardson, James T., Joel Best, and David G. Bromley. 1991. *The Satanism Scare*. New York: Aldine de Gruyter.

Rigsby, Bruce. 1977. "Some Pacific Northwest Native Language Names for the Sasquatch Phenomenon." In *The Scientist Looks at Sasquatch*, ed. Roderick Sprague and Grover S. Krantz, 31–37. Moscow: University of Idaho Press.

Rimmer, John. 1984. *The Evidence for Alien Abductions*. Northamptonshire, UK: Aquarian.

Roof, Wade C. 1999. *Spiritual Marketplace: Baby Boomer and the Remaking of American Religion*. Princeton, NJ: Princeton University Press.

Roof, Wade Clark, Jackson W. Carroll, and David A. Roozen. 1995. "Conclusion: The Post-War Generation-Carriers of a New Spirituality." In *The Postwar Generation and Establishment Religion: Cross-Cultural Perspectives*, ed. Wade Clark Roof, Jackson W. Carroll, and David A. Roozen, 243–55. Boulder, CO: Westview.

Roosevelt, Theodore. 1927. *Hunting Adventures in the West*. New York: Putnam.

Ross, Catherine, and John Mirowsky. 2002. "Households, Employment, and the Sense of Control." *Social Psychology Quarterly* 55:217–35.

Rosten, Leo. 1975. *Religions of America: Ferment and Faith in an Age of Crises*. New York: Simon and Schuster.

Russell, Jeffrey. 1991. "The Historical Satan." In *The Satanism Scare*, ed. James T. Richardson, Joel Best, and David G. Bromley, 41–48. New York: Aldine de Gruyter.

Sagan, Carl. 1997. *The Demon-Haunted World: Science as a Candle in the Dark*. New York: Ballantine.

Saler, Benson, Charles A. Ziegler, and Charles B. Moore. 1997. *UFO Crash at Ros-*

well: The Genesis of a Modern Myth. Washington, DC: Smithsonian Institution Press.

Saliba, John. 1995. "Religious Dimensions of the UFO Phenomenon." In *The Gods Have Landed: New Religions from Other Worlds,* ed. James R. Lewis, 15–64. Albany: State University of New York Press.

———. 2003. "The Earth is a Dangerous Place: The Worldview of the Aetherius Society." In *Encyclopedia Sourcebook of UFO Religions,* ed. James R. Lewis, 123–42. Amherst, NY: Prometheus.

Schieman, Scott, and Alex Bierman. 2007. "Religious Activities and Changes in the Sense of Divine Control." *Sociology of Religion* 68 (4): 361–81.

Schieman, Scott, Kim Nguyen, and Diana Elliot. 2003. "Religiosity, Socioeconomic Status, and the Sense of Mastery." *Social Psychology Quarterly* 66(3): 202–21.

Schieman, Scott, and Gabriele Plickert. 2008. "How Knowledge Is Power: Education and the Sense of Control." *Social Forces* 87(1):153–83.

Schieman, Scott, Tetyana Pudrovska, Leonard I. Pearlin, and Christopher G. Ellison. 2006. "The Sense of Divine Control and Psychological Distress: Variations by Race and Socioeconomic Status." *Journal for the Scientific Study of Religion* 45 (4): 529–49.

Schuessler, John F. 2000. *Public Opinion Surveys and Unidentified Flying Objects: 50+ Years of Sampling Public Opinions.* Morrison, CO: Mutual UFO Network (Retrieved from http://www.nidsci.org/pdf/schuessler2.pdf, March 3, 2008).

Scribner, Scott, and Gregory Wheeler. 2003. "Cosmic Intelligences and their Terrestrial Channel." In *Encyclopedic Sourcebook of UFO Religions,* ed. James R. Lewis, 157–71. Amherst, NY: Prometheus Books.

Scott, James C. 1977. "Protest and Profanation: Agrarian Revolt and the Little Tradition, Part I." *Theory and Society* 4 (1): 1–38.

Sherkat, Darren E. 2001. "Tracking the Restructuring of American Religion: Religious Affiliation and Patterns of Religious Mobility, 1973–1998." *Social Forces* 79 (4): 1459–93.

———. 2008. "Beyond Belief: Atheism, Agnosticism, and Theistic Certainty in the United States." *Sociological Spectrum* 28:438–59.

Sherman, Lawrence W., Douglas A. Smith, Janell D. Schmidt, and Dennis P. Rogan. 1992. "Crime, Punishment, and Stake in Conformity: Legal and Informal Control of Domestic Violence." *American Sociological Review* 57:680–90.

Shermer, Michael. 2002. *Why People Believe Weird Things: Pseudoscience, Superstition, and Other Confusions of Our Time.* New York: Holt.

Sjodin, Ulf. 2002. "The Swedes and the Paranormal." *Journal of Contemporary Religion* 17:75–85.

Slate, Bobbie Ann, and Al Berry. 1976. *Bigfoot.* New York: Bantam.

Smelser, Neil J. 1962. *Theory of Collective Behavior.* Glencoe, NY: Free Press.

Smith, Christian. 2003. *Moral, Believing Animals: Human Personhood and Culture.* New York: Oxford University Press.

Smith, James M. 2003. *Sasquatch: Alabama Bigfoot Sightings*. Wadley, AL: self-published.

Smith, Simon G. 2003. "Opening a Channel to the Stars: The Origins and Development of the Aetherius Society." In *UFO Religions*, ed. Christopher Partridge, 84–102. New York: Routledge.

Southall, Richard. 2003. *How to Be a Ghost Hunter*. Woodbury, MN: Llewellyn.

Sparks, Glenn. G. 2001. "The Relationship between Paranormal Beliefs and Religious Beliefs." *Skeptical Inquirer* 25:50–56.

Spencer, John. 1991. *The UFO Encyclopedia: A to Z Guide of Extraterrestrial Phenomena*. New York: Avon.

Spilka Jr., Bernard, Ralph W. Hood, Bruce Hunsberger, and Richard Gorsuch. 2003. *The Psychology of Religion: An Empirical Approach*. 3rd ed. New York: Guilford.

Stark, Rodney. 1996. *The Rise of Christianity*. Princeton, NJ: Princeton University Press.

———. 2001. "Gods, Rituals, and the Moral Order." *Journal for the Scientific Study of Religion* 40:619–36.

———. 2002. "Physiology and Faith: Addressing the 'Universal' Gender Difference in Religious Commitment." *Journal for the Scientific Study of Religion* 41 (3): 495–508.

———. 2004. *Exploring the Religious Life*. Baltimore: Johns Hopkins University Press.

———. 2008. *What Americans Really Believe*. Waco, TX: Baylor University Press.

Stark, Rodney, and William Sims Bainbridge. 1980. "Networks of Faith: Interpersonal Bonds and Recruitment to Cults and Sects," *American Journal of Sociology* 85:1376–95.

———. 1985. *The Future of Religion: Secularization, Revival and Cult Formation*. Berkeley: University of California Press.

———. 1987. *A Theory of Religion*. New York: Peter Lang.

Stark, Rodney, and Roger Finke. 2000. *Acts of Faith: Explaining the Human Side of Religion*. Berkeley: University of California Press.

Stark, Rodney, and Laurence Iannaccone. 1997. "Why the Jehovah's Witnesses Grow So Rapidly: A Theoretical Application." *Journal of Contemporary Religion* 12:133–57.

Steensland, B., J. Z. Park, M. D. Regnerus, L. D. Robinson, W. B. Wilcox, and R. D. Woodberry. 2000. "The Measure of American Religion: Toward Improving the State of the Art." *Social Forces* 79:291–318.

Steinman, William S., and Wendelle C. Stevens. 1987. *UFO Crash at Aztec: A Well Kept Secret*. Tucson, AZ: UFO Photo Archives.

Stevens, Phillip. "The Demonology of Satanism: An Anthropological View." In *The Satanism Scare*, ed. James T. Richardson, Joel Best, and David G. Bromley, 21–40. New York: Aldine de Gruyter.

Stiebing, William H. Jr. 1984. *Ancient Astronauts, Cosmic Collisions and Other Popular Theories about Man's Past*. Buffalo, NY: Prometheus Books.

Stinchcombe, Arthur. 1990. *Information and Organizations*. Berkeley: University of California Press.

Story, Ronald. 1980a. *The Encyclopedia of UFOs*. New York: Doubleday.

———. 1980b. *Guardians of the Universe?* New York: St. Martin's.

Stranges, Frank E. 1967. *The Stranger at the Pentagon*. Van Nuys, CA: I.E.C.

Strieber, Whitley. 1987. *Communion: A True Story*. New York: William Morrow.

Swatos, William H. 1988. "Picketing Satan Enfleshed at 7-Eleven: A Research Note." *Review of Religious Research* 30 (3): 73–82.

Taylor, Catherine, and Susan B. Sorenson. 2002. "The Nature of Newspaper Coverage of Homicide." *Injury Prevention* 8:121–27.

Thomas, William I., and Dorothy Swain Thomas. 1928. *The Child in America: Behavior Problems and Programs*. New York: Knopf.

Thurston County Sheriff's Office. 1988. Transcript interview with Paul Ingram conducted by Joe Vukich and Brian Schoening. Olympia, WA.

———. 1989a. Transcript of interview with Sandra Ingram conducted by Loreli Thompson. Olympia, WA.

———. 1989b. Transcript of interview with Chad Ingram conducted by Dr. Richard Peterson and Detective Brian Schoening. Olympia, WA.

Toby, Jackson. 1957. "Social Disorganization and Stake in Conformity: Complementary Factors in the Predatory Behavior of Hoodlums." *Journal of Criminal Law, Criminology and Police Science* 48 (May/June): 12–17.

Torres, Noe, and Ruben Uriarte. 2008. *The Other Roswell: UFO Crash on the Texas-Mexico Border*. Roswellbooks.com.

Trachtenberg, Joshua. [1939] 2004. *Jewish Magic and Superstition: A Study in Folk Religion*. Philadelphia: University of Pennsylvania Press.

Troeltsch, Ernst. [1912] 1932. *The Social Teaching of the Christian Churches*. New York: Macmillan.

Tumminia, Diana G. 2005. *When Prophecy Never Fails: Myth and Reality in a Flying-Saucer Group*. New York: Oxford University Press.

Valerian, Valdamar. 1988. *The Matrix*. Stone Mountain, GA: Arcturus Book Service.

Victor, Jeffrey S. 1993. *Satanic Panic: The Creation of a Contemporary Legend*. Chicago, IL: Open Court.

Vigil, Delfin. 2006. "Conspiracy Theories Propel AM Radio Show into Top 10." *San Francisco Chronicle*. November 12.

Vold, George B., Thomas J. Bernard, and Jeffrey B. Snipes. 1998. *Theoretical Criminology*, 4th ed. New York: Oxford University Press.

Wallis, Roy. 1974. "The Aetherius Society: A Case Study in the Formation of a Mystagogic Congregation." *Sociological Review* 22:27–44.

Warnke, Mike. 1972. *The Satan Seller*. South Plainfield, NJ: Bridge Books.

Weaver, Richard L., and James McAndrew. 1995. *The Roswell Report: Fact vs. Fiction in the New Mexico Desert*. Washington, DC: U.S. Government Printing Office.

Weber, Max. [1922] 1991. *The Sociology of Religion*. Trans. Ephraim Fischoff. Boston: Beacon.

Weeks, Matthew, Kelly P. Weeks, and Mary R. Daniel. 2008. "The Implicit Relationship Between Religious and Paranormal Constructs." *Journal for the Scientific Study of Religion* 47 (4): 599–611.

Whelan, Christopher. 1996. "Marginalization, Deprivation, and Fatalism in the Republic of Ireland: Class and Underclass Perspectives." *European Sociological Review* 12:33–51.

Wilcox, Clyde, Sharon Linzey, and Ted G. Jelen. 1991. "Reluctant Warriors: Premillennialism and Politics in the Moral Majority." *Journal for the Scientific Study of Religion* 30 (3): 245–58.

Williams, Peter W. 1980. *Popular Religion in America: Symbolic Change and the Modernization Process in Historical Perspective*. Englewood Cliffs, NJ: Prentice Hall.

Williamson, W. Paul, and Ralph W. Hood Jr. 2004. "Differential Maintenance of and Growth of Religious Organizations Based Upon High-Cost Behaviors: Serpent Handling within the Church of God." *Review of Religious Research* 46:150–68.

Williamson, W. Paul, and Howard R. Pollio. 1999. "The Phenomenology of Religious Serpent Handling: A Rationale and Thematic Study of Extemporaneous Sermons." *Journal for the Scientific Study of Religion* 38:203–18.

Willman, Skip. 2002. "Spinning Paranoia: The Ideologies of Conspiracy and Contingency in Postmodern Culture." In *Conspiracy Nation: The Politics of Paranoia in Postwar America*, ed. Peter Knight, 21–39. New York: New York University Press.

Wilson, Keith M., and Jennifer L. Huff. 2001. "Scaling Satan." *Journal of Psychology* 135 (3): 292–300.

Wlodarski, Robert, and Anne Powell Wlodarski. 2001. *A Texas Guide to Haunted Restaurants, Taverns, and Inns*. Plano, TX: Republic of Texas Press.

Woodberry, Robert D., and Christian Smith. 1998. "Fundamentalism et al.: Conservative Protestantism in America." *Annual Review of Sociology* 24:25–56.

Wright, Lawrence. 1994. *Remembering Satan*. New York: Knopf.

Wu, Zheng, and Randy Hart. 2002. "The Effects of Marital and Nonmarital Union Transition on Health." *Journal of Marriage and Family* 64:420–32.

Wuthnow, Robert. 1978. *Experimentation in American Religion*. Berkeley: University of California Press.

———. 1987. *Meaning and Moral Order: Explorations in Cultural Analysis*. Berkeley: University of California Press.

Yamane, David. 1998. "Experience." In *Encyclopedia of Religion and Society,* ed. William H. Swatos Jr., 179–82. Walnut Creek, CA: AltaMira.

———. 2000. "Narrative and Religious Experience." *Sociology of Religion* 61 (2): 171–89.

Zahn, Margaret A., and Philip C. Sagi. 1987. "Stranger Homicide in Nine American Cities." *Journal of Criminal Law and Criminology* 78 (2): 377–97.

Zeleney, Jeff. 2008. "Obama, in His New Role as President-Elect, Calls for Stimulus Package." *New York Times,* November 7.

Index

About the Authors

Christopher D. Bader is Associate Professor of Sociology at Baylor University and Associate Director of the Association of Religion Data Archives (www.thearda.com).

F. Carson Mencken is Professor of Sociology at Baylor University, where he is also Director of Research at the Institute for Studies of Religion.

Joseph O. Baker is Assistant Professor of Sociology at East Tennessee State University.